Human-Computer Interaction Series

T0137702

Human-Computer Interaction is a multidisciplinary field focused on human aspects of the development of computer technology. As computer-based technology becomes increasingly pervasive - not just in developed countries, but worldwide - the need to take a human-centered approach in the design and development of this technology becomes ever more important. For roughly 30 years now, researchers and practitioners in computational and behavioral sciences have worked to identify theory and practice that influences the direction of these technologies, and this diverse work makes up the field of human-computer interaction. Broadly speaking it includes the study of what technology might be able to do for people and how people might interact with the technology. In this series we present work which advances the science and technology of developing systems which are both effective and satisfying for people in a wide variety of contexts. The human-computer interaction series will focus on theoretical perspectives (such as formal approaches drawn from a variety of behavioral sciences), practical approaches (such as the techniques for effectively integrating user needs in system development), and social issues (such as the determinants of utility, usability and acceptability).

For further volumes:
http://www.springer.com/series/6033

Estefanía Martín • Pablo A. Haya • Rosa M. Carro
Editors

User Modeling and Adaptation for Daily Routines

Providing Assistance to People with Special Needs

 Springer

Editors
Estefanía Martín
Department of Languages
   and Computer Systems
Universidad Rey Juan Carlos
Madrid
Spain

Pablo A. Haya
IIC-Knowledge Engineering Institute
Universidad Autónoma de Madrid
Madrid
Spain

Rosa M. Carro
Department of Computer Science
   and Engineering
Universidad Autónoma de Madrid
Madrid
Spain

ISSN 1571-5035
ISBN 978-1-4471-6091-5   ISBN 978-1-4471-4778-7 (eBook)
DOI 10.1007/978-1-4471-4778-7
Springer London Heidelberg New York Dordrecht

Printed on acid-free paper

Springer is part of Springer Science+Business Media (www.springer.com)

Preface

This book arises from the motivation of bringing to attention how adaptive methods and techniques can benefit people with special needs in their everyday lives. Assistive technologies, adaptive systems and context-aware applications are three well-established research fields. There is, in fact, a vast amount of literature that covers HCI-related issues in each area separately. However, the contributions in the intersection of these areas have been less visible, despite the fact the potential impact of such synergies may have on improving daily living. In this context, the workshops on "User Modeling and Adaptation for Daily Routines: Providing Assistance to People with Special and Specific Needs (UMADR)", held at UMAP'2010 and UMAP'2011, respectively, sought to increase the visibility of these challenging works. The interest generated by these two editions gave the initial impulse of this book.

The works presented in this book seek to reduce the obstacles encountered by individuals with special needs. Furthermore, they share two particular characteristics: (1) they provide assistance by means of interactive computer systems that can be adapted or adapt themselves to their current users; and (2) they focus on daily life routines rather than virtual access and interaction. We expand the definition of special needs in such a way that the reader can find works that impact on users traditionally considered with special needs, such as those with psychological or cognitive limitations, or elderly people, as well as people facing unusual routines such as health treatments.

Regardless of the application-domain, the main goal here is to be able to provide a customizable assistance to users according to their context, that is, considering their capabilities, their preferences and needs, their location, or the available resources and devices (PDAs, smart phones, laptops, etc.). Clearly, modeling user's capabilities, situations, limitations and needs is an essential task for adapting the activities to each user. Thus, this is also one of the key topics of discussion.

This book pursues a comprehensive review of state-of-the-art practices on user modeling and adaptation for people with special needs, as well as the challenges to be addressed in order to achieve their actual deployment. Therefore, the book topics include analysis, design, implementation and evaluation of adaptive systems to assist users with special needs to take decisions and fulfill daily routine activities, with special emphasis on major trends in: modeling user features, limitations and special needs; representing daily activities, including potential difficulties and decisions to be taken; designing and building adaptive assistants for daily routines; and evaluating the use of this type of assistants.

Structure of This Book

The first chapter presents a succinct review of adaptive systems related with disabled people. The reader can get an idea of the related research work in this area, extracting the main opportunities and challenges. Next, the book is structured in three parts: Models and Theories, Design, Prototyping and Implementation and Evaluation.

The first part Models and Theories focuses on modeling different features (e.g. the user's personal traits, including the affective state; the task to be done; the user's context; etc.). Sometimes, these features are well-known when the user is located at a familiar environment. However, users can do sporadic interactions in unforeseen situations. In this case, the adaptation of the activities is performed by combining previous information from the same user in other environments or by inferring the user needs taking into account the knowledge about previous interactions of similar users in the same situations. These users' features will be considered to assist them in performing daily routines, both at home and in outdoor environments. Therefore, the integration and sharing of user's models, as well as deriving conclusions about them, are key factors when users can be in different environments and use different devices.

The second part presents how to "*design, prototype and implement applications*" for people with special needs. One of the most important challenges of adaptive systems is to define the key user features to be considered for adaptation, taking into account the activity to be done and the context where the user will carry it out. The variety regarding the type and potential ranges of disabilities makes it difficult to use the term "average disabled user". Thus, it is complicated to find which features would be more appropriate to be taken into account for task personalization. The awareness of the user needs, their capabilities, and limitations is necessary for a correct interface design, as well as for assisting the user in the task accomplishment. Bearing these factors in mind during system design leads to more usable systems, whose interfaces fit the user needs better, making the time needed to learn how to interact with it shorter. On the other hand, currently, one of the most popular types of adaptive systems are recommender systems, which try to deliver information to the users according to the interests, preferences and needs of each individual at every time. Related to the scope of this book, many current research works deal with recommender systems that assist people with special needs in health-related aspects during their daily lives. In this direction, the last chapter of this part presents a review of recommender systems emphasizing the design and implementation of health recommender systems.

Adaptive applications have the potential to assist users with special needs. However, evaluating the usability of such adaptive applications tends to become very complex. The "*evaluation*" part of this book is focused on the evaluation of usability from different points of view and applications. There are several evaluation procedures and metrics oriented to non-impaired users. However, understanding the behavior of people with special needs presents its own particularities. This difference is accentuated in field studies where traditional metrics (time to complete a task, errors made, workload, etc.) may not provide useful information.

Following this direction, the first chapter of this part presents a discussion of the challenges of field evaluation with impaired populations, explained through the experience of a research study with cognitively impaired people receiving mobile assistance while travelling. The next chapter is centered in the evaluation of recommender systems, covering a variety of tried and tested methods and metrics. Following with the topic of recommender systems for health, a case study that investigates the applicability of a suite of recommender algorithms in a recipe recommender system aimed to assist individuals in planning their daily food intake is presented. Finally, a proposal for automated usability evaluation of model-based adaptive user interfaces is presented in the last chapter of this book. This approach can be used at an early stage of the developments. User interactions are simulated and evaluated by combining a user model with other user interface models from a model-based development framework, which is capable of providing different adaptation alternatives based on the user attributes and the context of use. As a result, different design alternatives and adaptation variants can be compared under equal usability evaluation criteria.

Audience

This book targets technological and social researchers interested in user modeling and adaptation for people with special needs, enterprises who want to develop personalized technological products for everybody, practitioners who are interested in applying adaptation strategies for supporting people with special needs in their daily lives and HCI-oriented Ph.D. students working on the area of user modeling and adaptation for people with special needs. In addition, this book will be useful for the academic curriculum and will hopefully stimulate new research findings to advance the knowledge of how to help people with special needs in their life by providing the best adaptation to support their usual activities.

Madrid, Spain   Estefanía Martín
August 2012   Pablo A. Haya
                                                                                      Rosa M. Carro

Acknowledgements

We would like to thank all the authors for their valuable and outstanding contributions to this book. Without their effort, this book edition would have not been possible.

We would also like to thank the reviewers, who helped us to select the chapters for this book, and offered insightful and detailed comments on the selected ones. Their constructive feedback to authors contributed to the high quality of the book through. The reviewers are:

- Ryan S.J.d. Baker, Columbia University Teachers College (United States)
- Jesús G. Boticario, Universidad Nacional a Distancia (Spain)
- Manuel Freire, Universidad Complutense de Madrid (Spain)
- Serge Garlatti, Telecom Bretagne (France)
- Simeon Keates, University of Abertay Dundee (United Kingdom)
- Tsvi Kuflik, University of Haifa (Israel)
- Alexandros Paramythis, Cyberhouse Gmbh (Austria)
- Olga C. Santos, Universidad Nacional a Distancia (Spain)
- Richard Simpson, University of Pittsburgh (United States)
- Leon Urbas, Technische Universität Dresden (Germany)
- Yang Wang, Carnegie Mellon University (United States)
- Michael V. Yudelson, Carnegie Mellon University (United States)
- Floriano Zini, Free University of Bozen-Bolzano (Italy)

We would like to acknowledge to the Project ASIES (TIN2010-17344), funded by the Spanish Ministry of Science and Innovation, which supports the participation of the guest editors in this book.

We are grateful to Beverley Ford, Helen Desmond and Ben Bishop from Springer UK for their help and support.

Finally, our special thanks to our family and friends.

Madrid, Spain
August 2012

Estefanía Martín
Pablo A. Haya
Rosa M. Carro

Contents

Part III   Evaluation

Chapter 1
Adaptation Technologies to Support Daily Living for All

Estefanía Martín, Pablo A. Haya, and Rosa M. Carro

Abstract The goal of this chapter is to bring light about how adaptation technologies can ease daily living for people with special needs. Assistive technologies, adaptive systems and context-aware applications are three well-established research areas whose findings can be interestingly merged. In particular, adaptation methods and techniques support the adaptation of existing software to better suit each user's need. In the last years, the need of building applications that allow the inclusion of people with special needs in different fields has been emphasized. Along this chapter, we present different research works that contribute to the integration of this collective, by providing means to support either their personal development or the accomplishment of their daily tasks. The technological solutions chosen for this chapter are mainly related to three areas of application: activities of daily living, health and education. This chapter also summarizes the most widely used adaptation features and processes in this context.

E. Martín (✉)
Departamento de Lenguajes y Sistemas Informáticos I, Escuela Técnica Superior en Ingeniería Informática, Universidad Rey Juan Carlos, c/Tulipán s/n, 28933 Móstoles, Madrid, Spain
e-mail: estefania.martin@urjc.es

P.A. Haya
Instituto de Ingeniería de Conocimiento, Universidad Autónoma de Madrid, Av. Francisco Tomas y Valiente, 11, 28049 Madrid, Spain
e-mail: pablo.haya@iic.uam.es

R.M. Carro
Departamento de Ingeniería Informática, Escuela Politécnica Superior, Universidad Autónoma de Madrid, Av. Francisco Tomas y Valiente, 11, 28049 Madrid, Spain
e-mail: rosa.carro@uam.es

E. Martín et al. (eds.), *User Modeling and Adaptation for Daily Routines: Providing Assistance to People with Special Needs*, Human–Computer Interaction Series, DOI 10.1007/978-1-4471-4778-7_1, © Springer-Verlag London 2013

1.1 Motivation

Human-computer interaction studies have focused, since their origins, on making systems more usable and useful, aiming at providing users with experiences that fit their background knowledge and objectives [40]. In particular, the needs of people with disabilities, as well as those of the elderly [51], have been some of the main concerns of research on human-computer interaction. Universal access has become a mainstream issue and topic for accessible computing research [89]. The main goal can be summarized as providing an accessible interaction with products, applications, and services by anyone, anywhere, and at any time [94]. Technology and user diversity involves tempting challenges that have been attracting a multidisciplinary group of people with both academic and industry background.

Designing human-computer interfaces for users with disabilities is a complex task [7]. Brajnik [10] grouped the WCAG 1.0 guidelines by their impact on specific user groups: blind, low-vision, deaf, color blind and physical handicapped users, as well as people with cognitive disabilities. Currently, practitioners can access valuable guidelines [76] and handbooks [52, 75, 92] to ensure that systems are designed targeting as many users as possible. It is worth considering that the potential user population extends beyond users with special needs to all those people showing individual or cultural differences, for instance, or those in extraordinary situations [55]. Therefore, when designing systems and interfaces for all, both special and specific needs should be addressed.

There are two main approaches to implement universal design within computer-based systems in order to fulfill the user needs. The first one consists on designing unique interfaces for all, trying to address the needs of as many collectives as possible within the same interface. On the opposite, adaptive interfaces are those dynamically generated according to each user's needs, so that the most suitable interface is built for each of them according to their particular needs or preferences, also considering the adaptation criteria specified at the design phase. User modeling [57] and adaptation techniques are critical to provide suitable solutions for all the users, including disabled people [93].

Adaptation methods and techniques contribute to adapt existing software to better suit each user's needs [11], represented in user models [12]. This implies an effort to design products and applications that can adapt to suit the broadest possible end-user population. The initial contributions of adaptive methods and techniques focused on supporting adaptive access to multimedia contents through the Internet [29, 73]. Some of the first adaptive applications, supporting adaptive contents and adaptive navigation, were Web-based educational systems, information systems, help systems and institutional information systems [11].

Adaptation methods and techniques can be used with different purposes. They can be incorporated in any application to support, for example, individualized assistance or personalized recommendations, among others. It can be provided not only through personal computers, but also through mobile devices, in different situations. Nowadays, that the development of handheld devices has quickly evolved, and the access to wireless networks is more feasible, the number of persons that use online applications through mobile devices is growing exponentially. Mobile adaptive techniques facilitate the generation of individualized application interfaces on the fly, which can be delivered through the Internet to diverse users with different devices in a great variety of situations. These applications can be related to leisure, working or learning, among others.

Adaptive systems show a great potential for users with special needs. The first system that incorporated adaptive techniques to ensure accessibility and high-quality interactions for all the potential users was AVANTI [39]. It aimed to address interaction requirements of individuals with diverse abilities, skills, needs and preferences, using Web-based multimedia applications and services. Another example is presented in Kurhila and Varjola [61]. This adaptive e-learning system provides adaptation to users with problems in mental programming (i.e., showing difficulties in organizing tasks or in figuring out problem solving strategies). Regarding social abilities, Sc@ut [46] has been used for improving social integration of people with temporary or permanent communication difficulties, specifically autistic children. More recently, adaptive applications able to assist users with limitations in different activities of their daily living have been developed. Each day, all of us are involved in many activities related to housework, study or working tasks, urban-life, and so on. Within the day, there are a lot of decisions to be taken, either in regular situations or in unexpected ones. However, while some people can take these decisions easily, this may be difficult for others (for example, for those with physical or cognitive limitations).

Computer-based training applications can help people to improve their abilities (e.g., motor, sensory, memory, reasoning, communication, social, or emotional skills among others). As a complement to this training process, personalized assistants can help them to accomplish their activities in daily life, with the aim to overcome the specific difficulties that some people may have to manage them. Some examples of expected and unexpected issues that people daily face are: indoor and outdoor navigation; information searching, reading and understanding; daily schedule and task prioritization; health and personal care; cleaning or eating habits; mathematics in daily life; tool and device manipulation; safety and security issues; working tasks; sustainable habits; or living in society.

The first task to be carried out to build adaptive systems in this context relates to the identification of the main difficulties and potential solutions for helping the users to carry out routine tasks. More specifically, the first aspect to be decided is which user attributes (capabilities, preferences, personality, cognitive limitations, motor disabilities, affective states, context, etc.) should be taken into account to assist to users in their daily routines, considering different contexts (housework, learning, work, transport, leisure, etc.). In this direction, the user features, as well as the routine tasks and contexts, must be modeled somehow to be considered by the adaptive systems. Another question to be answered is which adaptation methods and techniques are more appropriate for providing adaptive assistance in daily activities, and how adaptive assistants and systems will be implemented and evaluated. Last but not least, adaptive systems' potential trade-offs, such as privacy, proactivity or predictability should also be managed. All these represent challenging issues to be addressed in this context of adaptive assistants for daily routines.

1.2 Adaptive Systems for People with Special Needs

Regarding the domain of adaptive systems focused on people with special needs, we can classify them in three different areas: activities of daily living, health and education. Next, some research works of each area are presented, emphasizing the adaptation features to adapt the systems for each user, and how to perform the adaptation process.

1.2.1 Activities of Daily Living

Independent living is a key requirement for many people with special needs. It can represent a significant increase in their quality of life, reflected on both social and private aspects of the individual. Many research works address issues appearing in daily-living situations. According to the location where the activities take place, we can distinguish between indoor and outdoor activities.

The home environment is the place where most of the basic activities essential for an independent living are performed (ex. personal hygiene, dressing, self-feeding, etc.). Smart homes [26] are technology-enhanced environments that constitute the basic hardware and software infrastructure for assisting people in their home [5]. Building smart environments that exhibit specific forms of social interaction is the goal of Ambient Intelligence [1]. Smart environments should be able to recognize the inhabitants, and adapt themselves to their individual preferences, capabilities, behaviors [21] and context [33].The combination of Ambient Intelligence and assistive technologies is also known as Ambient Assisted Living (AAL).

Caregivers and patients alike face the challenge of making medical decisions in dynamically changing environments, using whatever resources are available at home. The rapid and constant growth of senior population has targeted many of these AAL efforts to provide services for elderly people [59, 104]. Thus, home healthcare solutions are becoming, by necessity, more prevalent [88]. In addition there is also a social dimension of AAL that empowers awareness and communication, avoiding the isolation derived from living alone [44]. This social dimension can also be complemented by means of social robots [41] that act as both companions and mediators between the user and the smart environment [28].

Regarding outdoor activities, the widespread use of smart phones has created a new opportunity to address the daily challenges faced by those with disabilities. Handheld devices combined with appropriate middleware enable ubiquitous services for universal access [2]. Specifically, mobile applications developed with an understanding of the needs of a diverse set of users can be customized individually based on specific requirements [9].

Within mobile applications, cognitive assistants are commonly chosen solutions. These systems facilitate the performance of everyday activities either by reminding the user to do any task, or by supporting the execution of a complex one, or a combination of both. Complex activities can be broken up into elementary steps that the user should execute sequentially in order to accomplish the task. However, this division poses several issues for people with cognitive impairments. They may have difficulties on remembering even simple task splitting. Additionally, something like food preparing, for instance, can be performed in multiple manners. This further complicates the decision of which is the next step to follow. With this in mind, it becomes clear that skills training, such as meal preparing, have received plenty of attention [62]. Computers and, in particular, handheld devices can be used as virtual prompters, reducing the need of external prompts from a caregiver [98]. An example of such approach is given by Davies et al. [30], reporting the use of a visual assistant that enhances self-direction of persons with cognitive disabilities in performing community-based vocational tasks. In a similar vein, Gómez et al. [49] have experimented on how adaptive manuals can be successfully used for assisting people with acquired brain injury.

However, one drawback to consider in these works along with many others [72] is the use of bespoke applications hindering personalization and reusability. A promising approach is developing end-user tools that allow caregivers to define the sequence of steps that compose a task of everyday living, and to describe the instructions that should be followed in each step. During the task accomplishment, the system guides the cognitively disabled user reproducing the instructions for each step. A notable example is MAPS (Memory Aiding Prompting System) [17], a system that consists of a multimedia editing tool and a context-responsive handheld prompter.

A successful guidance in this direction implies overcoming several problems such as detecting the beginning and ending of a task, determining whether a step has been correctly accomplished, and deciding whether the user can finish the task even skipping some intermediary steps. There are no restrictions to suit a task sequence for each user, although caregivers may find it cumbersome when the number of users and/or tasks is high. A more challenging approach is allowing the caregiver to define a canonical task division, and the system intelligently adapts the sequence of steps to the user abilities and context.

One immediate issue arising from the need of delivering personalized instructions deals with selecting the correct mode to interact with each user. This is particularly important in both indoor [97] and outdoor [50, 85] wayfinding applications. The most common alternatives are audio, video, pictures or text. There are several studies focused on testing which interaction mode is more suitable for people with cognitive disabilities. The results are varied. Fickas et al. [38] studied different modes of prompting in route-following assistance, and reported that travelers with cognitive impairment performed best when given prompts via speech-based audio instructions. Likewise, GUIDE tested an auditory-verbal interface that simulates normal conversational prompting using voice recognition with positive results [77]. However, in González et al. [50] the visual interface worked better, in general, than the audio one when guiding a group of cognitively limited users through a university campus, with the aim to find out which type of interface better suits each user needs in relation to the scores obtained by them in different parts of the WAIS test (e.g., verbal or manipulative abilities). Chang and Wang [23] experimentally compared video and picture prompts reporting that travelers performed better using video prompts than audio ones but feeling slightly more rushed. Finally, Liu et al. [65] used a Wizard-of-Oz technique for testing three different modalities (images, audio, and text) of prompting directions. In this case, the three modalities were tested by all the users. They did not find a modality that was preferred over the others. On the contrary, they highlight that the difference on performances and preferences were due to individual differences rather than to the modality. All of these findings indicate the high variability on user preferences, and in turn, the necessity of incorporating personalization mechanism in this kind of systems. This variability is accentuated if the users are physically disabled. To mitigate this heterogeneity problem, one possible approach is to support a multimodal interaction [16].

Other relevant aspect to take into account is the autonomy and independence necessarily to entail the access to a job. For many people with disabilities, commuting can be a major issue that, at the end, may constitute a great barrier for their integration into the working world. Likewise, the difficulties to use public transport may also affect to their spare time [25]. Many of the studies and systems presented are part of wayfinding applications. These works focus on how the presentation of route information can be adapted to the user. Another important part that may require adaptation is the route calculation [3, 81], since the shortest path is not always the most suitable one. For instance, a user with motor disabilities should avoid a transit using an underground station if the premises are not accessible.

To conclude, user modeling and personalization techniques are critical research areas in the creation of these socio-technical environments that support daily living activities [18]. The outcome of this research produces theories and models about user behavior and needs in everyday life that, in turn, become an essential part of the adaptive systems. Nonetheless, despite the variety and quality of the aforementioned works and many others [47], it is also clear that there is still a significant need for upstream research in this field. As LoPresti et al. [68] summarized in their review of assistive technology for cognitive rehabilitation, there is still very little knowledge about the relationship between the clinical characteristics and the most suitable interventions. Similarly, de Joode et al. [34] call for "*matching user demands and suitable technology to optimize the therapeutic effect*". An emerging field of research that can benefit the realization of accurate user models is the automatic evaluation of adaptive applications at runtime [83]. This technique is based on evaluating the feasibility of different adaptation alternatives by means of the combining different user models and adaptation paths in a simulation.

1.2.2 Health

Adaptive systems have been applied successfully in medicine to inform patients about their conditions, to enable them to take decisions or to persuade them to be compliant with care plans. Different diseases such as diabetes [6], cardiovascular disease [31], and cancer [22] have been addressed by these systems. Depending on the target users of each health adaptive systems, they can be classified in two different types: recommender systems for doctors, nurses and caregivers; or adaptive systems to recommend treatments to people with specific diseases.

The goal of adaptive systems for health professionals is to provide personalized information to them according to the features and needs of their patients. Owing to the diversity of disabilities and features to be taken into account in each of them, building user models for these systems is complex.

The user model for this type of systems usually stores information related to the user personal data, personal health records, diagnoses or allergies. For example, PULSE [31] and PIGLIT [22] combine information from personal health records with adaptive Web-based presentation techniques to provide personalized learning materials. However, with the goal to provide personalized health recommendations concerning disabled people, adaptive systems need detailed and exhaustive user models and clinical guides that take in mind the specific aspects of many existing disabilities. In order to model the information managed by these systems, international terminologies and classifications are used to aid the users on what they ask for. One option for building user models for these systems is using the "*International Classification of Functioning, Disability and Health*" (ICF) established by the World Health Organization, which organizes health domains [104]. This classification includes aspects related to body functions (e.g. mental functions, sensory functions), structure (e.g. nervous system, eye), and social features such as communication, interaction or interpersonal interaction, among others. Furthermore, general documents about safety response, concerning the disabled, knowledge provided by expert health professionals or knowledge acquired from the associations of disabled people, can be used with the aim to extract basic rules about how to communicate and behave with disabled people such as blind, deaf, or mute people, and how to transport motor-impaired persons in emergency situations such as fires. Chittaro et al. developed an adaptive system whose user model combine personal information, personal health records, allergies, diagnoses, ICT features and expert health knowledge [24].

Some examples of adaptive systems that support personalized information and diagnosis are PRESYDIUM [24], EMSAVE [15] or DMSS-R [64], among others. The two first systems are focused on the domain of emergency medical assistance for disabled people. PRESYDIUM (*Personalized Emergency System for Disabled Humans*) is an adaptive information Web-based system that provides tailored operating instructions in the field, for helping medical first responders. In addition, this system allows health professionals, the disabled people themselves, and their families to accessing and managing personal medical profiles. The personalized instructions are provided thanks to the detailed patient model along with the expert medical knowledge basis. EMSAVE (*Emergency Medical Services for the disAbled Virtual Environment*) is a virtual reality system for training users in emergency medical procedures concerning disabled persons. In a first stage, this system does not contain adaptation. However, the authors are working to include adaptive modules that can automatically generate scenarios starting from the guidelines for the different disabilities. Moreover, the adaptive modules will suggest the procedures and disabilities with worst results so that the learner works on them. Finally, DMSS-R is a revised version of DMSS (*Dementia Management Support System*) [63] that supports clinical routines and reasoning processes as performed by individual health professionals in daily practice when they suspect cases of dementia. Data related to the user profile, activities used in the diagnosis process, expert knowledge about the types of dementia, and the interventions associated with each type of patient are managed by the system. The adaptation process is supported by a rule-based mechanism with structures and ontologies based on formal argumentation theories and activity theoretical analyses of clinical practices.

Regarding the adaptive systems intended to recommend treatments to people with specific diseases (e.g. diabetes, asthma, cancer) or to help to improve eating habits, different techniques are used in order to suggest items for specific users [67]. In the health domain, the most popular techniques are content-based filtering to recommend items similar to others, collaborative filtering, which considers the success of the recommendations previously made to users with similar interests, or hybrid approaches, combining these or other recommendation techniques [14]. Depending on the target user, it could be interesting to use certain techniques. Content-based filtering can be appropriated for people with chronic diseases such as diabetics or celiacs, since the recommended items will be similar or even the same. However, if the system tries to recommend different healthy products, not oriented to chronic patients, collaborative filtering could be a better option, since recommendations are more diverse in this case.

Some examples of recommender systems for people under treatments or for those hoping to improve healthy habits can be found in López Nores et al. [67] and De Rosis et al. [35], respectively. López Norés et al. present iCabiNET, whose goal is to promote medication adherence in contexts of daily life [66]. This system combines information about the user's prescription from personal electronic health records and his context. When the user is located at home, the user context can be obtained in two different ways: (a) automatically, with sensors-enhanced medicine containers that monitor whether the user has taken the medicines or (b) manually, when the user must annotate by him when he takes the drugs. When the user is outside, the system uses GPS technology and mobile devices. Once the system knows the required information, in the case that the user did not take his medicines, it generates issue warnings (e.g. reminder: you must take the pill for the diabetes) or provides alerts if the context of the user could be in conflict with the medicines he is taking (e.g. do not take alcohol in a restaurant if you have taken antibiotic). De Rosis et al. present the use of an embodied conversational agent in order to change dietary behaviors [35]. Many governments have made advertisements and efforts to encourage people to eat healthy (e.g. the consumption of fruits and vegetables play a key role in cancers, reduce the risk for heart disease and hypertension, or prevent the obesity [8, 103]). By understanding the food preferences and assisting users to plan a healthy and appealing meal, it is aimed to reduce the effort required from users to change their diet [42]. The system presented by De Rosis et al. focuses on recognizing the user mental state and providing healthy recommendations by adapting the dialog between the user and an agent accordingly. The information required to perform the adaptation is stored in the user and agent models. Depending on the user state, the agent's emotional reaction will be different. The system tries to detect whether the user behavior is right or wrong, the intention of the user to change non-appropriated behaviors, whether the internal and external conditions favor the change of this behavior, the user knowledge related to the dietary plan, and the level of achievement in following the healthy plan. When a wrong behavior is detected, the agent tries to persuade the user in order to change his eating habits. It suggests a personalized plan and offers support during its execution.

1.2.3 Education

Computer-based educational applications have shown to be a useful complement for learning since their creation. Internet brought the possibility of deploying Web-based educational applications to be spread all over the world. The development of collaboration technologies allowed the implementation of collaborative and cooperative learning environments too. There is a wide range of educational applications to support different theories and methodologies of teaching and learning.

On one hand, and focusing on users with special needs, technology offers them new opportunities to learn, share information and gain independence [87]. On the other hand, adaptation methods and techniques can be incorporated within learning applications to build enhanced learning environments that better suit each user needs [11]. Adaptive hypermedia has been widely used to support personalized learning. Web-based adaptive environments allow individualized learning, so that each user receives the instruction in the most suitable way according to his particular needs or preferences [13, 20, 32]. In addition, adaptation has been used to propose different collaborative activities to groups of users [19, 45]. Later, pervasive and ubiquitous computing has changed the ways that we will learn throughout our lives [54]. Students can access to digital learning contents using different devices from anywhere. Therefore, one of the key aspects is to allow learning to students on their own pace independently of the physical place and the device used. Some examples of mobile learning adaptive systems can be found in [27, 100] and [70]. Finally, with the peak of social networks, the social learning environments offer new opportunities to students. These environments must support the learner finds the right content, the student connect with the right people and increasing the motivation for learning [99].

According to Brusilovsky and Millán [12], the most popular features modeled and used by adaptive Web systems are the user knowledge, interests, goals, background, individual traits, and context of work. Specifically, the user's knowledge of the subject being taught and the users' individual traits (e.g. learning styles, cognitive factors, personality, emotional state, etc.) appear to be the most important user features in the context of adaptive learning environments, although other features can be included in the user model as well. For example, the user context (e.g. device used, physical place, environmental noise, etc.) is an interesting feature to consider when individuals use mobile devices [70]. All this information about the users must be captured and stored in the user model. The most traditional approach consists of using questionnaires [37, 53], more recently shortened adaptively according to the user answers [78]. Other approaches deal with inferring the user features from his actions. For example, information about the user learning style can be extracted from his interactions within the learning environment itself [91, 101]; data of his personality can be inferred from his interactions within social networks [48, 79]; and information about the user emotional state can be obtained by analyzing his writings through natural language processing techniques [71, 80]. All these features are relevant for adapting the systems to the users. In particular, recent research has pointed out the fundamental role that emotions play in human behavior. The emotional state of a user at a certain time can influence the way in which he interacts with the systems, as well as his particular needs at that time. According to the experts on cognitively impaired people training, one of the main limitations of this population relates to emotion identification and control. Therefore, providing them assistance adapted to their emotional state is crucial.

When the potential users of a system are people with special needs, some additional considerations must be done in order to provide effective adaptation. On the one hand, when users have physical disabilities (e.g. visual impairment, motor dysfunction or hearing impairment), the system interface, as well as the contents delivered, must be adapted to the user capabilities. Some examples deal with supporting voice recognition for users with limited mobility [82, 84]; text-to-speech [60] or haptic interfaces [95] for blind users; or changing the audio material for textual transcriptions for deaf users [58]. On the other hand, usually, users with cognitive disabilities have deficits or difficulties with memory, literacy skills, attention and problem solving [90], and often visual or motor impairments. People with cognitive limitations have troubles to comprehend and to perceive the environment. They have difficulties with the processes of learning acquisition and consolidation. For this reason, some activities, such as problem solving, should be contextualized to help learners to extrapolate knowledge to real situations. Furthermore, new concepts must be presented in a repeated and flexible way in order to facilitate their assimilation. Finally, they can feel frustrated and disoriented if the activities are monotonous or if their level of difficulty is higher than their capabilities to solve them. Therefore, unnecessary items should be deleted from the learning environment, and the difficulty of the tasks must be adapted to their knowledge and capabilities. Keates et al. [56] address the impact that cognitive and learning difficulties have on the user's ability to interact with information technology systems. Some guidelines related to the design of activities for cognitively disabled people can be found in [4] and [43]. In the context of educational environments for people with special needs, there exist two main types of systems: (a) flexible educational systems based on previous adaptation engines that include some accessibility facilities, and (b) ad-hoc adaptive applications, whose goal is domain-specific and are oriented to a specific disability.

e-Adventure [96] is a prototypical example of an adaptive educational learning environment that supports accessibility. Their authors have introduced recently interaction profiles for different stereotypes of users: unknown disabilities, limited vision, blindness, and reduced mobility. eAdventure includes a game adaptation engine that can modify the game experience according to the user profile [74]. If the user has limited vision, the graphical user interface is adapted, enabling a high contrast mode. Users with limited mobility will use the voice interface, and blind people use both voice and keyboard interface. Furthermore, e-Adventure also provides some support for people with cognitive disabilities (e.g. removing educational contents that are too challenging). Other example of adaptive learning system that considers some accessible capabilities was presented by Roldán et al. [86]. They show how to adapt individual and collaborative activities in inclusive learning environments using multitouch tabletops. The adaptation mechanism takes into account both personal user's information and collaborative aspects. The personal features are stored in the user model, which comprises both static information (e.g. background information, previous experience, motor functionality, visual impairments or index scores representing the major components of intelligence [102], etc.) and dynamic information (e.g. physical location of the users, activities performed, results obtained, etc.). The adaptation is based on a recommendation mechanism previously developed for adaptive mobile learning systems [70]. For disabled users, the adaptation mechanism allows to define the adaptation of both content visualization (e.g. multimedia elements will be enlarged if the user has visual impairments) and interaction modes (e.g. in pair-matching activities, gestures such as drag-and-drop can be simplified by clicking in the source and destination elements). Furthermore, the adaptation of collaborative activities is necessary when users are working together for solving them. In this work, an aggregation policy determines how group features are obtained as a combination of the individual ones and how they affect to the adaptation.

On the other hand, there are some adaptive ad-hoc training applications oriented to disabled users, more specifically, to cognitive disabled people. One example is the game "The big party", whose goal is to promote the development of social skills and personal autonomy for people with intellectual disabilities (e.g. Down syndrome) [36]. This game was developed within the eduWAI platform, which includes Moodle 2.0 for managing the educational courses. The game trains users for a social event organized by the company where they are working. To complete the game, the student must achieve five different goals related to personal hygiene, clothing, etiquette principles, principles of good behavior, and use of common resources. Each goal is split in a set of sub-objectives, each of them mapped to an assessment rule. Educators of these students can provide different levels of information in order to give the most suitable feedback to students. The student gender is used to adapt the game regarding the clothes and the hygienic items to be shown. Some students' interactions can modify the flow of the game depending on the achievement of the objectives. Figure 1.1 shows a screenshot from this game when the student is working on personal hygiene. Clicking in each item of the bathroom, the student can learn the functionality of each item.

Fig. 1.1 Screenshot of "The big party" game

The second example was presented by Martín et al. [69]. This game is focused on learning how to travel within the Madrid underground network. Users are trained to achieve simple tasks regarding travel planning. They can also learn to plan more efficient and effective trips. Furthermore, their decision making ability is expected to improve by interacting with the game when unexpected situations are simulated (e.g. there is a breakdown in a certain line). Activities of different complexity are proposed to distinct types of users, taking into account issues such as the trip duration or the number of stations and transfers involved. The game adapts the learning tasks to the users' personal abilities and needs, especially considering their cognitive disabilities and their progress during the game. The game adaptation is performed by means of a rule-based mechanism. Figure 1.2 shows two screenshots from different levels of this game.

1.3 Discussion

The collective of users with special needs embraces people under treatment (e.g. chronic patients), people with physical impairments, and cognitive disabled people, including the elderly. Depending on the user type of need, different adaptive support may be needed.

People under treatment, with no physical or cognitive impairment, can receive the corresponding instructions according to their disease and treatment. However,

Fig. 1.2 Game for trip planning and decision-making using Madrid underground

the adaptation of either the language used in these instructions or the navigational guidance is not required in this case, since they should be able to understand the instructions and follow them.

In the case of people with physical impairments, adaptive systems should provide different accessible user interfaces according to the user capabilities (e.g. text-to-speech for blind users). Furthermore, additional help can be incorporated (e.g. shortcuts to the most popular actions for expert users and blind people, sounds to enhance feedback for people with motor impairments or blind users, high contrast or option to enlarge elements for users with limited vision, and so on).

The adaptation process for cognitively disabled people is more complex, as they may also have some physical difficulties. Focusing on the cognitive limitations, the navigational guidance should be direct, so that the information is provided step by step. The user knowledge and skills are other key factors to consider, since these users may get very frustrated if they find a task excessively difficult for them, and may feel bored and unmotivated if it is too easy. The suitability of a system for this collective depends not only on the success of the content adaptation and the navigational guidance, but also on content clarity and simplicity.

Regarding the application fields, most of them center on supporting the users' personal autonomy in their daily life. In the previous section, adaptive applications dealing with activities of daily living, health and education have been presented. In these approaches, user limitations (physical impairment, cognitive disability and people under treatment) have been considered in different ways. On the one hand, both physical impairments and cognitive disabilities have been tackled in diverse research works dealing with providing adaptation for activities of daily living. Adaptive applications for cognitively disabled people to improve their personal autonomy through educational games or trainers have been developed (e.g., those related to hygiene, clothes, good behavior, travelling planning or decision-making). Finally, most of the adaptive solutions intended for chronic patients or people with eating disorders are implemented as recommender systems for healthy habits. Next, we summarize the most widely used adaptation features and processes for each area presented in the previous section.

In the context of activities of daily living, adaptation requirements can be found in two levels. First, the presentation of information appears as a main concern independently of the application domain. On one hand, visual and hearing impairments limit the election of the interaction mode, yet it should be adjusted according to the grade of disability. On the other hand, people with cognitive impairments have access to a broader range of interaction modes. However, there is less agreement than what it might be expected regarding which is the best manner to present the information. These results suggest that adaptive techniques should occupy a prominent role on assistive technologies for people with cognitive disabilities. Second, task sequencing allows the variation of the number of steps that must be given to accomplish a task, as well as of the order in which these steps must be executed. Some steps can be skipped as the user gains proficiency with the task, or depending on the user's background and grade of disability.

Related to health systems, nowadays people are getting more and more concerned about the importance of both their health and following healthy habits. A well-balanced diet contributes to reduce the probability of serious illnesses such as a heart disease as well as to prevent obesity. Owing to this fact, the number of health-related recommenders has increased during the last years. The goals of these systems can be summarize as: (a) informing the patients about their conditions, enabling them to take decisions and persuading them to be compliant with care and health plans; and (b) providing personalized information to physicians depending on each patient in order to help them within clinical routines, reasoning processes or training in emergency situations, especially when they are interacting with different types of disabled people.

Building user models for these recommender systems is complex, due to the diversity of disabilities and features to be taken into account for providing appropriate diagnosis, treatments, care and health plans. International standards, terminologies and classifications are required to share information between physicians from different countries. To support personalized recommendations, a detailed user model including user general data, personal health records, diagnosis, allergies, and prescriptions, is required. Recent research works incorporate the user physical location or his mental state to the user model. Apart from this model, recommender systems require an exhaustive domain model to describe the different illnesses, diagnostics or interventions, in order to provide the most appropriated treatments or plans in each case. Domain models can be built from the knowledge of health experts and professionals or even from that of the associations for disabled people. Finally, different recommendation algorithms and techniques, such as rule-based mechanisms, ontologies, Bayesian networks, recommendation algorithms or inference mechanisms, are used by health recommender systems. Since chronic patients, disabled people and people with eating disorders need different types of recommendations, the most suitable algorithms, techniques or hybrid approaches are used in each case.

Regarding educational systems, although many of them are not specifically designed for people with cognitive limitations, they use powerful adaptation engines that, sometimes, receive as input the course to be delivered, the types of users to which it is intended, and the adaptation criteria. This fact allows using these systems for training users with cognitive limitations, converting them into accessible and adaptive applications for this collective. In this case, the user models store the type of disabilities to be considered. In addition, the corresponding adaptation criteria must be specified to adapt both the contents and the training tasks to be presented at each time to each user.

On the one hand, contents should be adapted for each specific disability. In order to support content adaptation to diverse physical disabilities, the information should be available in different formats (e.g. audio for blind users or text for deaf people) and appropriated interfaces must be available to allow human-computer interaction (e.g. voice recognition should be supported for users with limited mobility). The designers of contents for people with cognitive disabilities should pay attention to: (i) the specific language used within the activity instructions, guarantying that it is clear and easy to read, (ii) the multimedia material used to present the information in a visual way, rather than using texts, and the possibility of combining different material formats to help users to process the information, (iii) the context of the activity in real situations, to facilitate knowledge transference and concept abstraction, and (iv) the difficulty of the activity, which must fit the knowledge and capabilities of the user, to avoid frustration when big challenges are proposed and to avoid user boredom when the task is too easy.

On the other hand, adaptive navigational guidance will lead each user with cognitive limitations to the most suitable training tasks to be accomplished at each time. For these users, the guidance between activities should be direct, and unnecessary elements must be removed from the interface, so that they do not lose the attention focus. Furthermore, repeating the same tasks several times under different variants using different information contributes to concept assimilation.

1.4 Conclusions

The goal of this chapter has been to show how adaptive methods and techniques can benefit people with special needs in their everyday lives. Assistive technologies, adaptive systems and context-aware applications are three well-established research fields. In the last years, the research community has emphasized the need of building applications that allow the inclusion of people with special needs in different fields. Furthermore, some adaptive systems targeting at this collective start to emerge, combining the previous knowledge from two main areas: human computer interaction, and adaptive and recommender systems. Along this chapter, some examples of adaptive systems focusing on people with special needs have been presented. Interdisciplinary researchers join efforts in all the works presented, with the goal of creating adaptive systems that fit these user needs.

Next, the following chapters of this book present a comprehensive review of state-of-the-art practices on user modeling and adaptation for people with special needs, and bring up the challenges to be addressed in order to achieve useful and usable environments. The book topics include analysis, design, implementation and evaluation of adaptive systems to assist users with special needs to take decisions and fulfill daily routine activities, with special emphasis on major trends in: modeling user features, limitations and special needs; representing daily activities, including potential difficulties and decisions to be taken; designing and building adaptive assistants for daily routines; and evaluating the use of this type of assistants.

The book is structured in three parts: "Models and Theories", "Design, Proto-typing and Implementation" and "Evaluation". In every part, current trends and solutions in each of these directions are presented. Furthermore, it is discussed whether the knowledge from previous research, including existing models and technologies, are useful for these target users or, otherwise, new models, methods or techniques should be developed in order to provide adaptation to this collective.

We expect that the contributions presented in this book bring light about how adaptation technologies can ease daily living for all, and promote the research in this direction to support sustainable high-quality healthcare, demographic ageing and social/economic inclusion.

Acknowledgments This work has been funded by the Spanish Government (ASIES project – Ministerio de Ciencia e Innovación, TIN2010-17344) and by Comunidad Autónoma de Madrid, project E-Madrid (S2009/TIC-1650).

References

1. Aarts E, de Ruyter B (2009) New research perspectives on Ambient Intelligence. J Ambient Intell Smart Environ 1(1):5–14
2. Ahmed S, Sharmin M, Ahamed SI (2008) Ubi-App a ubiquitous application for universal access from handheld devices. Univers Access Info Soc 7(4):273–283
3. Anglés-Alcazar L, Haya PA, Carro R (2010) WAI-ROUTES: a route-estimator system for aiming public transportation users with cognitive impairments. In: Proceedings of the sixth IASTED international conference advances in computer science and engineering (ACSE 2010), Sharm El-Sheikh, 15–17 March, pp 167–174
4. Aubrey C, Dahl S (2008) A review of the evidence on the use of ICT in the early years foundation stage. Early Childhood Research Unit, Institute of Education, University of Warwick
5. Augusto JC (2012) Smart homes as a vehicle for AAL. In: Augusto JC, Huch M, Kameas A, Maitland J, McCullagh P, Roberts J, Sixsmith A, Wichert R (eds) Handbook of ambient assisted living – technology for healthcare, rehabilitation and well-being. IOS Press BV, Amsterdam, Netherlands, pp 387–388
6. Binsted K, Cawsey A, Jones RB (1995) Generating personalised information using the medical record. In: Wyatt JC, Stefanelli M, Barahona P (eds) Lecture notes in computer science, vol 934. Springer, Heidelberg, pp 29–41
7. Biswas P, Robinson P (2008) Modelling user interfaces for special needs. Accessible Design in the Digital World (ADDW) 2008, York
8. Blanck HM, Gillespie C, Kimmons JE, Seymour JD, Serdula MK (2008) Trends in fruit and vegetable consumption among U.S. men and women, 1994–2005. Prev Chronic Dis 5(2):A35
9. Boisvert A, Paquette L, Pigot H, Giroux S (2009) Design challenges for mobile assistive technologies applied to people with cognitive impairments. In: Mokhtari M, Khalil I, Bauchet

J, Zhang D, Nugent C (eds) Proceedings of the 7th international conference on smart homes and health telematics: ambient assistive health and wellness management in the heart of the City (ICOST '09). Springer, Berlin/Heidelberg, pp 17–24

10. Brajnik G (2006) Web accessibility testing: when the method is the culprit. In: Miesenberger K, Klaus J, Zagler W, Karshmer A (eds) Computers helping people with special needs. Lecture notes in computer science, vol 4061. Springer, Berlin/Heidelberg, pp 156–163

11. Brusilovsky P (2001) Adaptive hypermedia. In: Kobsa A (ed) User modeling and user adapted interaction. Ten Year Anniversary Issue 11 (1/2):87–110

12. Brusilovsky P, Millán E (2007) User models for adaptive hypermedia and adaptive educational systems. In: The adaptive web: methods and strategies of personalization. Lecture notes in computer science, vol 4321. Springer, Berlin/Heidelberg, pp 3–53

13. Brusilovsky P, Schwarz EW, Weber G (1996) ELM-ART: an intelligent tutoring system on world wide web. In: Intelligent tutoring systems. Lecture notes in computer science, vol 1086. Springer, Berlin, pp 261–269

14. Burke R (2002) Hybrid recommender systems: survey and experiments. User Model User Adapt Interact 12(4):331–370, Kluwer Academic Publisher

15. Cabas Vidani A, Chittaro L (2009) Using a task modeling formalism in the design of serious games for emergency medical procedures. In: Proceedings of VS-GAMES'09: IEEE first international conference on games and virtual Worlds for Serious Applications. IEEE Computer Society Press, Los Alamitos, pp 95–102

16. Carbonell N (2006) Ambient multimodality: towards advancing computer accessibility and assisted living. Univers Access Info Soc 5(1):96–104

17. Carmien S (2005) End user programming and context responsiveness in handheld prompting systems for persons with cognitive disabilities and caregivers. In: Proceedings of ACM conference on computer-human interaction. Portland, pp 1252–1255

18. Carmien S, Dawe M, Fischer G, Gorman A, Kintsch A, Sullivan JF (2005) Socio-technical environments supporting people with cognitive disabilities using public transportation. ACM Trans Comput Hum Interact 12(2):233–262

19. Carro RM, Ortigosa A, Martín E, Schlichter J (2003) Dynamic generation of adaptive web-based collaborative courses. In: Decouchant D, Favela J (eds) Groupware: design, implementation and use. Lecture notes in computer science, vol 2806. Springer, Berlin/Heidelberg, pp 191–198

20. Carro RM, Pulido E, Rodríguez P (1999) Dynamic generation of adaptive internet-based courses. J Netw Comput Appl 22:249–257, Academic Press

21. Casas R, Blasco R, Robinet A, Roy A, Yarza A, Mcginn J, Picking R, Grout V (2008) User modelling in ambient intelligence for elderly and disabled people. In: Miesenberger K, Klaus J, Zagler W, Karshmer A (eds) Proceedings of the 11th international conference on Computers Helping People with Special Needs (ICCHP '08). Springer, Berlin/Heidelberg, pp 114–122

22. Cawsey A, Jones RB, Pearson J (2001) The evaluation of a personalized health information system for patients with cancer. User Model User Adapt Interact 10(1):47–72

23. Chang YJ, Wang TY (2010) Comparing picture and video prompting in autonomous indoor wayfinding for individuals with cognitive impairments. Pers Ubiquitous Comput 14(8): 737–747

24. Chittaro L, Carchietti E, De Marco L, Zampa A (2011) Personalized emergency medical assistance for disabled people. User Model User Adapt Interact 21(4):407–440

25. Consolvo S, Roessler P, Shelton B, Lamarca A, Schilit B, Bly S (2004) Technology for care networks of elders. IEEE Pervasive Comput 3(2):22–29

26. Cook DJ, Das SK (2005) Smart environments: technologies, protocols, and applications. Wiley, New Jersey

27. Corlett D, Sharples M, Bull S, Chan T (2005) Evaluation of a mobile learning organiser for university students. J Comput Assist Learn 21(3):162–170

28. Cozzolongo G, De Carolis B, Pizzutilo S (2007) Social robots as mediators between users and smart environments. In: Proceedings of the 12th international conference on intelligent user interfaces (IUI '07). ACM, New York, pp 353–356

29. Cremers A, Neerincx M (2004) Personalisation meets accessibility: towards the design of individual user interfaces for all. In: Stary C, Stephanidis C (eds) User-centered interaction paradigms for universal access in the information society. Lecture notes in computer science, vol 3196. Springer, Berlin/Heidelberg, pp 119–124
30. Davies D, Stock S, Wehmeyer M (2002) Enhancing independent task performance for individuals with mental retardation through use of a handheld self-directed visual and audio prompting system. Educ Train Ment Retard Dev Disabil 37(2):209–218
31. Davis S, Abidi SSR (2006) Adaptive patient education framework featuring personalized cardiovascular risk management interventions. In: Wade VP, Ashman H, Smyth B (eds) Proceedings of adaptive hypermedia 2006. Lecture notes in computer science, vol 4018. Springer, Heidelberg, pp 264–268
32. De Bra P, Aerts A, Berden B, De Lange B, Rousseau B, Santic T, Smits D, Stash N (2003) AHA! The adaptive hypermedia architecture. In: Proceedings of the 14th ACM conference on hypertext and hypermedia. ACM Press, New York, pp 81–84
33. De Carolis B (2005) Adapting home behavior to its inhabitants. In: Ardissono L, Brna P, Mitrovic A (eds) Proceedings of the 10th international conference on User Modeling (UM'05), Springer, Berlin/Heidelberg, pp 282–286
34. De Joode E, van Heugten C, Verhey F, van Boxtel M (2010) Efficacy and usability of assistive technology for patients with cognitive deficits: a systematic review. Clin Rehabil 24:701–714
35. De Rosis F, Novielli N, Carofiglio V, Cavalluzzi A, De Carolis B (2006) User modeling and adaptation in health promotion dialogs with an animated character. J Biomed Inform 39: 514–531
36. Del Blanco A, Torrente J, Moreno-Ger P, Fernández-Manjón B (2011) Enhancing adaptive learning and assessment in virtual learning environments with educational games. In: Jin Q (ed) IJDET – intelligent learning systems and advancements in computer-aided instruction: emerging studies. IGI Global, Hershey, Pennsylvania, USA, pp 144–163
37. Felder RM (1996) Matters of style. ASEE Prism 6(4):18–23
38. Fickas S, Sohlberg M, Hung P (2008) Route-following assistance for travelers with cognitive impairments: a comparison of four prompt modes. Int J Hum Comput Stud 66(12):876–888
39. Fink J, Kobsa A, Nill A (1998) Adaptable and adaptive information provision for all users, including disabled and elderly people. New Rev Hypermedia Multimed 4(1):163–188
40. Fischer G (2001) User modeling in human-computer interaction. User Model User Adapt Interact 11(1–2):65–86
41. Fong T, Nourbakhsh I, Dautenhahn K (2003) A survey of socially interactive robots. Robot Autonom Syst 42(3–4):143–166
42. Freyne J, Berkovsky S (2010) Recommending food: reasoning on recipes and ingredients. In: De Bra P, Kobsa A,Chin D (eds) Proceedings of the 18th international conference on user modeling, adaptation, and personalization. Lecture notes in computer science, vol 6075. Springer, Berlin/Heidelberg, pp 381–386
43. Friedman MG, Nelson BD (2007) Web accessibility design recommendations for people with cognitive disabilities. Technol Disabil 19(4):205–212, IOS Press
44. García-Herranz M, Olivera F, Haya PA, Alamán X (2012) Harnessing the interaction continuum for subtle assisted living. Sensors 12(7):9829–9846
45. Gaudioso E, Boticario JG (2002) Supporting personalization in virtual communities in distance education. Ser Innov Intell 1:327–362, World Scientific
46. Gea-Megías M, Medina-Medina N, Rodríguez-Almendros ML, Rodríguez-Fórtiz MJ (2004) Sc@ut: platform for communication in ubiquitous and adaptive environments applied for children with Autism, User-centered interaction paradigms for universal access in the information society. Springer, Berlin/Heidelberg, pp 50–67
47. Gillespie A, Best C, O'Neill B (2012) Cognitive function and assistive technology for cognition: a systematic review. J Int Neuropsychol Soc 18:1–19
48. Golbeck J, Robles C, Turner K (2011) Predicting personality with social media. In: Proceedings of the conference on human factors in computing systems (CHI). Vancouver, 7–12 May 2011, pp 253–262

49. Gómez J, Montoro G, Haya PA, Alamán X, Alves S, Martínez M (2012) Adaptive manuals as assistive technology to support and train people with acquired brain injury in their daily life activities. Personal and ubiquitous computing. Springer, London
50. González A, Carro RM, Haya PA (2012) Where should I go? Guiding users with cognitive limitations through mobile devices outdoors. In: Proceedings of the international conference Interaccion 2012. Elche
51. Gregor P, Newell AF, Zajicek M (2002) Designing for dynamic diversity: interfaces for older people. In: Proceedings of the fifth international ACM conference on assistive technologies (Assets '02). ACM, New York, pp 151–156
52. Helal A, Mokhtari M, Abdulrazak B (2008) The engineering handbook of smart technology for aging, disability and independence. John Wiley & Sons Inc., Hoboken, New Jersey, USA
53. Kaufman AS, Lichtenberger E (2006) Assessing adolescent and adult intelligence, 3rd edn. Wiley, Hoboken
54. Kay J (2008) Lifelong learner modeling for lifelong personalized pervasive learning. IEEE Trans Learn Technol 1(4):215–228, IEEE Computer Society Press Los Alamitos, CA, USA
55. Keates S (2009) Inclusive design for ordinary users in extraordinary circumstances. In: Proceedings of 5th international conference on universal access in HCI. San Diego, pp 525–534
56. Keates S, Adams R, Bodine C, Czaja S, Gordon W, Gregor P, Hacker E, Hanson V, Kemp J, Laff M, Lewis C, Pieper M, Richards J, Rose D, Savidis A, Schultz G, Snayd P, Trewin S, Varker P (2007) Cognitive and learning difficulties and how they affect access to IT systems. Univers Access Inf Soc 5(4):329–339
57. Keates S, Langdon P, Clarkson PJ, Robinson P (2002) User models and user physical capability. User Model User Adapt Interact 12(2–3):139–169
58. Kheir R, Way T (2007) Inclusion of deaf students in computer science classes using real-time speech transcription. In: Proceedings of the 12th annual SIGCSE conference on innovation and technology in computer science education. ACM, New York, pp 261–265
59. Kleinberger T, Becker M, Ras E, Holzinger A, Müller P (2007) Ambient intelligence in assisted living: enable elderly people to handle future interfaces. In: Stephanidis C (ed) Proceedings of the 4th international conference on universal access in human-computer interaction: ambient interaction. Springer, Berlin/Heidelberg, pp 103–112
60. Konecki M, Lovrencic A, Kudelic R (2011) Making programming accessible to the blinds. In: Proceedings of the 34th international convention. Croatian society for information and communication technology, electronics and microelectronics – MIPRO, Croatia, pp 820–824
61. Kurhila J, Varjola H (2002) Using adaptive hypermedia to evaluate basic arithmetic skills in special education. In: Proceedings of the 8th international conference on computers helping people with special needs table of contents. Lecture notes in computer science, vol 2398. Springer, London, pp 98–106
62. Lancioni GE, O'Reilly MF (2002) Teaching food preparation skills to people with intellectual disabilities: a literature overview. J Appl Res Intellect Disabil 15(3):236–253
63. Lindgren H (2007) Decision support in dementia care: developing systems for interactive reasoning. Thesis, computer science, Umeå University, UMINF, 07.02 (2007). http://urn.kb.se/resolve?urn=urn:nbn:se:umu:diva-1138. Last access Aug 2012
64. Lindgren H (2011) Towards personalized decision support in the dementia domain based on clinical practice guidelines. User Model User Adapt Interact 21(4–5):377–406
65. Liu AL, Hile H, Borriello G, Brown PA, Harniss M, Kautz H, Johnson K (2009) Customizing directions in an automated wayfinding system for individuals with cognitive impairment. In: Proceedings of the 11th international ACM SIGACCESS conference on computers and accessibility. ACM, New York, pp 27–34
66. López Nores M, Blanco-Fernández Y, Pazos Arias JJ, García Duque J (2012) The iCabiNET system: harnessing electronic health record standards from domestic and mobile devices to support better medication adherence. Comput Stand Interfaces 34(1):109–116
67. López Nores M, Blanco-Fernández Y, Pazos Arias JJ, Gil-Solla A (2012) Property-based collaborative filtering for health-aware recommender systems. Expert Syst Appl 39(8):7451–7457

68. LoPresti EF, Mihailidis A, Kirsch N (2004) Assistive technology for cognitive rehabilitation: state of the art. Neuropsychol Rehabil 14:5–39
69. Martín E, Calvo S, Carro RM (2010) An adaptive game to train users with special needs to make decisions: using public transportation. In: Adjunct proceedings of the 18th international conference on user modeling, adaptation, and personalization. Big Island of Hawaii, 20–24 June 2010, pp 25–27
70. Martín E, Carro RM (2009) Supporting the development of mobile adaptive learning environments: a case study. IEEE Trans Learn Technol 2(1):23–36
71. Martín JM, Ortigosa A, Carro RM (2012) SentBuk: sentiment analysis for e-learning environments. In: Proceedings of the XIV international symposium on computers in education. Andorra, Oct 2012, pp 277–282
72. Mechling LC (2007) Assistive technology as a self-management tool for prompting students with intellectual disabilities to initiate and complete daily tasks: a literature review. Educ Train Dev Disabil 42(3):252–269
73. Mohan R, Smith JR, Li C (1999) Adapting multimedia internet content for universal access. IEEE Transact Multimed 1:104–114
74. Moreno-Ger P, Sancho P, Martínez-Ortiz I, Sierra JL, Fernández-Manjón B (2007) Adaptive units of learning and educational videogames. J Interact Media Educ. North America. Available at: http://www-jime.open.ac.uk/jime/article/view/2007-5. Date accessed: 12 Dec. 2012
75. Nakashima H, Aghajan H, Augusto JC (2010) Handbook of ambient intelligence and smart environments. Springer Science + Business Media, LLC., New York, USA
76. Nicolle C, Abascal J (2001) Inclusive design guidelines for HCI. Taylor & Francis, London
77. O'Neill B, Gillespie A (2008) Simulating naturalistic instruction: the case for a voice mediated interface for assistive technology for cognition. J Assist Technol 2:22–31
78. Ortigosa A, Paredes P, Rodríguez P (2010) AH-questionnaire: an adaptive hierarchical questionnaire for learning styles. Comput Educ 54(4):999–1005
79. Ortigosa A, Quiroga JI, Carro RM (2011) Inferring user personality in social networks: a case study in facebook. In: Proceedings of the 11th international conference on intelligent systems design and applications. Córdoba, Nov 2011, pp 563–568
80. Pang B, Lee L (2008) Opinion mining and sentiment analysis. Found Trends Info Retr 2(1–2): 1–135
81. Patterson DJ, Liao L, Gajos K, Collier M, Livic N, Olson K, Wang S, Fox D, Kautz H (2004) Opportunity knocks: a system to provide cognitive assistance with transportation services. UbiComp 2004: Ubiquitous Computing, pp 433–450
82. Pereira BO, Expedito C, Firmino De Faria F, Vivacqua AS (2011) Designing a game controller for motor impaired players. In: Proceedings of the 10th Brazilian symposium on human factors in computing systems and the 5th Latin American conference on human-computer interaction. Brazilian Computer Society, Porto Alegre, pp 267–271
83. Quade M, Lehmann G, Blumendorf M, Roscher D, Albayrak S (2011) Evaluating user interface adaptations at runtime by simulating user interaction. BCS HCI 2011:497–502
84. Reena Sharma F, Geetanjali Wasson S (2012) Speech recognition and synthesis tool: assistive technology for physically disabled persons. Int J Comput Sci Telecommun 3(4):86–91
85. Repenning A, Ioannidou A (2006) Mobility agents: guiding and tracking public transportation users. In: AVI '06: proceedings of the working conference on advanced visual interfaces. ACM, New York, NY, USA, pp 127–134
86. Roldán D, Martín E, Haya PA, García-Herranz M (2011) Adaptive activities for inclusive learning using multitouch tabletops: an approach. In: Perez-Marin D, Kravcik M, Santos OC (eds) Proceedings of the international workshop on personalization approaches in learning environments. CEUR workshop proceedings, vol 732. Girona, 15 July 2011, pp 42–47
87. Seegers M (2001) Special technological possibilities for students with special needs. Learn Lead Technol 29(3):32–39
88. Serna S, Pigot H, Rialle V (2007) Modeling the progression of Alzheimer's disease for cognitive assistance in smart homes. User Model User Adapt Interact 17(4):415–438

89. Shneiderman B (2000) Universal usability. Commun ACM 43(5):84–91
90. Solheim I (2007) Personalisation of user interface for the cognitively disabled: how to test cognitive functions and ICT skills. In: First T4P conference technology for participation and accessible eGoverment services, pp 98–101
91. Spada D, Sánchez-Montañés M, Paredes P, Carro RM (2008) Towards inferring sequential-global dimension of learning styles from mouse movement patterns. In: Nejdl W, Kay J, Pu P, Herder E (eds) Adaptive hypermedia and adaptive web-based systems. Lecture notes in computer science, vol 5149. Springer, Berlin/Heidelberg, pp 337–340
92. Stephanidis C (2009) The universal access handbook (human factors and Ergonomics). CRC Press. Taylor & Francis Group, Boca Raton
93. Stephanidis C (2011) Adaptive techniques for universal access. User Model User Adapt Interact 11:159–179, Kluwer Academic Publishers
94. Stephanidis C, Savidis A (2001) Universal access in the information society: methods, tools, and interaction technologies. Universal Access Info Soc 1(1):40–55, Springer Berlin, Heidelberg
95. Toennies JL, Burgner J, Withrow TJ, Webster RJ (2011) Toward haptic/aural touchscreen display of graphical mathematics for the education of blind students. World Haptics 2011:373–378
96. Torrente J, Vallejo-Pinto JA, Moreno-Ger P, Fernández-Manjon B (2011) Introducing accessibility features in an educational game authoring tool: The <e-Adventure> experience. In: Proceedings of the 2011 IEEE 11th international conference on advanced learning technologies. IEEE Computer Society, Washington, DC, pp 341–343
97. Tsai S (2007) WADER: a novel wayfinding system with deviation recovery for individuals with cognitive impairments. In: Proceedings of the 9th international ACM SIGACCESS conference on computers and accessibility (Assets '07). ACM, New York, pp 267–268
98. Tsui KM, Yanco HA (2010) Prompting devices : a survey of memory aids for task sequencing. In: Proceedings of the 2nd international symposium on quality of life technology: intelligent systems for better living, held in conjunction with RESNA 2010, Las Vegas, 28–29 June
99. Vassileva J (2008) Toward social learning environments. IEEE Transact Learn Technol 1(4): 199–214, IEEE Computer Society Press Los Alamitos, CA, USA
100. Verdejo MF, Celorrio C, Lorenzo E, Sastre-Toral T (2006) An educational networking infrastructure supporting ubiquitous learning for school students. In: Proceedings of the 6th IEEE international conference on advanced learning technologies, IEEE Computer Society, Kerkrade, The Netherlands, pp 174–178. Wechsler D (1997) The Wechsler adult intelligence scale. Psychological Corporation, San Antonio
101. Villaverde J, Godoy D, Amandi A (2006) Learning styles' recognition in e-learning environments with feed-forward neural networks. J Comput Assist Learn 22:197–206
102. Wechsler D (1997) The Wechsler adult intelligence scale. Psychological Corporation, San Antonio
103. World Health Organization (2012) Chronic disease information sheet. http://www.who.int/mediacentre/factsheets/fs311/en/index.html. Last access Aug 2012
104. World Health Organization (2012) International classification of functioning, disability and health (ICF). http://www.who.int/classifications/icf/en/. Last access Aug 2012

Part I
Models and Theories

Chapter 2
Extending In-Home User and Context Models to Provide Ubiquitous Adaptive Support Outside the Home

Amaia Aizpurua, Idoia Cearreta, Borja Gamecho, Raúl Miñón, Nestor Garay-Vitoria, Luis Gardeazabal, and Julio Abascal

Abstract Ubiquitous Computing has proved to be an excellent way of providing technological support for the daily life of people within its range. Ambient Assisted Living (AAL), which is largely based on Ubiquitous Computing, aims at tutoring and supervising elderly people and users with physical, sensory or cognitive disabilities in the performance of routine household activities. AAL's main aim is to increase the autonomy of dependent people in their daily life by providing them with supportive instructions for everyday routines and warnings about home safety issues. This concept can be extended to public spaces, where ubiquitous accessible services allow people with disabilities to access location-dependent web services (providing maps, addresses, transport schedules, etc.) and local intelligent machines (such as information kiosks or ATMs). This approach allows existing knowledge about the users, their common activities, and their environment to be used to extend the in-home AAL concept to the support of common routines performed outside the home. This chapter surveys the modelling techniques used inside the home and discusses the methodologies required for their extension for out-of-home use, including interoperation and sharing of models.

2.1 Introduction

In recent years, considerable effort has been devoted to research on systems that support dependent people so that they can live at home independently. The main objectives of supportive systems are to provide the information needed

A. Aizpurua (✉) • I. Cearreta • B. Gamecho • R. Miñón • N. Garay-Vitoria • L. Gardeazabal •
J. Abascal
EGOKITUZ: Laboratory of HCI for Special Needs, School of Informatics, University of the
Basque Country/Euskal Herriko Unibertsitatea, Manuel Lardizabal 1, 20018 Donostia, Spain
e-mail: amaia.aizpurua@ehu.es; idoia.cearreta@ehu.es; borja.gamecho@ehu.es;
raul.minon@ehu.es; nestor.garay@ehu.es; pedrojoseluis.gardeazabal@ehu.es;
julio.abascal@ehu.es

E. Martín et al. (eds.), *User Modeling and Adaptation for Daily Routines: Providing Assistance to People with Special Needs*, Human–Computer Interaction Series,
DOI 10.1007/978-1-4471-4778-7_2, © Springer-Verlag London 2013

to autonomously perform common everyday tasks and to detect situations that might compromise the users' safety. Obviously both objectives depend on people's location and therefore its solution is based primarily on context-aware computing. The indoor location of people is achieved through various types of sensors that can determine people's position more or less accurately. The context-sensitive help requires models that gather information about users, the tasks they perform and where they perform these tasks. These models may include restrictions on certain actions in certain places, as well as information about potentially dangerous situations. If there is a risk, specific actions need to be generated for the control of safety. Personalized interaction is also required because, depending on her or his characteristics, each user may need individual tutoring to perform a specific task in a specific place.

Most systems that support dependent people are designed to be installed in the home. All potential users are registered in the system and their characteristics are well known, so that accurate user models can be built and used. The support provided to dependent people can be extended to spaces outside the home that are provided with ubiquitous technology, such as public service buildings (e.g. day care centres). If the user is registered in these places the same modelling schema can be used as that adopted at home. However, the expansion of ubiquitous technology suggests the extension of support for dependent people to places where services for unregistered users are provided; e.g. smart environments in malls or administration buildings, where a number of services are ubiquitously offered to all potential users within its scope. These are also context-dependent services where, unlike in the previous cases, the users are occasional. In these cases the system does not have a model of each user because they have not previously been registered. This situation decreases the ability to provide personalized tutoring suited to the needs and characteristics of each person.

A more valuable extension of in-home support to out-of home support would require each ubiquitous service provider system to be able to access each model (e.g. user, task or context) or at least the part that is relevant to each specific interaction. This chapter presents and discusses diverse approaches for sharing models between in-home and out-of-home supportive environments. To begin, the following paragraphs briefly survey the equipment needed to set up an intelligent environment.

2.1.1 *Technology for Supportive Ubiquitous Interaction*

It is well known that Ubiquitous (or Pervasive) Computing aims to integrate into the environment computers and software that are carefully adjusted to provide discreet assistance for the activities taking place within that context. This aid should be "proactive" but not intrusive. Ubiquitous Computing spaces require some underlying technologies, principally the processors and sensors deployed in the environment that can interact with each other and with mobile devices through wireless or wired networks. Since most of these elements (including network protocols, operating systems, etc.) are heterogeneous, a new layer of software (called middleware) is required to ensure interoperability[1] between them. One particular interoperability problem is the inclusion of incoming devices in the system. Pervasive computing allows the provision of ubiquitous services to mobile computers when these are located within the range of the system. It is therefore necessary to have a way of managing the discovery, presentation, and the integration into the system of unknown mobile processors entering the pervasive space. Universal accessibility of ubiquitous services requires the use of open and compatible interoperability frameworks[2].

One of the most important characteristics of Ubiquitous Computing is context awareness. According to Dey, a system is context-aware if it uses context to provide relevant information and/or services to the user, where relevancy depends on the user's task [18]. Both in-home and out-of-home supportive systems are context dependent. In the first case, diverse contextual parameters (temperature, state of windows, doors, lights, gas, etc.) are collected by sensors deployed in the environment. The indoor location of people is achieved through various types of sensors that can determine people's position more or less accurately, depending on the requirements of the system. The triangulation of diverse types of radio-frequency signals (including RFID, Bluetooth and Wi-Fi), mobile phones[3], and the processing of video images are technologies[4] commonly used for this purpose.

When the user is outside, his or her location depends exclusively on general-purpose location systems. Currently, a mobile device can be located with varying degrees of precision by means of diverse technologies, such as: the Global Positioning System (GPS), General Packet Radio Services/Global System for Mobile Communications (GPRS/GSM), and Radio Frequency Identification (RFID)[5]. The context models have to take into account that outdoor location is usually less accurate than indoor location. However, it is generally sufficient to supervise the expected type of tasks performed outside the home, such as orientation, finding lost people, etc.

---

[1]Interoperability requirements are essential because Ubiquitous Computing involves a large diversity of hardware and software, which implies dealing with different combinations of devices, protocols and services. It cannot be forgotten that interoperability failures typically lead to problems that users will not be able to solve [31].

[2]Many European projects in the area of supportive intelligent environments have adopted URC/UCH (Universal Remote Console/Universal Control Hub), which is an ISO standard that acts as a middleware for ubiquitous interaction: Universal Control Hub 1.0 (DRAFT), http://myurc.org/TR/uch

[3]For instance, Taher et al. [54] propose an indoor wayfinding support system that includes using personal mobile phones.

[4]For more information about indoor location systems the Survey of Indoor Positioning Systems by Gu et al. [25] can be consulted.

[5]More information about outdoor people location technologies can be found in the book "Location-based Services: Fundamentals and Operation" by Küpper [38].

Up to now we have reviewed the technology used to support dependent people at home. The current challenge is how to extend the same type of support to out-of-home intelligent environments. In order to give an idea of the type of user interaction envisaged in this chapter let us propose an illustrative scenario.

2.1.2 Supporting People at Home and Outside the Home: A Possible Scenario

Antonia is an elderly person with poor memory, acquired hardness of hearing and slightly reduced vision. These restrictions present major challenges to her as she carries out her everyday activities. She lives alone at home in the same city as her children. To minimize the problems she encounters in living autonomously and to support her with her daily routines, her home has been equipped with supportive ubiquitous technology. A network of diverse sensors locates her position in the house and detects her body posture (standing, sitting, lying). In addition, some physical constants such as her heart rate and blood pressure are periodically measured. The information collected by these sensors is used to provide warnings and to trigger alarms when something unexpected or unauthorized happens. The system is also able to provide her with assistance with everyday tasks such as cooking or using home appliances. Reminders for routine tasks (meals, medicines, etc.) and for her personal schedule (visits to the doctor, calls to the family, etc.) can be also generated. The system also helps her to use communication and entertainment services such as chat and video chat with family and friends, and television and radio services. These are all provided via natural user interfaces adapted to Antonia's characteristics, needs and likes, based on the information collected about her in different models.

When she leaves home, the situation is different. She can access generic services (such as guidance and orientation, information on public transport, smart ticketing, etc.) through her mobile device (e.g. a smartphone). When she accesses these services the interface is automatically adapted to her capabilities either by using the profile that has been previously stored on her mobile device or by importing it from a repository in "the cloud". For instance, once a week she goes to the outpatient clinic using public transport. The underground station is equipped with an intelligent environment that provides various services, such as interactive transport maps, metro ticket dispenser, and arrival information. All these services are announced on her mobile device and Antonia selects the service she wants to use: "to buy a ticket". The appropriate interface is then downloaded to her mobile. The user interface has been adapted to her, using the profile information contained in the user model provided by her own device. The outpatient clinic is also equipped with several ubiquitous services. The system retrieves Antonia's profile from a centralized health information repository in order to adapt the services that are provided to her.

Thus, the intelligent support provided to Antonia is seamless: all these adaptations are transparent to her. Her device interacts with the intelligent environment without interrupting her. After leaving the house and encountering new ubiquitous services, Antonia has the same user experience that she has at home.

Therefore a key issue in seamless adaptive support is how to obtain, maintain and use the information about the user. The next two sections describe the modelling techniques used inside and outside the home respectively. In Sect. 2.4 the different proposals for changing from in-home to out-of-home use are described.

2.2 In-Home Context-Aware Modelling

Closely related to Ubiquitous Computing, the Ambient Intelligence (AmI) paradigm focuses on providing intelligent support to users by means of environment-embedded devices. "AmI systems are sensitive and responsive to the presence of people" [1]. One of the most promising areas within the paradigm of AmI is Ambient Assisted Living (AAL), which is focussed on helping people with special needs (mainly elderly people) to pursue an autonomous life. Smart Homes designed using AAL principles cover the private context, while other AAL implementations are used for shared spaces.

This section focuses on modelling the different features used by smart environments to assist users in performing daily routines in their own homes. In this case the users and the places are known, allowing the design of systems tailored to their needs. However these techniques are not restricted to in-home systems. Modelling of known users is also valid for other intelligent out-of-home environments where users are previously registered. The next section covers sporadic interaction with environments where users are not known.

The most common requirement of the projects surveyed in this section is to support the elderly in the performance of everyday routines. As a consequence, the design for home support must devote special attention to key issues such as usability, utility, social acceptance, privacy protection, low cost and non-requirement for administrative tasks. It is also necessary to bear in mind that household activities are different from those performed in the workplace [19]. In particular, Meyer and Rakotonirainy note that household activities are informal, not necessarily structured, and focus on tasks that make people's lives safer, convenient, enjoyable, entertaining, relaxing, etc. [43].

The following subsection describes a number of proposals that meet these criteria, analysed from the modelling point of view.

2.2.1 Context-Aware Modelling for Ambient Assistive Living

Let us review the proposals and results of a number of AAL projects and research papers, in relation to the models used for Smart Homes.

Amigo[6] (2004–2008): The Amigo project developed a middleware layer that
dynamically integrates heterogeneous systems to achieve interoperability between services and devices. For example, home appliances, multimedia players
and renderers, and personal devices are connected to the home network to work
in an interoperable way [23, 55].

Easy Line +[7] (2007–2009): This is a European project aimed at creating prototypes
of home devices that try to compensate for the loss of cognitive or physical
abilities of older people. It includes the creation of an AmI kitchen that can be
adapted to the user, to avoid the frequent home accidents involving white goods
appliances [11].

Semantic Matching Framework (SMF): Although this framework was not designed for an in-home AAL project, it is relevant to our survey because it deals
with daily routines at home for people with special needs. Ontologies are used
in SMF to describe user model semantics using the OWL-DL (Web Ontology Language – Description Logic) language. These ontologies also represent
devices (e.g. doors, windows, sensors, etc.) as "effectors", each containing a
set of characteristics defined as environment attributes. In SMF, adapting the
environment to people with special needs is based on detecting handicapping
situations that limit users' capabilities and providing adapted processes to
personalize service delivery [30].

VAALID[8] (2008–2011): The VAALID project (Accessibility and Usability Validation Framework for AAL Interaction Design Process) aims at creating a
framework to model and validate the AAL. It provides tools for authoring AAL
models and simulating these models for further validation. It allows editing and
configuration of the user, environment and device models and also handles the
interaction [46, 47].

SensHome[9] (2010–2011): As Frey et al. comment, SensHome is an attempt to create
an infrastructure and a methodology for recording, modelling, annotating and
analysing activities in Smart Environments, initially focusing on Smart Homes.
The result of this effort is the SensHome Activity model. Two real and virtual
environments were created that are synchronized with each other, representing a
house and a kitchen. Standard models are embraced to define the context [21, 53].

SOPRANO[10] (2007–2010): This is a European project that evolved to OpenAAL[11].
SOPRANO (Service-Oriented Programmable smart environments for older Eu-
ropeans) developed an AAL system aimed at enhancing the lives of frail and
disabled older people. The project uses a middleware called SAM (Soprano
Ambient Middleware), which is used to control the home context for people who
need assistance [33, 51, 58].

---

[6]http://www.hitech-projects.com/euprojects/amigo/

[7]http://www.easylineplus.com/

[8]http://www.vaalid-project.org/

[9]http://www.dfki.de/senshome/

[10]http://www.soprano-ip.org/

[11]http://openaal.org/

Table 2.1 Mapping of projects and research papers to the reviewed models

Project	Target population	Room	User model	Task model	Context model
Amigo	A	Generic	X	X	X
Easy-Line+	E and D	Kitchen	X	–	–
SMF	D	Kitchen and Living room	X	X	X
VAALID	A	Generic	X	X	X
SensHome	A	Kitchen and Living room	–	X	X
SOPRANO	E	Generic	X	X	X

E elderly people, *D* people with disabilities, *A* all people

When analysing and classifying the various projects and research papers presented in recent years there is a clear differentiation between those aimed at providing a solution to the problem of heterogeneity of devices and services, as explained in Sect. 2.1.1 (Amigo, SOPRANO), and those that are intended to provide a more seamless user experience necessary for the scenario in Sect. 2.1.2 (SensHome, VAALID, Easy Line+). While the first group focuses on issues such as middleware and interoperability between different networks in a Smart Home, the main aim of the second group is to best define the world around the users of Smart Homes, following the principles of "calm technology". These differences are also reflected in the models presented in the types of works for each, although they generally contain the same elements: person/user, environment/location, behaviour, activity/task, device/service/sensor, etc. Each project expands each of these fields in greater depth (and with more attributes) depending on which aspects are more relevant to the project. Table 2.1 summarizes the main characteristics of the surveyed research.

The names, structure and composition of the diverse models vary greatly between the different approaches. Some systems maintain separate models, while others tend to combine all the information available in a single model. Although the models vary greatly and depend very much on the characteristics and purpose of the system, they include some common structures. In the following paragraphs some of the most notable features of the models reviewed are briefly discussed.

2.2.1.1   User Modelling

User modelling[12] is a well-known technique that is essential for user-adapted interaction. According to Carmagnola et al. [9], the user model is a key component of

---

[12]The seminal paper [35] can be consulted for a deeper insight into the User Modelling. In this paper Kobsa describes the purposes of generic user modelling systems, their services within user-adaptive systems, and the different design requirements. Brusilovsky provides details on the application of user modelling to adaptive hypermedia in another influential paper [7].

an adaptive system. It maintains the user's properties, such as preferences, interests, behaviours, knowledge, goals and other events that are relevant to user adaptation. Adaptive applications usually have a specific user-modelling component, which is in charge of incrementally constructing a user model by storing, updating and deleting entities and supplying the other components with assumptions about a user. In fact, the quality of personalized services provided to the user depends largely on the characteristics of the user models, including their precision, the amount of data stored, whether these data are up to date, etc.

For users with disabilities, or elderly users, some of the user features are permanent (e.g. the type of disability), while others may gradually change (e.g. the ability to use a specific input device). In addition, certain user features can change quickly over short periods of time, such as dexterity, strength, motivation, mood, and interest. This is similar to the *Ser* and *Estar* models presented in Chap. 3 of this book [10]: *Ser* refers to essential user characteristics, while *Estar* refers to the condition or potentially temporary attributes. The user model must be able to cope with all the changing characteristics in order to provide a well-adapted interaction. For instance, in Chap. 4 of this book, De Carolis et al. [17] state that modelling cognitive and affective human factors is essential in order to provide assistance to elderly people in smart environments. They propose an embodied social agent NICA (Natural Interaction with a Caring Agent), which acts as a virtual caregiver, to assist elderly users in a smart environment.

In the field of Ambient Assisted Living, the user model can contain diverse types of data, such as:

- Demographic data.
- Physical, sensory and cognitive characteristics (including disabilities and restrictions).
- Preferred Language (but also including other languages known).
- Likes and preferences (e.g. temperature, lighting, schedules, etc.).
- Interests, moods.
- User location.
- Allowed and restricted tasks (which can include indication or restriction of the place and time they can be performed).
- Preferred mode of interaction (voice, text, icons, signed video, etc.).
- Specification of devices (operating system, browser, processor, memory, etc.) used to interact with the system.
- Specification of networks (bandwidth, range, etc.) used to interact with the system.
- Etc.

The user model implemented for home support is quite similar in the different projects that have been reviewed. Unfortunately, detailed information about the models is not always available, but there is information on how they are built. Most projects start from existing studies on older people. For instance, Casas et al.

use data obtained information from statistics published by Eurostat[13] [11]. They also use interviews to extract the most relevant information for the context. Vildjiounaite et al. use, as a starting point, stereotypes of the characteristics of a specific user, to be completed with other users' personal information [55]. Another method is to adopt one or more Personas[14]. Many projects have used Personas to model the users acting in a particular environment; e.g. Casas et al. [11] and I2Home[15]. In order to build their user model, Mocholí et al. [46] use the "Design for All" ICT Guidelines for ICT products and services of the ETSI[16]; the International Classification of Functioning, Disability and Health (ICF[17]); and the Common Accessibility Profile (CAP[18]).

2.2.1.2 Task Modelling

Task models[19] are logical descriptions of the activities to be performed to achieve users' goals. Although they were predominantly created for user interaction design, they can be useful for characterizing, monitoring and supporting the user in his/her everyday activities.

In the field of Ambient Assisted Living, the task modelling can include:

- User's goals and objectives.
- Description of the steps to perform each specific task (including the information that can be provided to help the user to perform that task).
- Ability to perform each task (which can change quickly over short periods of time) can be used for "mixed initiative" or "shared control" task scheduling.
- Etc.

It is important to model the user's behaviour to predict his/her next move or to validate the current task. The support for everyday routines requires checking that every task is being performed correctly. In this sense, Frey et al. [21] use an extended model of Leontiev's Activity Theory [40] to model activities, actions and operations. This leads to a model for controlling the behaviour and the tasks performed in system. The Amigo project [55] keeps an interaction history in order to monitor the status of a task by means of Machine Learning techniques, while Naranjo et al. use Workflow technology with the same purpose [47]. These two projects

---

[13]http://epp.eurostat.ec.europa.eu

[14]"Personas are not real people, but they represent them throughout the design process. They are hypothetical archetypes of actual users" [15].

[15]http://www.i2home.org/

[16]http://www.etsi.org

[17]http://www.who.int/classiffications/icf/en/

[18]Common Accessibility Profile is the basis of the ISO/IEC 24756:2009, http://www.iso.org/

[19]Paternó presents the main concepts underlying task models and discusses how they can be represented and used for designing, analyzing and evaluating interactive software applications [50].

use dynamic modelling to keep information about user behaviour and preferences. There are also attempts to model tasks at the user interface level; e.g. Stahl et al. used an implementation of ANSI/CEA-2018[20] to describe the tasks required to cook food in a kitchen [53].

2.2.1.3   Context Modelling

Context modelling[21] includes gathering, evaluating and maintaining context information within a formal representation, which is necessary for consistency checking, as well as ensuring that sound reasoning is performed on context data. According to Bettini et al. [6], the overall goal of formal context information modelling is to develop evolvable context-aware applications. Since context-modelling maintenance is expensive, the reuse and sharing of context information between context-aware applications should be also considered.

Context models applicable to Ambient Assisted Living can include data on:

- Conditions that affect the interaction in specific places (noise, light, privacy, etc.).
- Places allowed and restricted (with indication of the possible tasks and time).
- Parameters collected by the environmental sensors.
- Etc.

An important issue in modelling to support dependent people is the guarantee of connecting the hardware layer and the ubiquitous applications with the rest of the system. There are two important aspects to be addressed:

1. The abstraction of the different sensors that can be found (brand, model, family, etc.). This is the case with the SensHome system presented by Frey et al., which introduces a platform that provides a model-based approach to represent home devices and services [21]. Similarly, the OpenAAL consortium uses a set of ontologies to model the characteristics of the sensors (given the wide variety of brands and types that exist). These models can be used in the sensor fusion layer to establish the basis of the context modelling of an AAL system [58]. This is also similar to the SMF system, where an environmental model ontology specifies devices as effectors, each containing a set of characteristics for environmental attributes [30].
2. The interoperability between the different technologies (UPnP: Universal Plug and Play, WSDL: Web Service Description Language, etc.) through which devices are supported and services are provided in a ubiquitous environment.

---

[20]ANSI/CEA-2018 (American National Standards Institute/Consumer Electronics Association) defines an XML-based language for task model descriptions. http://www.w3.org/2005/Incubator/model-based-ui/wiki/ANSI/CEA-2018

[21]For more details about context modeling, the paper from Bettini et al. [6] discusses and compares the requirements that context modelling and reasoning techniques should meet.

To solve this problem the Amigo project extended a previous service model for interoperability, with syntactic and semantic descriptions as well as non-functional properties associated with services [23]. Another example of an interoperable architecture that includes the use of models for sharing information between different technologies is SAMBA (Systems for Ambient Intelligence enabled by Agents) [5].

The set of sensors provides the information necessary to ensure proper monitoring of user behaviour and the information about the task that they are performing. The use of models helps context-aware systems to create an abstract layer that provides a structured path to the information obtained through the sensors.

2.2.1.4 Reasoning with Models

The models can be provided with rules that allow inconsistencies to be detected and probably solved, new data to be inferred, or decisions to be taken when a specific combination of entries occurs. For example, the reasoning in SMF uses a set of first order rules involving user and environment characteristics to infer all handicapping situations and personalize services [30]. The reasoning module iteratively processes semantic matching rules and OWL-DL user and environment class instances in order to update the values of handicapping situations.

As previously mentioned, context-sensitive support uses models that gather information about users, the tasks they can perform and where they can perform them. These models can include restrictions on certain actions in certain places, as well as information about potentially dangerous situations. Table 2.2 shows a fragment of reasoning using information from the user, environment and task models used in the PIAPNE (Prototype of Ambient Intelligence for People with Special Needs) environment [2]. By applying the rules provided by the user/task/context models to the information provided by the sensors, the system is able to infer the tasks that are being performed by the user (washing_up, watching_TV). The set of rules in the user model indicates any incoherence between one of the tasks and the user's location. This allows the detection of possible dangers (potential flooding) and the implementation of contingency actions (alarm generation).

2.2.2 Discussion

In AAL, Smart Homes are intended to ensure the quality of life of elderly people who often also have some disabilities. As described in the previous section, in recent years many projects have been working on platforms capable of monitoring tasks and daily routines, and have suggested different solutions to these problems.

Table 2.2 Reasoning with PIAPNE models

Model	Status	Parameter/rule
User model: Sensors_Time	16:00	Time_daytime
Context model: Sensors_Kitchen	Tap is turned on Light is switched on	Tap_on, Light_on
Context model: Sensors_Living_room	TV is switched on Light is switched on	TV_on, Light_on
Context model: User_Location	User is at: Living_room Posture: sitting	User_location_ living_room User_posture_sitting
Task model: inferred task	Washing_up	Washing-up (Sensors_Kitchen: Tap_on, Light_on, Gas_off, Time_daytime)
Task model: inferred task	Watching_TV	Watching_TV (Sensors_Living_room: TV_on, Time_anytime)
User model: inferred danger	Medium level danger (potential flooding)	If Task (washing-up) and Not [User_location (kitchen)] → trigger_danger (severity: medium, type: flooding)
User model: action	Generate warnings and/or alarms	Trigger alarm (severity: medium, type: flooding, warning: flooding_message)

There have recently been initiatives (AALOA[22]) to unify and defragment this situation. The impact it could have on the acceptance of specific models by the scientific community in AAL is still unknown, but it is worth analysing the types of models and projects included in these initiatives [20]. The most interesting project is perhaps UniversAAL[23] [26], which involves consolidation and standardization to obtain an open platform for AAL. This platform is based on completed European projects, such as SOPRANO and PERSONA. UniversAAL includes the previously mentioned OpenAAL, an open source framework available for download, which is able to implement context-aware environments for AAL.

SmartHouse uses modelling for both the user and the available services, but context-aware performance also requires other models. It is necessary to have a task model (and other models) to store accurate data about the tasks: location, time etc. It is also necessary to have a behaviour model that is able to record user activities and to relate these to the other models. The extension of model and the pathways between models (including those that may exist outside the home) will provide more complete information, which is essential in order to avoid blind spots in monitoring daily routines.

[22]AAL Open Association http://www.aaloa.org/

[23]UniversAAL, UNIVERsal open platform and reference Specification for Ambient Assisted Living http://www.universaal.org/

2.3   Modelling Out-of-Home Ubiquitous Support

In this section, models designed for intelligent environments deployed outside the home are reviewed. This analysis is focused particularly on user modelling for ubiquitous systems that do not require previous registration. Similarly to the in-home systems in the preceding section, their objective is to support dependent people in performing routine tasks, but on this occasion in environments containing ubiquitous computer-based services.

Context is also a key factor in out-of-home systems, but a differentiating characteristic is the uncertainty about the services available. In in-home contexts the services and devices available to the user are well known and therefore the information required to adapt them to the user can be adequately modelled. In contrast, the services offered and requested outside the home are sporadic and it is therefore more complex to model the context of user interaction. In this case the applications and services are much more varied and there are also many more dynamic factors related to the physical environment that need to be modelled and taken into account (e.g. meteorological factors, noise, outdoor location, lighting, etc.).

2.3.1   Out-of-Home Context Modelling

The supportive out-of-home approach is based on three main areas: support for daily routines, ubiquitous computing and access to information for people with special needs. Few studies have been found that take into account these three areas of research and report on how to build their corresponding models. In this section, some of the works that best fit this approach are briefly described. These works have been ordered from greatest to least connection with the proposed approach. Table 2.3 summarizes the relationships between the areas of research and each model studied.

Table 2.3 Mapping the research areas and reviewed models

	Daily routines	Ubiquitous computing	Support for people with special needs
Sus-IT	X	X	X
INREDIS	X	X	X
Affinto	X	X	X
ViMos	X	X	–
CALA-ONT	X	X	–
Mobiday	X	X	–
mPersona	X	–	–
Ontology-based context model	–	X	–

2.3.1.1 Sus-IT

The Sus-IT project[24] was intended to generate new knowledge to understand changes due to aging, as well as linking these changes to the flexibility provided by information technology. Its aim was to investigate current and potential barriers to a sustainable and effective use of ICT by the elderly and to explore possible solutions in relation to socio-technological barriers. Sloan et al. [52] highlighted the difficulties encountered by the elderly as their skills become progressively worse over time. They proposed automatic or semi-automatic accessibility adaptations as a possible solution for the particular challenges they encounter. The authors established the need to model a user profile for this purpose. This profile needed to include a precise description of the individual, taking into account the capabilities of the users and their changes over time, their preferences, the level of experience of the system and certain social characteristics. Atkinson et al. [3] proposed a set of guidelines for an outdoor pervasive environment and pointed out the relevance of the context, which should include features such as the physical environment, light and noise levels, the capacities of users, their preferences and their devices. They also state that the diverse accessibility adaptations must be modelled and related to different interaction modalities. They consider four areas of interaction: auditory, visual, motor and cognitive. They also take into account two other communication parameters: time (since the devices can impose restrictions and users may have disabilities that alter the time required or available for certain interactions) and the volume of information (because the restrictions and conditions may alter the amount of information a user can receive or process).

2.3.1.2 INREDIS

The INREDIS[25] project aimed at creating a platform to provide ubiquitous access to ubiquitous services adapted for people with disabilities. While the Sus-IT project focused on the elderly, INREDIS took into account users with different disabilities. The main scenario was an intelligent environment where users with disabilities were able to access various services provided by local machines (such as information kiosks, vending machines, ATMs, etc.) using their own, appropriately adapted, mobile devices.

The generation of tailored interfaces in INREDIS was based on modelling techniques that use a Knowledge Base (KB) formed by different ontologies [45] in OWL. The KB was responsible for storing the ontologies and using rule-based

---

[24]Sus-IT project. Using ITs for a better and more independent future. http://sus-it-plone.lboro.ac.uk/

[25]INREDIS project: INterfaces for RElations between Environment and people with DISabilities. http://www.inredis.es/Default.aspx

reasoning on existing information to extract new knowledge. There were three main ontological models:

1. User model: containing information about the capabilities of users, their possible types of interaction, interests, hobbies and preferences, and socio-demographic data.
2. Context model: including the user's goals, the task, the environment, socio-cultural environment, the space-time environment and the services available in that context.
3. User device model: split into hardware (screen size, peripherals, etc.) and software (mark-up languages supported, programs installed, etc.).

2.3.1.3   Affinto

The Affinto ontology allows the creation and access of user and context models from different services provided by ubiquitous environments, as explained by Cearreta [12]. According to her, people very often perform routine tasks using interactive systems. Therefore, these interactions should be as natural and intuitive as possible. The inclusion of emotions can improve the interaction by increasing a user's level of understanding and decreasing the ambiguity of the messages (as happens in human conversations). The use of multi-modal interfaces makes it possible to include affective cues in the messages emitted by the system. Similarly, it is possible to recognize the users' emotions and to adapt the interactions to their actual circumstances. This allows a choice to be made on the best mode of communicating with users with communication restrictions (e.g. people with certain disabilities).

The Affinto ontology models interactions between users and systems by means of the OWL language, also taking into account emotional and modality issues. Affinto is built on a generic ontology base. The ontology thus defines the context as a whole, including the following properties: context subject (for both the user and the system), environment, social, task, and spatial-temporal. It must be noted that the subject property corresponds to any physical, cognitive or affective property of the subject:

- Physical properties: these define the communication parameters used by the subject (for example voice parameters).
- Cognitive properties: sensory (e.g. auditory) and perceptual (e.g. speech perception) processes that the subject can use.
- Emotional properties: these define and classify the emotions of the subject (using different theories and classifications of emotions, such as dimensional theory).

A specific version of Affinto for emotion recognition in multimodal systems was developed taking this generic ontology as the start point [12]. Subsequently, an updated version was built to support adaptive interaction based on users' capacities [13].

2.3.1.4 ViMos

Hervás and Bravo presented an interesting model for both user and context in ubiquitous systems [29]. This model defines the context from two perspectives: information visualization and ambient intelligence. The first viewpoint refers to perceptual and cognitive aspects, as well as graphical attributes and data properties. The second perspective includes characteristics of the environment and the display of information. Three OWL ontologies were created to model all these aspects:

- User ontology: describing the user's profile, the status (including location, activities, roles and objectives, among others).
- Device ontology: formally describing relevant devices and their characteristics, associations and dependencies.
- Physical environment ontology: defining the physical space.

These ontologies allow the establishment of communication between the user environment and the user interfaces. According to these authors, the information that can be found in people's everyday environment comes from several heterogeneous sources. It is therefore important to determine the best way to deliver and display this information. For this purpose, it is necessary to identify and describe the previously mentioned features in connection with the user and the context. They propose a framework called ViMos (Visualization Mosaics) that analyses the user context in order to provide a suitable interface, which is dynamically generated.

2.3.1.5 CALA-ONT

CALA-ONT is a Context Ontology Model for Ubiquitous Learning Environments. This model, proposed by Cho and Hong, described an ontology-based conceptual architecture and a context model, aimed at providing context-aware learning services in ubiquitous environments [14]. It was used to supply user-centric pervasive education services in smart schools provided with several embedded interoperable computing devices that enable learning whenever and wherever.

The context ontology model proposed consists of four upper classes and subclasses. It contains 12 main properties that describe the relationships between individuals from the upper class and their properties. The CALA-ONT model defined: individuals (*Person*), sites, activities, and computational entities in a *top-level* class. The *Person* class, which defines the general characteristics of the person, has a student, teacher and office worker as sub-classes. The *Place* class, which defines the general properties of a site, has an outdoor campus and an indoor campus as subclasses. The *Activity* class, which defines general school activities, contains a formal activity and other activity subclasses. The *ComEntity* class defines entities and contains general computing device, application software, and content as subclasses.

2.3.1.6 Mobiday

Mobiday [39] is a system implemented in a hospital to improve the effectiveness of communication between patients and doctors. Its aim was to assist the user in the tasks carried out in a day hospital. Mobiday used ubiquitous technologies and contextual information in an oncology unit to provide up-to-date updated information to patients and to allow context-dependent access to information on their status. The ultimate goal was that users learn from their actions and acquire certain routines. In order to carry out this approach, Mobiday takes into account the user's location using RFID technology, identifying their location (in key hospital rooms such as the waiting room or the laboratory) and recognizing their current activity. Based on this information, the system can decide if the context is appropriate for the user to receive certain messages. The flow of tasks carried out in a day hospital is modelled to guide the patient and to provide information about the next step to be followed. The system also uses other data, such as demographic information and information about diseases. The next version of the system is intended to take into account the patient's psychological status and to collect feedback on this [59].

2.3.1.7 mPersona

mPersona [49] is a web portal personalization system for wireless users, based on user modelling. It is aimed at mobile rather than ubiquitous environments. The system uses mobile agent technology to provide personalized content according to the user preferences and the local environment. It takes into account not only the users' profile but also their mobile devices. Users can thus get personalized wireless portals, based on their preferences and interests, which are adapted to the capabilities of their mobile devices. Its architecture includes a component for user registration and profile management. The user profile is split into two parts: "theme profile" and "device profile". According to the authors, the creation and management of these profiles is implementation specific. In the case of "theme", the profile can be created simply using a collection of keywords that represent thematic interests or using a complicated schema based on the user history. mPersona adopted the keywords approach. In relation to the device profile, there are two options: a simple collection of device features or a standard format such as CC/PP (Composite Capability/Preference Profiles). mPersona took the first option. Apart from modelling the user, the system requires that the content of web sites be described in some way. The structure of the website content provider in the wireless environment is usually a hierarchy of information types, represented by a tree structure. Users can thus get personalized wireless portals based on their preferences and interests and adapted to the capabilities of their mobile device.

2.3.1.8 An Ontology-Based Context Model in Intelligent Environments

Gu et al. presented a context model based on an ontology written in the OWL language [24]. This model enables semantic representation of context by defining an upper common ontology for general background information and a series of low-level ontologies that can be applied in different sub-domains. The context ontology defines a common vocabulary to share context information in a ubiquitous computing environment. By sharing the interpretation of the structure of context information between users, devices and services, semantic interoperability is achieved. Building a large ontology by integrating different ontologies that describe portions of the broad context enables the reuse of domain knowledge. The upper ontology defines basic concepts such as *Person*, *Location*, *Computational Entity* and *Activity*. The details of these basic concepts are defined in domain-specific ontologies that can vary from one domain to another. The authors defined all the descendant classes for a specific-use case, which is a Smart Home environment. They also classify a variety of contexts in two main categories: direct and indirect context. The direct context is acquired from a context provider, which can be an internal source (indoor location provider) or external source (weather information server). The direct context can be classified into perceived context and defined context. The perceived context is obtained from physical sensors, while the defined context is often specified by a user. The indirect context is obtained by performing context aggregation and reasoning processes to the direct context.

2.3.2 Discussion

Having reviewed the literature we can conclude that there are few works that combine all the aims: to support the elderly or people with disabilities in performing routine tasks in ubiquitous environments outside their homes. Only three of the previously mentioned eight research works directly address the issues: Sus-It, INREDIS, and Affinto. For instance, the user models of these different projects could be extended to describe the user capabilities (as in the INREDIS project) and these user capabilities could be related to different adaptations (as in the Sus-IT project).

All of the works model both the user and the context, but they follow different approaches. Some works model the user, the mobile device and the context separately; e.g. INREDIS. Others include both the user and the device within a global context (e.g. Sus-IT and Affinto). In other cases, task modelling is necessary in order to provide the user with the appropriate information for the current activity (e.g. CALA-ONT, Mobiday). Unfortunately, most papers focus on describing the purpose and implementation of the system rather than explaining the aspects of modelling. Thus, important details about the implementation of the models are lacking: such as structure, technology used, information storage, etc.

The diversity in the modelling is largely due to the lack of standards and the dependence on the application domain. When designing for out-of-home interaction, very diverse applications and services can appear. The variety of approaches taken leads to different requirements for information about the user and the context of interaction. Despite this, and based on the previously mentioned classification, it is clear that some are application-oriented models designed for a particular system (e.g. mPersona and Mobiday), while others (such as the work of Gu et al. in [24] or Affinto) are general purpose ontology-based models. Specific application-oriented models are usually implemented using simple structures such as a set of keywords, as in mPersona. This may work for specific context-sensitive applications, but it is not suitable for ubiquitous access to different applications or services. In this line, some recent projects (such as INREDIS and Sus-IT) have attempted to go beyond the model for a given system. Instead of designing a model for a specific application, user and context, these projects have tried to use models that are valid for various services provided by a common architecture. In this regard ontology-oriented modelling might be the best approach, because it provides a high level of expressivity and formality based on Semantic Web technologies. These models can potentially share knowledge and are capable of reasoning using context information. This type of context modelling seems promising for advancing in the development of ubiquitous systems. This applies not just to offering services ubiquitously within the same architecture, but also to going further and ensuring access to ubiquitous services belonging to different environments and different ubiquitous architectures.

Supporting out-of-home routine tasks requires the modelling of new elements that were not present in in-home support.

- Modelling the user: Out-of-home sporadic interactions with ubiquitous services require dynamic user modelling that can include collecting information about the user, which may be obtained either from his or her access device or from a remote repository. In addition to expanding the parameters used at home, such as likes and preferences, the extended user model needs to include information about allowed and restricted spaces (including how far the user can go without generating an alarm). Similarly, the list of allowed and restricted tasks needs to be adapted.
- Modelling the context: The way in which certain activities are performed and the permissions to do them or warnings against doing them depend on the characteristics of the place where they are performed. Out-of-home interaction requires an extension of the context modelling to include detailed descriptions of the physical and social constraints, in order to determine the feasibility of each task. For instance, specific environmental conditions (such as lighting or noise) could make it impossible to read or hear instructions. Therefore the way in which the interaction is performed needs to be adapted to these conditions.
- Modelling the user device (or access device) is important in order to ensure that the out-of-home interaction is interoperable. In order to establish suitable interactions, the user device has to provide a complete description of its technical (hardware and software) characteristics. This includes modelling hardware

aspects[26], such as the size of the screen, or the software installed (e.g. the web browser). Most systems include modelling the user device in other models, such as the context model, avoiding the need for creation of a specific model for this purpose.

- Modelling other features: some projects mention the need for modelling other key features. For instance, the Sus-It project claims that accessibility adaptations must be modelled and related to the users' modalities.

Focusing on modelling for the elderly to support them in ubiquitous out-of-home environments, it must be borne in mind that the context changes may be frequent. In addition a large number and wide range of services may be accessible. It is therefore important that the model is both extensible and dynamic; i.e. the model must allow new information to be added and the information currently contained to be updated. The users must also have access to the information contained about them in the models.

2.4 Combination and Extension of In-Home Models for the Provision of Out-of-Home Services

The extension of in-home support systems to out-of-home ubiquitous support services requires that the models be enhanced and expanded in order to contain sufficient information, for instance, about: the users' characteristics and preferences outside the home (when these are different to those at home); the new tasks that can be carried out by the user; the characteristics of the environments where they are performed; and any rules that condition or restrict these activities. In most cases this requires models to be shared between different supportive ubiquitous systems. In fact, this is one of the major challenges for out-of-home ubiquitous environments. Heckman uses the concept of Ubiquitous User Modelling to refer to the modelling and exploitation of user behaviour data when interacting with a variety of systems to share their models (see Fig. 2.1) [27]. For example, let us imagine an elderly user with sight restrictions who uses a home support service to control the oven via voice. There is probably a basic model that contains information about his or her capabilities. If this same user wants to use a support system to control an elevator outside the home it would be very useful if the two supportive systems could share their user models. In this way, the user would not need to again communicate his/her preference for using voice, for example, to interact with the system. If the two systems were able to communicate with each other, or the user models of both systems were interoperable and capable of exchanging information, the user would be able to use the elevator with complete transparency. Even if the latter did not have

---

[26]For instance, CC/PP is a RDF-based data exchange language that allows representing information about the user's device. http://www.w3.org/TR/CCPP-struct-vocab/

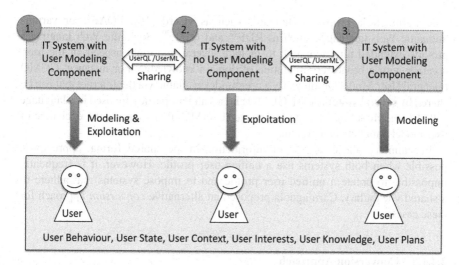

Fig. 2.1 An abstract view of Ubiquitous User Modelling, aimed at modelling, sharing and exploiting user data [27]

a user modelling component it could exploit the model provided by the first system (see box 2 in Fig. 2.1).

It is therefore necessary to understand how the systems can exchange heterogeneous user data or models so that they do not have to provide information about their characteristics or preferences each time they first use services outside the home. To achieve this it is necessary that the models and the data are interoperable. Carmagnola proposed two approaches to achieve interoperability, depending on whether or not the different systems share a single model [8]. A summary of these two approaches is presented in the next subsection.

2.4.1 Two Approaches for Achieving Interoperability

Carmagnola identified two main approaches to achieving syntactic and semantic interoperability, *shared format* and *conversion*. A third approach would be the combination of both approaches [8].

2.4.1.1 Shared Format Approach

The shared format approach utilizes user profiles to represent and exchange data from the user model and thus achieve a unified user profile. This unified profile is easily interchangeable between and interpretable by different systems. To achieve this, Carmagnola proposed standards such as vCard [16], FOAF[27] or various Semantic Web languages, such as RDF[28] and OWL[29]. Semantic Web languages provide extended representation to include several important aspects of the user, together with a broad representation of domain knowledge. For instance, GUMO (General User Model Ontology) is a user model available via the Internet that can be shared by several systems [27]. GUMO classes and properties are used in a language called User Modeling Markup Language (UserML) that supports the exchange of user model data between systems.

In summary, the exchange of information in the shared format approach is possible when both systems use a unified user profile. However, it is frequently impossible to create a unified user profile and to impose systems that adhere to a shared vocabulary. Carmagnola proposed an alternative *conversion* approach for these cases.

2.4.1.2 Conversion Approach

This approach excludes the use of a semantic or shared representation for the user model. Instead, algorithms and techniques are created to convert the syntax and semantics of user model data used in a system for use in another system. In this line, Carmagnola highlights the work of Berkovsky et al. [4] who defines hybrid recommendation algorithms to bootstrap user models in a system using information from other systems. However, this approach does not consider the semantic richness and the domain-specific knowledge on the user that the different systems have accumulated.

2.4.1.3 Combined Approach

Carmagnola proposes a solution combining the benefits of both approaches to allow flexibility in representing user models and to provide semantic mapping of user data from one system to another. The author developed a user model interoperability framework that does not impose sharing a common model [8]. The systems have the freedom to represent their models according to their specific requirement. However, to ensure interoperability they have to adhere to a standard in order to be able to exchange semantically rich data. The RDF language is used for this purpose. Carmagnola also considers that system providers (i.e. systems that the user encounters outside the home) should be required to participate in the interoperability

---

[27]FOAF: Friend of a Friend vocabulary specification 0.91 2007. http://xmlns.com/foaf/spec/ 20071002.html

[28]Resource Description Framework (RDF). W3C Recommendation, 10 Feb 2004. http://www.w3. org/TR/rdfconcepts/

[29]Web Ontology Language (OWL) - W3C Recommendation, 10 Feb 2004. http://www.w3.org/ 2004/OWL/

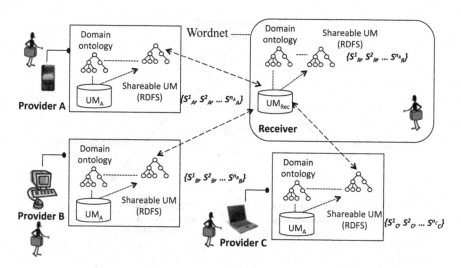

Fig. 2.2 Architecture framework for user model interoperability [8]

effort in order to maintain a shareable user model. This model should include some basic pieces of the user model that can be shared with other systems (in this case, using RDF statements). These fragments can only be shared if the user has previously given consent. In the presented scenario (Fig. 2.2) and depending on the interoperability process proposed, a *"receiver"* (R) application may request data about the user *"user"* (U) from other system *"providers"* (P). To this end a sharable model is linked to a domain ontology. When a system R needs to keep information about the user an interoperability process is performed: firstly it retrieves the shared model for the suppliers A, B and C, so that the system can interact with the fragments S_A, S_B and S_C, and then the specific data needed from these fragments is searched for.

Ontologies are well-suited to the creation of user models because they provide sufficient mechanisms for incorporating semantics in these models. In addition, ontology definition languages (e.g. RDF, OWL) are highly recommended in order to achieve interoperability between the models (to be able to exchange information). Thus, the idea of semantic mapping proposed by Carmagnola can be applied using ontologies (i.e. *ontology mapping*).

In the following paragraphs two architectures for performing ontology mapping are presented. They differ in whether or not upper ontologies are used.

2.4.2 Architectures for Ontology Mapping

According to Mao, "ontology mapping is finding correspondences between similar semantic elements in different ontologies" [42]. If these elements correspond to

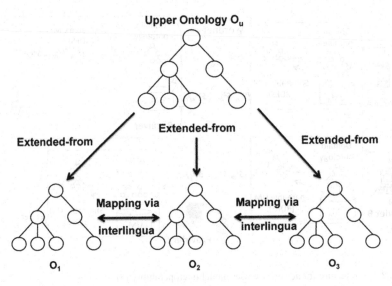

Fig. 2.3 Ontology mapping via an upper ontology [42]

concepts, partial mapping will be obtained. However, complete mapping will be achieved if, in addition to concepts, similarities between their relationships are searched for [41]. In Mao's work, the authors propose two architectures (centralized and decentralized) for searching for correspondences between ontologies.

2.4.2.1 Centralized Architecture

The centralized architecture uses upper ontologies for mapping heterogeneous ontologies. There are several upper ontologies that use very general taxonomies, universal and independent of the domain, which are able to guarantee the expressiveness and representation of concepts in any domain, precisely due to their generality. These ontologies have two main objectives: to help building specific ontologies based on general concepts and, principally, to assist in the union, mapping or integration of two independent domain ontologies. The latter is possible because, although they are independent, their root (and maybe other) concepts coincide with some of the general concepts of the upper ontology. It is thus possible to know the semantics of the union and exchange information between two or more ontologies.

These domain ontologies can use the same terms but with different meanings because of the context they come from. Alternatively, they may use terms that are different but refer to the same concept. Therefore, ontologies such as WordNet [44] can be used for union and consistency, maintaining the semantics and the coherence of the initial ontology. Figure 2.3 shows a simple example of the mapping of three ontologies using the same upper ontology. The mapping between these ontologies can be established via interlingua information provided by the upper ontology.

Among the suitable upper ontologies the following can be highlighted. DOLCE (Ontology for Linguistic Description and Cognitive Engineering) [22], OpenCyc[30], and SUMO (Suggested Upper Merged Ontology) [48]. The latter was created by the IEEE Standard Upper Ontology Working Group. Although in the beginning it was considered an upper ontology, its main objective was to build a single, consistent and complete ontology (now combined with a mid-level ontology called MILO[31]) and several other domain ontologies (such as the Communications and Economics ontology [28]). SUMO is composed of about 1,000 well-defined and documented concepts, which are linked within a semantic network with a large number of axioms, using the OWL language. Krüger et al. developed an ontological model of user context and situations (called UbisWorld). This can represent any part of the real world, be it an office, shop or an airport, or it can represent people, objects or locations, or time or events, and the properties and characteristics of all these entities [37]. This ontology therefore conceptualizes any real world entity, but it also integrates a mid-level ontology (the above mentioned GUMO) to represent the concepts related to the user.

Thus, starting from an upper ontology such as SUMO, concepts related to a more specific area such as user modelling can be specified and detailed.

There are ontologies or middle-level models, such as GUMO, representing the user and context but still remaining independent of a specific domain, thus facilitating the search for similar items. In some cases GUMO is considered an upper ontology. It is often not easy to categorize models as high-level or more specific based on their generalization, since many models cover broad areas but are also able to represent specific domains. GUMO uses OWL as the ontology language, but has been designed following the approach of the UserML language. The idea is to identify the general concepts of the user model using upper or mid-level ontologies. The previously mentioned SUMO and UbisWorld ontologies are suitable choices for this purpose. The representation of more specific knowledge could be left to the existing specific ontologies. This view leads to a modular approach, which is a key feature of GUMO. The reason for Hechman proposing this upper ontological user model was the lack of adequate alternatives at that time [27].

As we have seen, relating different ontologies to the same upper ontology can facilitate mapping. However, a suitable upper ontology may not be found or is simply not wanted. Mao therefore defines a second architecture, which is described below.

2.4.2.2 Decentralized Architecture

An alternative approach involves a decentralized architecture, which, instead of using an upper ontology interlingua, performs mappings by using different types of

---

[30]OpenCyc ontology, http://www.opencyc.org/

[31]MILO (Mid-level Ontology), http://sigmakee.cvs.sourceforge.net/viewvc/sigmakee/KBs/Mid-level-ontology.kif

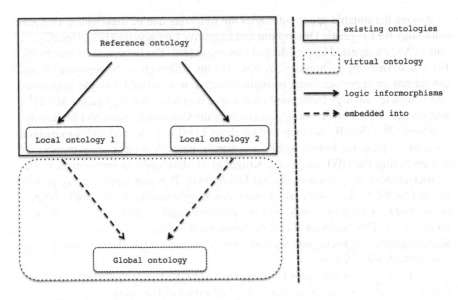

Fig. 2.4 IF-Map scenario for ontology mapping [32]

information from diverse ontologies. Mao provides several examples of these types of information: structural information (e.g. subclass and superclass relationships, domain properties, etc.) can provide an idea about the ontologies; lexical information (e.g. names, definitions, etc.) can help to re-rank the results of the mapping; auxiliary information (e.g. WordNet) provides semantics for the ontology elements; and, finally, instance information, if available, is especially useful for learning techniques which require training data. To accomplish this decentralized approach, the author proposes five mapping methods: heuristic and rule-based, machine learning-based, graph-based, probabilistic, and reasoning and theorem proving.

Other Ontology Mapping Techniques

With regard to the term ontology mapping, and depending on how we represent the result of the mapping, we can find other definitions such as *integration*, *merging*, *articulation*, *alignment*, *morphism*, *logic infomorphism*, etc. [32, 41]. Based on the *logic infomorphism* term, Kalfoglou and Schorlemmer developed an automatic method, called IF-Map (Information-Flow-based method for ontology mapping), to perform ontology mapping between a variety of different ontologies in a distributed environment. Figure 2.4 shows the IF-MAP scenario for establishing such mappings.

"Local ontology 1" and "Local ontology 2" are existing ontologies, populated and used by different communities, while "Reference ontology" is an agreement that promotes the exchange of knowledge and is supposed not to be populated.

The purpose of the reference ontology would be similar to an upper ontology but more specific than it, in order to facilitate the mapping. "Global ontology" is an ontology that does not exist, but that will be built "on the fly" to perform the merging.

Wang et al. propose a similar approach, using a reference ontology to handle service-oriented ontologies [56]. The proposed reference ontology is specified in such a way that it facilitates the mapping of ontologies. The main objective of the proposed methodology is to use a basic knowledge of the industrial domain. This knowledge is included in the reference ontology to improve the performance of the ontology mapping process. In this way, we first map the terms from the different local ontologies to the terms defined in the intermediate reference ontology, with subsequent mapping based on the semantic relationship of the intermediate terms.

2.4.3 Discussion

One of the main challenges presented in this chapter is to find the best way for systems to communicate with each other in order to exchange information about the user. The systems can then interpret this information and even deduce new features to avoid the user being continuously requested for data.

Sharing user models would improve the support provided by the various support systems in ubiquitous environments. Some of the information needed about the user by new ubiquitous services may already be stored in the user model for the home environment. This information can therefore be reused by the systems found outside the home, whenever these are interoperable.

Therefore, a highly recommended option is the use of languages that can add semantics to data and, also, the use of ontologies for representing these data. The communication needed for the exchange of information can then be carried out by mapping ontologies.

Returning to our earlier example where an elderly user with sight restrictions wants to use an elevator outside the home. As presented in this section, the procedure would be for the model of the supportive system for the lift to communicate with (i.e. to be mapped to) the base model previously created by the home system. An example of this communication is described below. The aim of this example is to show the most common characteristics used for modelling in-home and out-of-home activities. Some of the characteristics match up in both models; i.e. they have the same meaning but they are represented using different terminologies. The use of different terminologies for referring to the same concepts is something that often happens when the models are created by different service providers. The example could be also useful for explaining the process of reusing the information from an in-home model in an out-of-home model.

Some of the characteristics corresponding to the in-home model for an elderly user with sight restrictions could be the following (see Fig. 2.5): the user's likes have been described taking some contextual features into account. For instance,

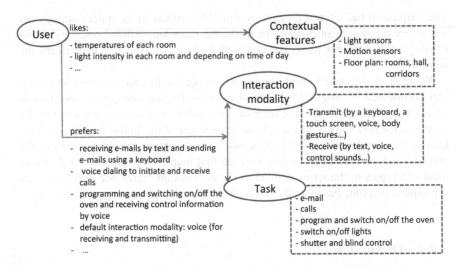

Fig. 2.5 An in-home model's instance that corresponds to an elderly user with sight restrictions

the user likes certain temperatures in each room (he/she likes a higher temperature in the living room, but a lower temperature in the kitchen). This can be described using the floor plan included in the context model. The user's preferences are also described. In this case, the characteristics of interaction modalities and tasks are considered. Thus, different methods of receiving and transmitting information can be indicated, depending on the task to be performed by the user. In this specific case, he/she prefers to use voice as the mode of interaction in almost all the tasks.

The characteristics relating to in-home models are usually more personalized and custom designed. Thus, the preferences about modalities of interaction can be directly indicated. However, in out-of-home modelling the ubiquitous services must provide a more extended model for describing the preferences and abilities of extremely diverse users. For instance, Fig. 2.6 shows an out-of-home model that includes some user abilities in order to describe the way that the user can interact with the assistance service of an elevator. In addition, a system that automatically generates interfaces could offer a tailored interface based on the characteristics provided by the model. Apart from the user's abilities, the model could describe the functionalities offered by the services (e.g. knowing which floor the elevator is on or indicating which floor the user wants to go to) and the contextual features (e.g. environmental noise), since these could change the way of interacting.

Communication between the service model and the user model must then take place in order to automatically create an instance of the interface for the user with sight restrictions using the elevator. As we can see in Figs. 2.5 and 2.6, each model describes, using its own terminology, the way that the user has to interact with the services. As stated earlier in this section, it is possible to map these models using different types of techniques. Thus, the component of the system responsible for performing this communication and generating a tailored interface would be able to

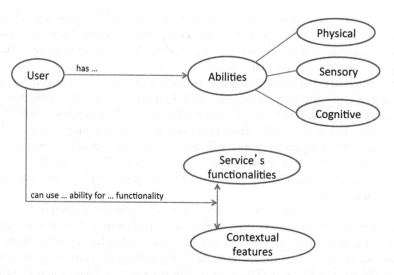

Fig. 2.6   An example of an out-of-home service model

deduce that the user is unable to see (or, at least, that he/she does not usually use the visual modality of interaction). It can also deduce that the user is able to hear and that he/she prefers to use voice as the modality of interaction for accessing the service's functionalities. Therefore, when the user requires this service it will transmit voice (for example, to indicate which floor the elevator is on). The description of some contextual features could also be useful, for instance to provide the information at a suitable volume because there is a lot of environmental noise.

Another important issue is where or how to store the results of the mapping between the different domain models. Two main approaches are possible: (a) the models are stored on a server that can be accessed from different ubiquitous environments and the necessary information extracted; (b) the information is stored in the user's device. In the latter approach, the user device can share the user model with ubiquitous services. For the implementation, either a user ontology can be designed that retains information each time a different service is used, or multiple distributed ontologies can be designed that store information about each of the domains.

The storage of models leads to ethical and legal responsibilities that must be respected. This includes provision of the necessary measures to ensure data security and privacy [36].

2.5   Conclusions

Diverse implementations of the Ubiquitous Computing paradigm allow the provision of context-aware services to people with mobile devices. These intelligent environments have proved to be extremely valuable in helping people with different degrees of physical, sensory or cognitive disabilities to live autonomously. For instance, a number of European projects working in the area of Ambient Assisted Living have demonstrated its validity in extending the length of time that elderly people are able to continue to live at home.

It is expected that the availability of out-of-home Ubiquitous Computing services will increase rapidly. These environments will provide very diverse context-aware services to occasional users. It is very likely that many of these services will prove to be supportive to users with disabilities. For instance, they may provide access to a range of intelligent machines that are currently unavailable to people with disabilities because their interfaces are not accessible. The provision of access to these services through the user's own mobile device would overcome most accessibility barriers.

In order to ensure their accessibility, access to any type of ubiquitous service requires the provision of user-adapted interfaces, based on modelling diverse factors such as the tasks, the environment and the user's own characteristics. In-home intelligent services create and maintain their own models, thus providing better and better adaptation to the user. In contrast, occasionally accessed out-of-home services do not have accurate models to adapt to each user. The most promising approaches to resolving this issue are:

- Adaptation for sporadic simple interactions can be resolved by the creation of standardized profiles that are stored in the user's mobile device and are uploaded to the ubiquitous service provider in order to obtain an adapted interface.
- More complex interactions may require the creation of standardized larger models available "in the cloud".

In both cases, two main problems must first be solved. Firstly, the structure of the models must be standardized in a way that allows the knowledge collected and stored to be understood, shared and utilized. The recent works published by Carmagnola et al. [9] on user model interoperability may provide significant guidance in this challenge. Secondly, this information must be shared in a way that ensures the privacy of the user. Recent research in this field by Wang and Kobsa [57] and Knijnenburg and Kobsa [34] show very promising approaches for the creation of privacy-aware model disclosure.

Abbreviations

AALOA	AAL Open Association
ANSI/CEA	American National Standards Institute/Consumer Electronics Association
CAP	Common Accessibility Profile
CALA-ONT	Context Ontology Model for Ubiquitous Learning Environments
CC/PP	Composite Capability/Preference Profiles
DOLCE	Ontology for Linguistic Description and Cognitive Engineering

FOAF	Frienf Of A Friend
GUMO	General User Model Ontology
ICF	International Classification of Functioning Disability and Health
IF-Map	Information-Flow-based method for ontology mapping
INREDIS	INterfaces for RElations between Environment and people with DISabilities
MILO	Mid-level Ontology
NICA	Natural Interaction with a Caring Agent
OWL-DL	Web Ontology Language – Description Logics
PIAPNE	Prototype of Ambient Intelligence for People with Special Needs
SAMBA	Systems for Ambient Intelligence enabled by Agents
SMF	Semantic Matching Framework
SOPRANO	Service-Oriented Programmable smart environments for older Europeans
SUMO	Suggested Upper Merged Ontology
UniversAAL	UNIVERsal open platform and reference Specification for Ambient Assisted Living
UCH	Universal Control Hub
URC	Universal Remote Console
UserML	User Modelling Markup Language
VAALID	Accessibility and Usability Validation Framework for AAL Interaction Design Process
ViMos	Visualization Mosaics

Acknowledgments This research work has been partly funded by the Department of Education, Universities and Research of the Basque Government. In addition, A. Aizpurua, B. Gamecho and R. Miñón enjoy PhD scholarships from the Research Staff Training Programme of the Department of Education, Universities and Research of the Basque Government.

References

1. Aarts E, Wichert R (2009) Ambient intelligence. In: Bullinger H-J (ed) Technology guide principles–applications–trends. Springer, London
2. Abascal J, Fernández de Castro I, Lafuente A, Cia JM (2008) Adaptive interfaces for supportive ambient intelligence environments. In: Proceedings of the international conference on computers helping people with special needs 2008. Lecture notes in computer science, vol 5105. Springer, London, pp 30–37
3. Atkinson M, Machin C, Li KY, Sloan D (2010) Towards accessible interactions with pervasive interfaces, based on human capabilities. In: Miesenberger K, Klaus J, Zagler W, Karshmer A (eds) Proceedings of the international conference on computers helping people 2010. Lecture notes in computer science, vol 6180. Springer, Heidelberg, pp 162–169
4. Berkovsky S, Kuflik T, Ricci F (2008) Mediation of user models for enhanced personalization in recommender systems. User Model User-Adapt Interact 18(3):245–286
5. Berre AJ et al (2007) SAMBA – an agent architecture for ambient intelligence elements interoperability. In: Jardim-Gonçalves R, Müller JP, Mertins K, Zelm M (eds) Enterprise interoperability II – new challenges and industrial approaches. Springer, Heidelberg

6. Bettini C, Brdiczka O, Henricksen K, Indulska J, Nicklas D, Ranganathan A, Riboni D (2010) A survey of context modelling and reasoning techniques. Pervasive Mobile Comput (Elsevier) 6(2):161–180
7. Brusilovsky P (2011) Adaptive hypermedia. User Model User-Adapt Interact 11:87–110
8. Carmagnola F (2009) Handling semantic heterogeneity in interoperable distributed user models. In: Kuflik T, Berkovsky S, Carmagnola F, Heckmann D, Krüger A (eds) Advances in ubiquitous user modelling. Lecture notes in computer science, vol 5830. Springer, Heidelberg, pp 20–36
9. Carmagnola F, Cena F, Gena C (2011) User model interoperability: a survey. User Model User-Adapt Interact 21:285–331
10. Carmien SP, Martínez Cantera A (2013) Diagnostic and accessibility based user modelling. In: Martín E, Haya PA, Carro RM (eds) User modeling and adaptation for daily routines. Springer, London, pp 61–88
11. Casas R, Blasco R, Robinet A, Roy Delgado A, Roy Yarza A, McGinn J, Picking R, Grout V (2008) User modelling in ambient intelligence for elderly and disabled people. In: Proceedings of the international conference on computers helping people with special needs. Lecture notes in computer science, vol 5105. Springer, Heidelberg, pp 114–122
12. Cearreta I (2010) Affinto: Ontología para la definición y creación de sistemas de interacciones afectivas sensibles al contexto. Dissertation, University of Basque Country
13. Cearreta I, Garay N (2011) Toward adapting interactions by considering user emotions and capabilities. In: Proceedings of the 14th international conference on human-computer interaction (HCII). Lecture notes in computer science, vol 6763. Springer, Heidelberg, pp 525–534
14. Cho DJ, Hong MW (2008) A design of ontology context model in ubiquitous learning environments. In: Mastorakis NE, Mladenov V, Bojkovik Z, Simian D, Kartalopoulos S, Varonides A, Udriste C, Kindler E, Narayanan S, Mauri JL, Parsiani H, Man KL (eds) Proceedings of 12th WSEAS international conference on computers. World Scientific and Engineering Academy and Society (WSEAS), Wisconsin, pp 844–848
15. Cooper A (2006) The inmates are running the asylum: why high tech products drive us crazy and how to restore the sanity. Sams Publishing, USA
16. Dawson F, Howes T (1998) Vcard mime directory profile. RFC 2426, Internet Engineering Task Force. http://www.ietf.org/rfc/rfc2426.txt. Last accessed on 17 Dec 2012
17. De Carolis B, Mazzotta I, Novielli N, Pizzutilo S (2013) User modeling in social interaction with a caring agent. In: Martín E, Haya PA, Carro RM (eds) User modeling and adaptation for daily routines. Springer, London, pp 89–116
18. Dey AK (2001) Understanding and using context. Pers Ubiquitous Comput 5:4–7
19. Edwards W, Grinter R (2001) At home with ubiquitous computing: seven challenges. In: Abowd GD, Brumitt B, Shafer S (eds) Ubicomp 2001: ubiquitous computing, international conference, Atlanta, GA, September 30–October 2 2001. Lecture notes in computer science, vol 2201, Springer, Heidelberg, pp 256–272
20. Fagerberg G, Kung A, Wichert R, Tazari M (2010) Platforms for AAL applications. In: Lukowicz P, Kunze K, Kortuem G (eds) Smart sensing and context, 5th European conference, EuroSSC 2010, Passau, Germany, 14–16 November 2010. Lecture notes in computer science, vol 6446. Springer, Heidelberg, pp 177–201
21. Frey J, Neßelrath R, Schulz C, Alexandersson J (2010) SensHome: towards a corpus for everyday activities in smart homes. In: Proceedings of the multimodal Corpora: advances in capturing, coding and analyzing multimodality. International conference on language resources and evaluation (LREC), Malta, 19–21 May
22. Gangemi A, Guarino N, Masolo C, Oltramari A, Schneider L (2002) Sweetening ontologies with DOLCE. In: Gómez-Pérez A, Benjamins VR (eds) Knowledge engineering and knowledge management: ontologies and the semantic web, 13th international conference, EKAW 2002, Sigüenza, Spain, 1–4 October 2002. Lecture notes in computer science, vol 2473. Springer, Heidelberg, pp 166–181

23. Georgantas N, Issarny V, Mokhtar SB, Bianco S, Thomson G, Raverdy PG (2010) Middleware architecture for ambient intelligence in the networked home. In: Nakashima H, Aghajan H, Augusto JC (eds) Handbook of ambient intelligence and smart environments. Springer, Boston, pp 1139–1169
24. Gu T, Wang XH, Pung HK, Zhang DQ (2004) An ontology-based context model in intelligent environments. In: Znati T, McDonald AB (eds) Proceedings of the communication networks and distributed systems modeling and simulation conference, San Diego, CA, 18–22 Jan 2004, pp 270–275
25. Gu Y, Lo A, Niemegeers I (2009) A survey of indoor positioning systems for wireless personal networks. IEEE Commun Surv Tutor 11(1):13–32
26. Hanke S, Mayer C, Hoeftberger O, Boos H, Wichert R, Tazari MR, Wolf P, Furfari F (2011) universAAL – an open and consolidated AAL platform. In: Wichert R, Eberhardt B (eds) Ambient assisted living, 4. AAL-Kongress 2011, Berlin, Germany, January 25–26, 2011. Springer, Heidelberg
27. Heckman D (2005) Ubiquitous user modeling. Dissertation, Saarland University
28. Hella L, Krogstie J (2010) A structured evaluation to assess the reusability of models of user profiles. In: Bider I, Halpin T, Krogstie J, Nurcan S, Proper E, Schmidt R, Ukor R (eds) Enterprise, business-process and information systems modeling, 11th international workshop, BPMDS 2010, and 15th international conference, EMMSAD 2010, held at CAiSE 2010, Hammamet, Tunisia, 7–8 June 2010. Lecture notes in business information processing, vol 50, part 2. Springer, Heidelberg, pp 220–233
29. Hervás R, Bravo J (2011) Towards the ubiquitous visualization: adaptive user-interfaces based on the semantic Web. J Interact Comput 23:40–56
30. Kadouche R, Abdulrazak B, Giroux S, Mokhtari M (2009) Disability centered approach in smart space management. Int J Smart Home 3(2):13–26
31. Kaikkonen A, Kaasinen E, Ketola P (2009) Handheld devices and mobile phones. In: Stephanidis C (ed) The universal access handbook. CRC Press, Boca Raton
32. Kalfoglou Y, Schorlemmer M (2003) Ontology mapping: the state of the art. J Knowl Eng Rev 18(1):1–31
33. Klein M, Schmidt A, Lauer R (2007) Ontology-centred design of an ambient middleware for assisted living: the case of soprano. In: Towards ambient intelligence: methods for cooperating ensembles in ubiquitous environments (AIMCU), 30th annual German conference on artificial intelligence (KI 2007), Osnabrück
34. Knijnenburg B, Kobsa A (2012) Making decisions about privacy: information disclosure in context-aware recommender systems. Institute for Software Research Technical Report # UCI-ISR-12-1. http://www.isr.uci.edu/tech_reports/UCI-ISR-12-1.pdf. Last accessed on 17 Dec 2012
35. Kobsa A (2007) Generic user modeling systems. In: Brusilovsky P, Kobsa A, Nejdl W (eds) The adaptive web: methods and strategies of web personalization. Lecture notes in computer science, vol 4321. Springer, Heidelberg, pp 136–154
36. Kobsa A (2007) Privacy-enhanced web personalization. In: Brusilovsky P, Kobsa A, Nejdl W (eds) The adaptive web: methods and strategies of web personalization. Lecture notes in computer science, vol 4321. Springer, Heidelberg, pp 628–670
37. Krüger A, Baus J, Heckmann D, Kruppa M (2007) Adaptive mobile guides. In: Brusilovsky P, Kobsa A, Nejdl W (eds) The adaptive web: methods and strategies of web personalization. Lecture notes in computer science, vol 4321. Springer, Heidelberg, pp 521–549
38. Küpper A (2005) Location-based services: fundamentals and operation. Wiley, Chichester
39. Lamber P, Girardello A, Ricci F, Mitterer M (2009) Mobiday: a personalized context-aware mobile service for day hospital workflow support. In: Grasso F, Paris C, (eds) Proceedings of the AIME09 International Workshop on Personalization for e-Health, 19 July 2009, Verona, Italy, pp 15–19 http://cgi.csc.liv.ac.uk/~floriana/Pers4eHealth09/Pers4eHealth09.pdf. Last accesed on 17 Dec 2012
40. Leontiev A (1978) Activity, consciousness, personality. Prentice Hall, Englewood Cliffs

41. Li L, Yang Y (2008) Agent-based ontology mapping and integration towards interoperability. J Expert Syst 25(3):197–220
42. Mao M (2008) Ontology mapping: towards semantic interoperability in distributed and heterogenous environments. Dissertation, University of Pittsburgh
43. Meyer S, Rakotonirainy A (2003) A survey of research on context-aware homes. In: Johnson C, Montague P, Steketee C (eds) Proceedings of the Australasian information security works conference on ACSW Frontiers'03, vol 21. Australian Computer Society, Inc., Australia, pp 159–168
44. Miller GA (1995) WordNet: a lexical database for English. J Commun ACM 38(11):39–41
45. Miñón R, Abascal J, Aizpurua A, Cearreta I, Gamecho B, Garay N (2011) Model-based accesible user interface generation in ubiquitous environments. In: Campos P, Graham TCN, Jorge JA, Nunes NJ, Palanque PA, Winckler M (eds) Human-computer interaction – INTERACT 2011, 13th IFIP TC 13 international conference, Lisbon, Portugal, 5–9 September 2011, Proceedings, part IV. Lecture notes in computer science, vol 6949. Springer, Heidelberg, pp 572–575
46. Mocholí JB, Sala P, Naranjo JC (2010) Ontology for modelling interaction in ambient assisted living environments. In: Bamidis PD, Pallikarakis N (eds) XII Mediterranean conference on medical and biological engineering and computing 2010, 27–30 May 2010, Chalkidiki, Greece. IFMBE proceedings, vol 29. Springer, Heidelberg, pp 655–658
47. Naranjo JC, Fernandez C, Sala P, Hellenschmidt M, Mercalli F (2009) A modelling framework for ambient assisted living validation. In: Stephanidis C (ed) Universal access in human-computer interaction. Intelligent and ubiquitous interaction environments, 5th international conference, UAHCI 2009, held as part of HCI international 2009, San Diego, CA, 19–24 July 2009. Proceedings, part II. Lecture notes in computer science, vol 5615. Springer, Heidelberg, pp 228–237
48. Niles I, Pease A (2011) Towards a standard upper ontology. In: Proceedings of the international conference on formal ontology in information systems 2001 (FOIS '01), vol 2001. ACM, New York, pp 2–9
49. Panayiotou C, Samaras G (2004) mPERSONA: personalized portals for the wireless user: an agent approach. Mob Netw Appl 9(6):663–677
50. Paternó F (2002) Task models in interactive software systems. In: Chang SK (ed) Handbook of software engineering and knowledge engineering, vol 1: Fundamentals. World Scientific Publishing Co, Singapore
51. Sixsmith A, Meuller S, Lull F, Klein M (2009) SOPRANO – an ambient assisted living system for supporting older people at home. In: Mokhtari M, Khalil I, Bauchet J, Zhang D, Nugent C (eds) Ambient assistive health and wellness management in the heart of the city, 7th international conference on smart homes and health telematics, ICOST 2009, Tours, France, 1–3 July 2009. Lecture notes in computer science, vol 5597. Springer, Heidelberg, pp 233–236
52. Sloan D, Atkinson MT, Machin CHC, Li K (2010) The potential of adaptive interfaces as an accessibility aid for older web users. In: Ferres L, Shelly C, Takagi H, Asakawa C (eds.) Proceedings of the 2010 International Cross-disciplinary Conference on Web Accessibility W4A, Raleigh, NC, 26–27 April 2010. ACM Press, New York
53. Stahl C, Frey J, Alexandersson J, Brandherm B (2011) Synchronized realities. J Ambient Intell Smart Environ 3:13–25
54. Taher F, Cheverst K, Harding M (2010) Exploring mobile phones and digital display systems to support indoor navigation by formative study methods. Int J Handheld Comput Res 1(3):32–50
55. Vildjiounaite E, Kocsis O, Kyllönen V, Kladis B (2007) Context-dependent user modelling for smart homes. In: Conati C, McCoy K, Paliouras G (eds) User modeling 2007, 11th international conference, UM 2007, Corfu, Greece, 25–29 July 2007. Lecture notes in computer science, vol 4511. Springer, Heidelberg, pp 345–349
56. Wang S, Brown KP, Lu J, Capretz M (2011) A reference ontology based approach for service oriented semantic interoperability. Int J Web Portals (IJWP) 3(1):1–16
57. Wang Y, Kobsa A (2012) A PLA-based privacy-enhancing user modeling framework and its evaluation. User Model User-Adapt Interact. doi:10.1007/s11257-011-9114-8

58. Wolf P, Schmidt A, Otte JP, Klein M, Rollwage S, Konig-ries B, Dettborn T, Gabdulkhakova A (2010) openAAL – the open source middleware for ambient-assisted living AAL. In: Proceedings of AALIANCE conference, Malaga, Spain, 11–12 Mar 2010
59. Zini F, Ricci F (2011) Guiding patients in the hospital. In: Proceedings of the 2nd international workshop on user modeling and adaptation for daily routines (UMADR): providing assistance to people with special and specific needs, pp 35–42

Chapter 3
Diagnostic and Accessibility Based User Modelling

Stefan P. Carmien and Alberto Martínez Cantera

Abstract This chapter discusses application driven user modelling by dividing user model applications into two broad categories: to provide access for the user with a device and to derive conclusions about the user. Both imply different requirements and different algorithms. The chapter starts by reviewing user modelling literature. Next, the chapter focuses on a discussion of design work in providing accessible documents to deliver accessible educational materials to students, matched to their needs and the capabilities of the device that they are using, so modelling components need to be considered. Next is a presentation of user models supporting the diagnosis of cognitive states, employing a user model that is expressed as fusion of sensor data. With a baseline created, the system captures sensor data over time and compares it with 'normal' pattern, to identify indications of Mild Cognitive Impairment (MCI). Finally, a novel framework for User Models design is shown, dividing user data into static and dynamic types.

3.1 Introduction

Our chapter will discuss application driven user modelling. Here we will discuss application based modelling in contrast to generic user modelling [23]. Context and location dependent applications, typically, will require the sort of specialized partitioning of the user models discussed here; however much that is said in application based user modelling can be applied to generic user modelling systems.

In this chapter we will look at user models as task driven systems, driven by the pull of the application and the availability of content. Because these models are used as terms of selection or as the source for classification their structure is

S.P. Carmien (✉) • A.M. Cantera
Tecnalia Research and Innovation, Mikeletegi Pasealekua 1-3, E-20009 Donostia, Spain
e-mail: stefan.carmien@tecnalia.com; alberto.martinez@tecnalia.com

E. Martín et al. (eds.), *User Modeling and Adaptation for Daily Routines: Providing Assistance to People with Special Needs*, Human–Computer Interaction Series,
DOI 10.1007/978-1-4471-4778-7_3, © Springer-Verlag London 2013

pre-determined rather than emergent and any inferences should be drawn solely from the user data itself.

We will discuss user model applications in two broad categories: User models used to provide access for the user with a device and user models used to derive conclusions about the user. Each of these has different requirements and uses different algorithms to accomplish their goals. We will discuss each of these approaches in terms of a worked out example.

Finally the chapter will close with a novel way to approach user models from the perspective of changing user attributes. This is driven by a relational database approach to users and contexts, and inspired by several experiences with projects and models where the two were conflated. By keeping data that never changed in the same 'table' as attribute values that change frequently, the system is forced to either keep multiple copes of a user model for a single person, or to constantly change the model as the context of use changes. In the chapter we will discuss the ramifications of these approaches.

3.2   Theoretical Background

User models have been used as diagnostic tools when combined with reasoning engines in expert systems [23], as configuration aids in systems with stereotype patterns [12, 31], as recommender systems in collaborative filters [27], and as tools for properly fitting assistive technology to real users needs [20]. User models that provide support for interface presentation, in terms of what, how, and when information is presented [12] are well suited to presentation of educational materials as discussed in Sect. 3.3.

The initial uses of user models supported simple lists of attribute value pairs and some kind of logic formalism. Stereotypes made user modelling possible by limiting the vocabulary that the user was described with thus allowing inferences and contradiction detection [25]. Some user models did consider the difference between static and dynamic user model attributes [19], but from the perspective of the user as a solitary unit, not part of a dynamic system. There has been a great amount of work done on user model servers, along with the architecture of the system to modularise the functions as well as supporting reuse [24]. The great advantages of these systems, abstraction and generality, is a shortcoming in designing systems that are context and history sensitive, because they typically do not retain the changing states of the users interactional and current context. In general, user modelling systems [22] need to:

- Store information about users in a non-redundant manner.
- Provide support for classification of users as belonging to one or more of these subgroups, and the integration of the typical characteristics of these subgroups into the current individual user model;

- Support recording of users' behaviour, particularly their past interaction with the system.

Additionally, user modelling systems often have these characteristics (from Fink and Kobsa [11]):

- Expressiveness and strong inferential capabilities
- Support for quick adaptation.
- Extensibility.
- Import of external user-related information.
- Management of distributed information.
- Support for open standards.
- Load balancing.
- Failover strategies.
- Transactional consistency.
- Privacy support.

There are several kinds of architecture that support novel kinds of user modelling, particularly in the field of ubiquitous and mobile computing where numerous environmental and usage history data drive the systems output to the user. In some cases having a central server provides too much reliance on robust network connection, on the other hand local devices may not have computational resources to provide real-time system response. At times, in response to security concerns, using a local desktop computer for specific data processing is the only (secure) way to guarantee the privacy and intimacy of personal information, so the decision of what/how to protect this critical information must be tackled *ad hoc* and agreed to by the end user and legal stakeholders.

User models can also be a support for interface presentation, in terms of what, how, and when information is presented [12]. This approach is well suited to presentation of educational materials as discussed in Sect. 3.3.

The World Wide Web Consortium [28, 49, 50] has provided several useful frameworks for integrating user, device and content. Substantial thought and prototyping effort has been done to produce systems [46–48] that (1) are standards based and (2) use robust technologies (RDF, existing device metadata) that formed a basis for much of the thought in Sect. 3.3.

Probably one of the most complex fields for user modelling is related to the daily activity user profiling. To tackle this challenge several projects were started on the second half of last decade: MavHome project [53], the Gator Tech Smart House [15] the iDorm [8], the Georgia Tech Aware Home [1], and the University of Colorado Adaptive Home [33]. This type of user modelling is based on sets of sensors of various types deployed across an unconstrained environment where the person performs his or her daily activity, which allows knowing what the person is doing at any moment, specially regarding activities of daily living (ADL [21]). The environment consists of various smart objects and a human being and the interactions amongst which constitute different events. The sequence of these events can tell us the when, what with and how, i.e. the person is cooking, taking breakfast, personal care, tiding the house or just sleeping. Events may have strong dependence on preceding events over multiple durations [34], and this really compounds the daily routine. A majority of previous approaches for activity representation requires explicit modelling of activity structure [32, 40]. Because such models are not at a hand or existing *a priori*, representations that can encode activity structure with minimal supervision are needed [14]. To this end, there has been recent interest in extracting activity structure simply by computing their local event-statistics (see e.g. [41], using Vector Space Model [37, 54]; using Latent Semantic Analysis [7], and [13]; using n-grams [29] respectively), but there the concept of activity is closely related to automatic document processing, natural language processing or video imaging processing, which are most times far from the peculiarities that human activities of daily living might show. Also, by adapting Latent Dirichlet Allocation graphic models [4] and Author-Topic Models from document interpretation to out- door human activity analysis, some authors have generated plausible explanations for the similarity of some parts of the data (topics) obtained from cell phones and Bluetooth devices [10, 42]. More complex but also more accurate for human activity recognition for this kind of user modelling is the use of Markov models which can better accomplish the successful detection of ADL initiation and completion. While this method is effective at distinguishing between simple tasks, handling real-world task recognition is more challenging [39]. The CASAS project [38] added some temporal information to the models to make the models more robust. Based on Markov Models and Finite State Machines, Aztiria et al. developed an algorithm to obtain frequent behaviours by means of learning user's patterns taking into account the special features of intelligent environments [3]. Based on this algorithm, Aztiria et al. propose in [2] a process to discover sequences of user actions in a system based on speech recognition. In this approach, patterns are used not only to automate actions or devices, but also to understand users' behaviour and act in accordance with it. The speech recognition system allows user to interact with the patterns in order to use his/her acceptance to automate actions. This learning machine for frequent behaviours while performing activities of daily living is a common topic in both Aztiria's research and BEDMOND project [30] but with a different interpretation focus on the user model created: Aztiria's work deals with automated assistance for implementing personal preferences (frequent activities), while BEDMOND project looks for changes in those personal preferences to be interpreted with neurology criteria. Due to those important similarities and the ability of Markov Models for ticketing and activity classification (in general) the BEDMOND project decided to follow this technique for user modelling in regard to activities of daily living.

3.3 User Models for Content Accessibility

A current topic in European research is systems supporting universal access to distance learning[1,2,3], the specifics described here came out of initial design work in the EU4ALL project [9]. These projects emphasise the use of content fitted to stereotypical sensory, and to a lesser degree, cognitive disabilities. Adding to the complexity of the problem is the rising popularity of mobile platforms, where previously a reasonable assumption was that the material would be accessed through 'typical' PCs, now material may be presented on screens as small as a smartphone and in the pad format. The rise of ubiquitous and embodied computational services adds to the complexity of delivery of the right content, in the right way, and via the right medium [12].

This kind of personalization is a special case of a broad range of applications and systems that will be tailored to a user's needs and capabilities and with respect to the context at the time and place of use. Scenarios of use may include searching and accessing schedules and real-time location of buses in transit services non-visually on a smartphone [43]; reading medical records on a wall display closest to the users current location and printing them on the nearby printer; locating a friend in a crowded shopping district, locating a film centre nearby and purchasing tickets, and using a mobile pad to present a text version of a lecture given as part of a distance learning university course.

This kind of deep personalization is dependent on three things: the end user, the context (which includes the device used for input and output) and the content. Each end-user presents a unique set of abilities and needs; sometimes this may be as broad as a preferred language or as deep as sensory and motoric disabilities with preferred alterative presentation mode (e.g. low visual acuity & synthesized text) and preferred input mode (i.e. voice commands, scan and select input). The context of the application has two dimensions: the actual environment, including the history of the users interactions with the computer (in general) and earlier sessions with this application; and the device with which the user interacts with the system, including the device constraints (i.e. small screened smartphones) and the device capabilities (i.e. speakers, text synthesiser). The third part of the personalization is the content that is presented to the user; this may be one of a set of identical 'content' expressed in different modalities, or a server that adapts the content to the needs and capabilities of the user/device.

Although this chapter and book is focused on user models, it is difficult to discuss a system that uses user models without considering the context in which the user models provide leverage. Here we will start with considering the user herself, the User Model (UM). While the specifics discussed here are concerned with the needs

---

[1]http://www.aegis-project.eu

[2]http://adenu.ia.uned.es/alpe/index.tcl

[3]http://www.eu4all-project.eu/

and abilities that differ from 'typically' abled users, looking at the problem with this lens makes it easier to highlight the salient issues for all users. Each person brings to the problem space a unique set of abilities and needs, and it is important to consider both the disability *and* the preferred mode of adaptation that this user has. Because of the unique set of attributes that the user brings to the application the use of simple stereotypes, while initially appealing, may cause a poor fit (due to the too large granularity of the stereotype) between document, applications and user. For these reason these user models have attributes that describe discretely individuals to the adaptation system. Examples of these discrete attributes may include various levels of visual disability, where describing their visual sense with a binary blind/not blind may not capture the large percentage of partially sighted persons who could gain some advantage from a custom form of visual interface. Similarly motoric and cognitive disabilities both require a wide range of attribute-value pairs to describe them. Further, a given person may have a *combination* of sensory/motoric/cognitive abilities that makes them unique. Ontologies and hierarchical description schemas may be useful, both as a support for attribute names but also in that nodes that are not leafs may also provide goals for places to base accessibility support. Finally, this part of the user modelling system should only concern itself with those attributed to the user which never change, or change very slowly monotonically down an axis of ability. By this we mean that if a user condition pertinent to the application waxes and wanes, in contrast to only decreasing over time, this should be captured as a part of the context/device model as described below.

The next element in this user modelling system is the device model (DM), which in a larger sense is the context. By this we mean several things: (1) the actual context which includes the current time and place and various other details that constitute the environment (2) the device used to access the material and (3) the changing attributes of the user. To describe the actual physical context existing ontologies and frameworks may prove both useful and a way to access existing data sources. Part of the captured context includes resources as well as static descriptions, i.e. network accessibility, temperature, light. Chapter 2 of this text nicely lays out the advantages of device modelling in discussion the problems of interoperability.

Device as context makes sense if you talk about context as everything on the outside of the user that affects, or is pertinent to, the user. In the case of the users device this provides an inventory of capabilities to the system. The inventory of device abilities can include local availability of resources (i.e. printers, Java, browser) I/O capabilities such as a list of compatible mime types [16] and input affordances (touch screen, speech synthesiser and verbal recognition). These qualities can be represented in existing schemas (frameworks or ontologies) such as UAProf and CC/PP [35, 49]. A more dynamic approach for device description can be taken with systems like the examples of V2 [44] and URC [45], or the aria initiative [51] where the device can self configure to match the needs of the applications user controls.

Finally context can be considered as the history of the user and application. History as context can be built from system history, application history, and users history (as captured for example in bookmarks and previous preferred configurations). The user modelling system can use these as both local support for making inferences, i.e. he is doing this task and has just finished this subtask, and as a basis for inferring conditions of importance to the successful completion of the goal-at-hand. An example of this could come from a task support application [5] where the user may have paused for a long time at this point in previous trials (and might trigger additional help from the system) or where the user is going over the sub task prompts very rapidly, from which the application may infer that the user has these sub-tasks memorised in a chunk and therefore might flag compression of many prompts for a set of sub-tasks into one single prompt for a larger sub-task.

The last part of this user modelling system is the content itself. It may be easier to think of the content as a participant in the accessibility process to talk about it in process terms. In this case we could use the term Digital Resource Description (DRD), a set of metadata associated with documents. In the educational example we are discussing every document or 'chunk' of digital material in an educational process has a DRD record. This approach comes out of the work that has been done in learning object metadata (LOM – IEEE 1484.12.1-2002 Standard for Learning Object Metadata) [17]. A LOM is a data model, usually encoded in XML, used to describe a learning object (a chunk of content).

The provision of appropriate material results from this set of attributes and values fitting together with the needs of the user as expressed in her user model and the capabilities of the user current device as express in the DM. This approach can take two forms: selection and delivery, and adaption. Both of these have network bandwidth requirements for successful use, which are part of the information on the DRD record. The selection and delivery approach finds the existing right content based on the user and device/context and presents this to the user. The adaption approach takes a meta document representing the content and creates the accessible content on the fly.

Select and deliver requires the system to create and store different versions of the same material, and this leads to authoring and on-going revision problems. The advantage of replacement it that it is relatively easy to implement, after the matching infrastructure in the UM and DM are in place. The problem with this approach is that content authors have the burden of many adaptations and later modifications of material will make sets of the same content out of synch. Adaptation forces the author to write in a kind of markup language, which may be mitigated by authoring support tools. Adaptation also requires another layer of software to take the marked up content as input and produce the appropriate content; this may either be done on the server or at the client. Also adaptation may support interface adaptation like ARIA [51] and URC/V2 [18], taking motoric issues in accessibility into account.

Adaption, while a complete solution, requires standardizing and built-in functionality like cascading Style sheets (CSS), which have been used in this fashion

Table 3.1 Existing personalized distance learning standards	LOM (IEEE)
	Dublin Core (DC-education extensions)
	IMS
	ACCLIP
	ACCMD
	ISO 24751−1,2,3
	DRD, PNP

with some success. Select and deliver can use existing systems but adaptation requires a whole new infrastructure, and more relevantly, the adoption of this infrastructure by all content developers.

Having described all the parts of the user modelling for accessibility system we can now describe it in short hand as:

$$UM + DM + DRD = CP$$

which we will call the Content Personalization formula.

Where UM is the user model. DM refers here to the Device Model, remembering that we have included context and history in the DM. The DRD refers to the metadata that describes the content that we have, which may take many different forms pointing to the same concepts. Finally the CP stands for content personalized for the user and context. In order for this to work we must have a tightly controlled vocabulary which is often domain specific, so that UM and DM and DRD must have matching attributes and ranges of values. It is important to ensure adoption of such systems by building on existing standards such as shown in Table 3.1.

Here are existing standards that we use in the following example:

- User Modelling (UM): PNP (personal needs and preferences from part 2 ISO 24751 draft 2007)
- Device modelling (DM): CC/PP (from W3C Composite Capabilities/Preference Profiles: Structure and Vocabularies 2.0 (CC/PP 2.0))
- Content Metadata: DRD (from Part 3: Access for All ISO 24751 (draft 2007))

So the content personalization formula then becomes:

$$PNP + CC/PP + DRD = CP$$

Here is an example of the process, in our prototypical remote learning accessibility system (Fig. 3.1). First there is a request for content object (CO) in learning process, to do this the user agent (browser) uses a proxy that inserts device model ID into the header of http request containing the request for a CO in the form of the device identifier. Then the virtual learning environment (VLE) passes these (the content ID, the UM-ID and the DM-ID) to a content personalization module

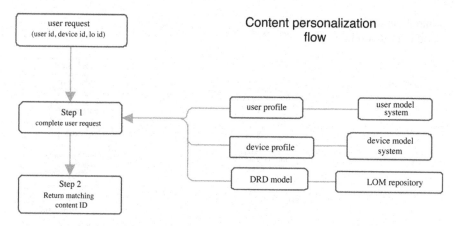

Fig. 3.1 Content personalization flow in select and deliver model

(using web service calls from here to the return to the VLE). Content personalization module then gets:

1. User profile from user modelling subsystem
2. Device profile from device modelling system
3. CO accessibility metadata-digital resource description (DRD) from Learning Object Metadata Repository
4. It matches them and returns the right one (if there is one)

An alternative process flow, using the adaptation model is below (Fig. 3.2).

Following that are examples of both the select and deliver approach and the adapt approach; to deliver accessible educational materials to students, matched to their needs and the capabilities of the device that they are using. To effect this the three parts of the CP equation need to be considered. This can be expressed as shown in Table 3.2.

This process is further broken down in Tables 3.3, 3.4, 3.5, 3.6, 3.7, 3.8, 3.9, and 3.10a. Table 3.3 showing the Adaption Preference from PNP; Table 3.4 containing Preferences from PNP; Table 3.5 giving an example of DM Attributes from CC/PP; Table 3.6 laying out the pars of a Media Meta Record from DRM; Table 3.7 explicating how Table 3.6 is comprised of the Access Mode Record Template; Table 3.8 expand on Table 3.7 into an Adaptation Template; Table 3.9 illustrates the use of the Adaptation Template; and finally Table 3.10a showing the whole process in the Content Selection Matrix.

The PNP record in the user model stores the users preferences of content presentation. The index into the preferences table:

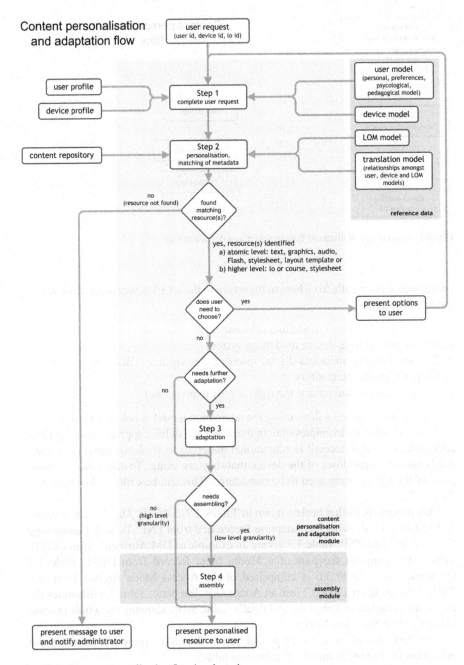

Content personalisation and adaptation flow

user request
(user id, device id, lo id)

user profile

device profile

Step 1
complete user request

user model
(personal, preferences, psycological, pedagogical model)

device model

content repository

Step 2
personalisation, matching of metadata

LOM model

translation model
(relationships amongst user, device and LOM models)

reference data

no
(resource not found)

found matching resource(s)?

yes, resource(s) identified
a) atomic level: text, graphics, audio, Flash, stylesheet, layout template or
b) higher level: lo or course, stylesheet

does user need to choose?   yes

present options to user

no

needs further adaptation?

no

yes

Step 3
adaptation

needs assembling?

no
(high level granularity)

yes
(low level granularity)

content personalisation and adaptation module

Step 4
assembly

assembly module

present message to user and notify administrator

present personalised resource to user

Fig. 3.2 Content personalization flow in adaptation process

Table 3.2 Three parts of CP equation

No.	Table	Example	Orig. access mode (s)	Adaptation type
1a	Auditory	Tape of talk	Audio	Transcription
1b	Visual	Text of lesson	Text	Audio tape
2	Visual	Physics lecture on video tape	Visual and Auditory-Two entries in metadata pointing at the same original content object: Visual and Auditory	
2_{visual}	Visual	Demonstration part of above	Visual part	Audio description
$2_{auditory}$	Visual	Lecture part of video	Auditory part	<none > NOTE: this is an *.avi
3	Visual	Photo caption	Visual	OCR
4	Visual	Text (a book)	Visual	Text to audio DM transformation

Table 3.3 Adaption Preference from PNP

Attribute	Allowed occurrences	Data type
Adaptation pref.	Zero or more per Content	Adaptation_Preference

The preferences table:

Table 3.4 Preferences from PNP

Attribute	Allowed occurrences	Data type
usage	Zero or one per Adaptation Preference	Usage_vocabulary Pg. 80
adaptation type	Zero or one per Adaptation Preference	Adaptation_type_vocabulary Pg. 64
original access mode	One per Adaptation Preference	access_mode_vocabulary pg. 63
Adaptation_preference_ranking = not DM or DRD	Zero or more per Adaptation Preference (i.e. multiple adaptation types for the same original access mode could exist)	Integer – the preference rank of the possible adaptation

Having gotten the user needs from the above, the personalizing process continues with the Device Model (in this simple case there are no context or historical data, but this is where they would go). Here the DM is based on the CC/PP record from UAProf [52]:

Table 3.5 DM attributes from CC/PP

Attribute	Description	Sample values
Mime_Type	List of the IANA mime type(s) that can be 'played' on this device	"Audio.MP3" See IANA mime type listings for vocabulary
AT-Transformation type	A bag of literal each literal represents a given transformation (scenarios)	Could be integers could be audio-to-text

where the mime types are:

- .aif   audio/aiff
- .aos   application/x-nokia-9000
- .asm   text/x-asm
- .eps   application/postscript
- .gif   image/gif
- .html   text/html
- .java   text/plain
- .jpg   image/jpeg

and the transformation type could be:

- Text → audio
- Audio → text
- HTML → correct colour contrast

Finally we have the metadata attached to each chunk of content. This is taken from the ISO 24751 part 3, the DRD record template. The media META record:

Table 3.6 Media meta record from DRM

Attribute	Allowed occurrences	Data type
Media_Object_ID	One time per Access For All Resource	EU4ALL Identifier
access mode statement	Zero or more per Access For All Resource	Access_Mode_Statement
has adaptation	Zero or more per Access For All Resource	EU4ALL Identifier
is adaptation	Zero or one per Access For All Resource	Is_Adaptation
adaptation statement	Zero or more per Access For All Resource	Adaptation_Statement
Mime_type – DM	Zero or more per Access Mode Statement	IANA Mime type

An Access Mode Record:

Table 3.7 Access mode record template

Attribute	Allowed occurrences	Data type
original access	One per Access Mode Statement	access_mode_vocabulary
access mode usage	Zero or one per Access Mode Statement	access_mode_usage_vocabulary

Disability	Example	Orig. access mode (s)	Adaptation type	PNP attribute / values	DRD Attribute / values	DM Attribute / values
Visual impairment	Physics lecture on video	Visual and Auditory Two entries in metadata pointing at the same original content object: Visual and Auditory				
Demonstration part of above	Visual part	Audio Description	Orig. access. Mode = Visual Adaptation type = Audio_Description Adaptation_ preference _ranking = 1	In the adaptation stanza Orig. access. Mode = Visual Adaptation type = Audio description Mime_type = audio.mp3	Mime_type = audio.mp3
Lecture part of video	Auditory part	<none> NOTE: this is an *.avi	Orig. access. Mode = Auditory Adaptation type = <no entry>	Mime_type = video.avi (we are only dealing with the audio side of the avi)	Mime_type = video.avi

Fig. 3.3   A more complex example of selecting content

An 'is adaptation' record:

Table 3.8   Is adaptation template

Attribute	Allowed occurrences	Data type
is adaptation of	One per Is Adaptation	EU4ALL Identifier
extent	One per Is Adaptation –	extent_vocabulary

And finally, the Adaptation Statement (AS):

Table 3.9   Adaptation template

Attribute	Allowed occurrences	Data type
adaptation type	Zero or one per AS	adaptation_type_vocabulary
original access mode	One per AS	access_mode_vocabulary
extent	Zero or one per AS	extent_vocabulary
Mime_type	Zero or more per AS	Mime type vocabulary from IANA site –

Putting them altogether we have:

Here is a more complex example requiring multiple adaptations. In this example there is a video of a physics lecture and a demonstration (Fig. 3.3). The video has two parts: audio and visual:

Finally, an example using device based transformation (Table 3.10b):

The above brief introduction to the complex domain of personalized content delivery is but one of many possible implementations of the UM + DM + DRD = CP formula. In this authors opinion the content selection and delivery approach is seriously flawed due to the authoring and updating requirement. By this I mean that although a given 'chunk' of content may exist in many different media, covering most possible needs and disabilities, any updating of the content requires simultaneous updating of all variations, a condition that has a very low probability of happening. On the other hand the adaptation approach, while complete, requires

Table 3.10a Content selection matrix

Disability	Original access mode	Adaptation type	PNP attribute/values	DRD attribute/values	DM attribute/values
Needs replacement for auditory	Audio	Transcription	Orig. access. Mode = Auditory // Adaptation type = Text represent-ation // Adaptation_preference _ranking = 1	Adaptation stanza: Orig. access. Mode = Auditory // Adaptation type = Text representation // Mime_type = Text.plain	Mime-type = text.plain
Needs replacement for visual	Text	Audio tape	Orig. access. Mode = Text Adaptation type = Audio representation //Adaptation _ranking = 1	Orig. access. Mode = Text Adaptation type = Audio representation Mime_type = Audio.MP3	Mime_type = Audio.MP3

Table 3.10b Content transformation example

Disability	Visually impaired
Example	Text (a book etc.)
Orig. access mode	Screen reader
Adaptation type	Orig. access. Mode = Text
	Adaptation type = Audio representation
	Adaptation_ preference _ranking = 1
PNP attribute/values	In the adaptation stanza
	Orig. access. Mode = Text
	No matching Adaptation type
DRD attribute/values	In the adaptation stanza
	Orig. access. Mode = Text
	No matching Adaptation type
DM attribute/values	DM has transformation attribute that maps from text
	to audio (i.e. has jaws or the like)

the adoption of a meta-language and adaption engines across the domain, which requires an integrated system to be designed, implemented and widely adopted. Because of the difficulty of doing this current efforts are typically focused on the select and deliver approach.

3.4   User Modelling for Diagnosis (the BEDMOND Project)

3.4.1   Project Background

The BEDMOND project uses user modelling with a very specific focus: how to early detect neurodegenerative diseases on the basis of human behavioural changes.

Despite controversies in neuro-cognitive and neuropsychological research, there is a general consensus that cognitive decline (CD) occurs in a high proportion of the older population (10–20%) causing discomfort in their daily performance and influencing negatively their quality of life. Though this CD can be considered a normal consequence of ageing process, it sometimes manifests in a pathological manner, progressing beyond the MCI state, which is considered to be a boundary stage between ageing and dementia. Persons with MCI have a higher risk of developing Alzheimer's Disease (AD) compared with older persons without discernable cognitive impairment [36]. When CD becomes pathological and transforms into a neuro-generative disease, it produces very high expenses to our Public Health Systems and Services, expenses that could be vastly diminished if the disease were detected at its earliest stage (Fig. 3.4).

The study of the early detection of neurodegenerative diseases is being widely carried out by investigating the root and causes of the brain degeneration, through several biomedical brain-centred fields, namely through genomic and proteomic

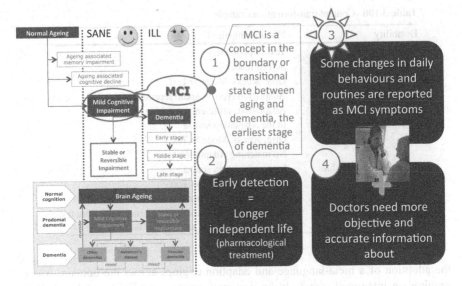

Fig. 3.4 Early stage of neurodegenerative diseases (MCI) can be detected through behaviour pattern changes

fields and modern ICT-based equipment for neuro-imaging. These fields of scientific research are still in initial phases and quite far from providing useful diagnostic tools efficacious in the short term. On the other hand, much less has been done in the detection and analysis of different early symptoms (prodromes) that can show externally, through behavioural changes in the person, the consequences of its affect on the cognitive domains of executive function (memory, disorientation, in-home activity, social affairs, etc.). These symptoms are related to specific mood changes and behaviours that strongly influence the performance of the activities of daily living. The severity of these symptoms are fairly well classified and range across several international scales for CD screening, running from a typical elder profile up to a pattern with very severe CD.

Using user models to diagnose medical/cognitive states is in its infancy, but consequently, if we are able to build a behavioural pattern for the person while being at home and still cognitively intact, which afterwards we can use in monitoring daily activity and matching it against the baseline pattern – and it is at that time user modelling becomes be crucial. In this way a system would be able to track the divergence from the original pattern. Then, these deviations are classified into different levels of danger and this classifying of the severity of the changes detected may be used to inform the doctor periodically with intelligent warnings (the intelligence must be provided by the health professional expertise to correctly interpret detected changes and deviations). This way, the doctor can get real-time objective information about the possible appearance of a neurodegenerative disease at its earliest stage.

A complete set of symptomatic behaviours, detailed by health professionals as to appear at MCI stage, where collected at the requirements specification phase of BEDMOND. Some of those symptomatic behaviours are related to activities of daily living and others to specific moods and behaviours not closely concerned with daily living (oversights, disorientation issues, etc.). For both groups of symptomatic behaviours, some of them, where feasible, can be detected through a home sensor network, taking into account that these sensors had to be necessarily low-cost and unobtrusive devices.

BEDMOND platform intelligence progresses through three main sequential steps before the last level, machine based intelligent inferences. Following is a presentation of this three-step processed information for quick understanding and easy interaction, and consequently for real usefulness and acceptance. These three steps proceed through layers of raw and derived data for knowledge processing before an early diagnostic result can be produced: (1) **data acquisition**, (2) **situation recognition** and (3) **situation interpretation**. All three steps rely on user modelling for daily activities.

This process uses a user model that is expressed as sets of sensor data. With a baseline created, the system captures sensor data over time and compares it with 'normal' events expressed as sensor data sets and uses them to classify indications of MCI.

In this first step the user model is made of a sequence of daily activities which all together build the daily routine pattern of the person. It is built from sensor events information, so this is the first step. Algorithms for user modelling and deviation calculation have been developed, pending of adjusting and optimizing the daily activity pattern for some relevant activities (meals taking, personal care). Also algorithms for deviation interpretation and user interface for presenting information to the doctor are tested and ready to be used. Four sheltered houses for field trials have been equipped with the complete infrastructure. They will serve for real testing of BEDMOND platform for about 6 months.

3.4.2   Modelling and Intelligence

Here we will describe in detail the process for creating and using user modelling in BEDMOND.

3.4.2.1   First Step: Data Acquisition

The sensors used within the smart home network for activity detection are commercial-off-the-shelf and low-cost, namely conventional Konnex (KNX) home automation sensors [26] and other wireless sensors with a proprietary protocol.

The system uses primarily low-cost and off-the-shelf sensors to monitor presence, pressure, furniture (open/close, reed switches), power consumptions (mainly for white and brown goods) and technical alarms (water, gas leak). A phone call detector for incoming and outgoing calls and a piezoelectric sensor for pressure

Table 3.11 List of sensors and home location

Room	Furniture	Sensor
Bathroom		Presence/motion sensor
	Cabinets and drawers	Reed switch
	Shower panel	Reed switch/temperature sensor
	Toilet (floor)	Pressure sensor
	Plug (shaver, hairdryer)	Power plug sensor
Kitchen		Presence/motion sensor; smoke sensor
	Refrigerator, freezer	Reed switch
	Microwave and oven	Power plug sensor/reed switch
	Cooker, toaster, ...	Power plug sensor
	Washing machine	Power plug sensor
	Cupboard and drawers	Reed switch
All	Chairs	Pressure sensor
Bedroom		Presence/motion sensor
	Bed	Pressure sensor
	Wardrobes and drawers	Reed switch
Living room		Presence/motion sensor
	TV, VCR, DVD, CD	Power plug sensors
	Sofa, chairs	Pressure sensor
	Phone	Phone sensor
Hall		Presence/motion sensor
	Drawers, entrance door	Reed switch

detection which also allows tracking the heart and respiratory rates while resting in bed are examples of some new sensors developed and integrated within an off-the-shelf telecare system, are part of the platform. The acquisition of a base line, let's call it the *behavioural pattern for daily activities*, is a complex process, partially automatic and partially manual. First, a large amount of sensor event data must be produced and stored from a real user in a real environment. Then, a manual classification and ticketing process must be applied, just to gather those events related to each of daily activities, and finally the routine or 'standard' sequence of activities. With part of that event data, typically 60–70%, a first behavioural pattern for daily activities is generated. The rest of data are later used to confirm and adjust the behavioural pattern up to the moment we get an optimized pattern, what means that about 90% of real data (events) confirm the pattern designed.

Table 3.11 lists some of the inexpensive and non-invasive sensors integrated in the current BEDMOND acquisition system prototype.

3.4.2.2 Second Step: Situation Recognition

The reasoning layer deepens into several levels, regarding the different sensors involved and the information provided by them. As shown in next Fig. 3.5, first raw description divides the set of rules of the BEDMOND system into a couple of main blocks: low level and high level layers, two consecutive reasoning steps.

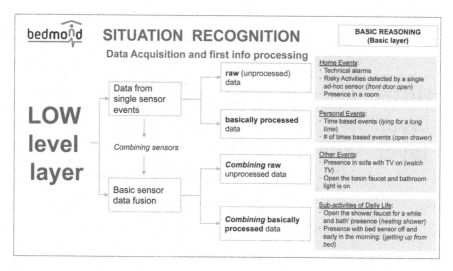

Fig. 3.5 Basic level of reasoning for situation recognition

Low level layer is related to information retrieved directly from sensor events or a basic data fusion. It is what BEDMOND calls the basic step in "Situation Recognition" phase. Some specific sensor events are able to provide relevant information by themselves; this is the case, for example, for the events triggered by the technical alarms (smoke and water leak). A single alarm event is informative enough to make the system react automatically to prevent the user about a potentially risky situation. A next level of processing could include counting of the number of alarm events registered; for example, if the system receives a certain number of alarms in a certain period of time, the system could reason in this way to detect a hazardous behaviour of the person living at home based on this "basically processed data". Another sub-level in this basic main block concerns the combination of data provided from several sensors. With a pressure sensor detecting the person in the sofa and a power consumption plug sensor activated by the TV set, the BEDMOND system can determine that the person is currently watching TV at that moment ("combining raw unprocessed data"). If those events are further processed, for example taking into account the moment of day when they are triggered and their repetition during several days of the week, a type of sub-activity of daily living being performed by the person can be inferred ("combining basically unprocessed data").

3.4.2.3 Third Step: Situation Interpretation

The previous steps are not enough to build a model or pattern of the daily activity of the person. In BEDMOND's scope, a daily routine pattern is highly relevant and thus has to be built – any single deviation might be useful support for the physician to make an early diagnosis of a neurodegenerative disease.

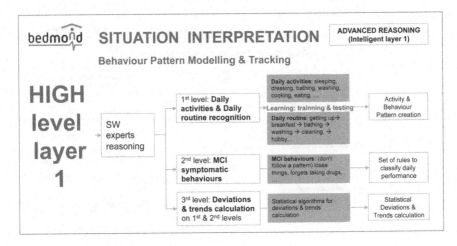

Fig. 3.6 Basic level of reasoning for situation recognition

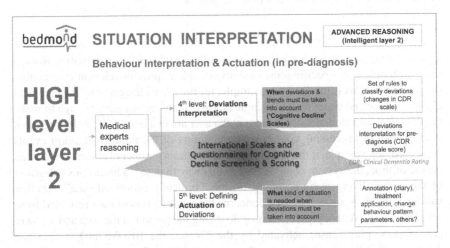

Fig. 3.7 Intelligent layer for situation interpretation with clinical criteria during pre-diagnosis stage

This is implemented in the highest level layer of reasoning, which BEDMOND calls the "Situation Interpretation" layer. It is divided into two main blocks: on the one hand, **behaviour modelling and tracking** (layer 1, in Fig. 3.6) and, on the other hand, **behaviour interpretation and actuation**. This latter main block supports generation of modules for both the pre-diagnosis assistance phase (layer 2, in Fig. 3.7) and the treatment assistance phase (layer 3, in Fig. 3.8).

Rules regarding the first main block can be considered as "software developers" rules whilst the second one is directed to the health professional's knowledge and

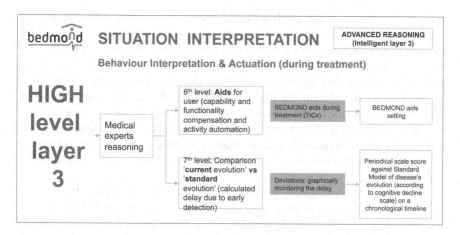

Fig. 3.8 Intelligent layer for situation interpretation during treatment stage

experience. Both include several sub-levels. As shown in Fig. 3.6 and starting from the previous basic reasoning level, BEDMOND learns and sets up an activity of daily living (ADL) profile like, for instance, having breakfast. This concrete ADL is made up of a sequence of several sub-activities: open the cabinet and take a cup → open the refrigerator and take the bottle of milk → ... This reasoning level for ticketing the sub-activities and subsequent ADL is really relevant for the early detection of a neurodegenerative process because any change on the sequence or the duration of certain sub-activities in such ADL may provide salient information for the doctor. In a similar way the next step of BEDMOND reasoning is built up with a high level model of the daily routine of the person as a new sequence of ADLs (sleep → get up → breakfast → personal care → home tiding → lunch → ...), taking into account that any deviation, change or even disappearance of an ADL in the daily routine sequence is a *prodrome* or early symptom of MCI too.

After this level of information interpretation, the behavioural pattern is created. Then, the daily tracking starts, getting the whole set of daily events from sensors and once known how to classify them into daily activities integrated in the pattern. Deviations from the pattern and trends from the daily monitoring are obtained as a last step at layer 1.

However, a second level, a set of rules, is designed to support the goals to which this project is aimed: MCI detection as the indicator of the onset of a pathological cognitive decline. As shown in next Fig. 3.7, this level will try to interpret the deviations amongst the patterns and daily performance.

When matching the daily information obtained from the home sensor network against the pattern BEDMOND proceeds to the "situation interpretation" stage. This matching includes inferring the existence (or not) of each sub-activity and daily activity, the duration of each and the sequence. The intelligence to interpret parameters (when a sub-activity or activity is missing, when an activity duration is shorter or longer, or when the sequence is altered), is provided by the doctor and introduced in the platform through the configuration module for behaviour interpretation. Depending on the user model and the expertise of the health professional, any change or deviation that has appeared in any of these parameters can be relevant for the early diagnosis. For a timely interpretation, the doctor is provided with three ranges or severity indexes, to present the processed information using a traffic-light colour strategy: green meaning there's nothing of concern happening, yellow means a warning and a recommendation of investigation of a slight deviation and red indicates that a strong deviation has been detected.

Apart from some changes in the daily routine (the aforementioned deviations), some specific behaviours of the person are considered as potential MCI symptoms too. This detection is not directly correlated with deviations in a behaviour pattern, though some of them can be attributed, to a certain extent, to changes in the way that some ADL are performed. There is no behavioural pattern for reminding appointments, for example, but this kind of forgetfulness may allow an early detection of MCI. This level is linked to sensor data fusion and to an imaginative but reliable way of detection. For example, BEDMOND algorithms detect the "loses things" behaviour (memory and/or disorientation problem) by considering a kind of erratic or compulsive period of search: many room presence detectors triggered, joint to many drawers opening / closing actions, in a short period of time or prolonged for a long while. The third level of reasoning for this first main block deals with the deviation calculation when comparing the behavioural pattern versus the daily tracking, which is a statistical matter.

The next level occurs after measuring deviations over the pattern, initially regarding the interpretation of those deviations and finally the actuation required after such interpretation. Health professional criteria are now brought into the generation of rule settings. These rules define the domains of the personality related to the executive function where the changes or deviations should be included (memory, disorientation, social affairs, etc.) but comprise setting the limits for the deviations in order to be considered in a range from mild to critical. This is the most complicated but flexible reasoning layer in BEDMOND platform.

There is also another level of intelligence in BEDMOND platform – as shown in next Fig. 3.8, which is related to consequences that could be automatically applied after deviation interpretation but it is not a matter of this chapter.

Next Fig. 3.9 recapitulates the whole set of reasoning levels approached by BEDMOND platform.

Next steps are to take into account seasonal changes of patterns due to the relevance that this segmentation might provide. This means that new patterns in future work will not be represented as a simple mean value but as a curve or a graph with mean values per month. BEDMOND is just a first approach to check the importance of the information provided, but surely not as profound as it can be.

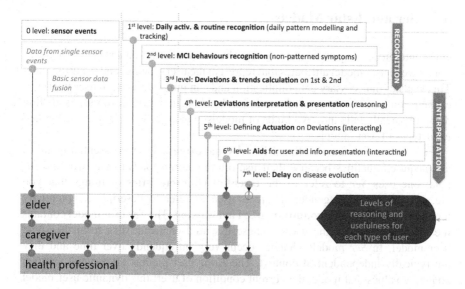

Fig. 3.9 Whole set of reasoning levels addressed by BEDMOND platform

3.4.3 Algorithmic Approach

We decided to work on ruled-based coding due to the complexity of rules to apply for some daily activities. Perhaps one of the most interesting patterns to describe relates to the "having lunch" activity. First, we had to rule out similar activities like occasional snacking (taking a piece of fruit) and others with low levels of meal preparation. Basically, in terms of cognitive deterioration, we wanted to determine if the person is starting to eat with a lower level of planning, shortening preparation activities or just rejecting some of them. We consider as relevant nutrition activities those related to (1) taking and using cutlery, (2) getting food items, (3) heating a meal and (4) sitting on a chair to eat. All of these are sensorized, though not in a very precise manner. Algorithms take events from sensors when those four activities appear in a sequence over a certain period of time. We take into account the sequence, time of day, number of times, and duration of events. Additionally we also consider what we call a 'confidence indicator' for each of those four activities. This confidence indicator reveals a likeliness of the activity appearance correlated with the "having lunch" activity and increases and decreases with triggers and time respectively, in a weighted way (not linear). Finally we apply a global confidence indicator for the whole group of partial indicators. All these indicators have been set up and validated through real experimentation. To detect deviations, the global indicator obtained at daily monitoring is compared with that one at the model. Then, each of the partial ones are considered to exist or not and compared with their correspondents in the general pattern. Certain ranges of deviations are interpreted as warnings for the doctor.

3.5 Ser and Estar Models

One common design problem encountered by user model systems is not distinguishing between user model attributes that represent the users 'being' and the users state. This leads to unnecessary data duplication and can migrate up to the user interface, causing confusion in the system's end-user. Looking at the whole of user modelling data, it basically falls into two kinds of models, which we will label as the *ser* and *estar* types of user models.

I have chosen to use two Spanish verbs that express to be as essential qualities and acquired qualities because their use roughly corresponds to the two kinds of data: one uses *Ser* to refer to the **essential characteristics** of things that you are, your name, your gender; *Estar* is used to refer to descriptive, potentially temporary attributes, the **condition**, like I am walking. The *Ser* user model contains the information about the users – these essential characteristics form the static user model. In *Ser* models changes occur very infrequently over time and they are typically independent of context. The *Estar* user models, in contrast, contain changing values that model the current condition of user; this dynamic user model may change over time, or there may be multiple copies that are linked one at a time to the ser model of the user. *Estar* models are often context dependent or reflect the different devices that are used at different times. *Estar* data type is used to keep histories of user actions.

This novel user model framework is driven by a relational database approach to users and contexts (i.e. normalization [6]), and inspired by several experiences with projects and models where the two were conflated, with problematic consequences. By keeping data that never changed in the same 'table' as attribute values that change frequently, the system is forced to either keep multiple copes of a user model for a single person, or to constantly change the model as the context of use changes. Also, conflation of the two types makes keeping histories complicated and causes redundant data to be stored. In the chapter we will discuss the ramifications of these approaches. This is not a 'new' approach *per se* (see the discussion of stable and temporary user characteristics in Chap. 4 and also in the discussion of modelling users with disabilities in Chap. 2 of this text), but by explicitly creating a framework that holds these two models design and performance advantages can be accrued.

Another advantage of discriminating between ser and estar models is that this provides a nice way to separate the actual data, so that applications with large amounts of sensor data can store it locally, making a mobile system less dependent on reliable high bandwidth connectivity.

3.6 Conclusion

Section 3.4 described a two part user model that comprises the ser user model for biographical modelling of the end-user and the estar part of the model stored with the device model. It is intended to be used by very many users simultaneously, and transparently deliver appropriate content in real-time. In contrast with this is the system in Sect. 3.3, which is designed to be used by only one person at a time (with the potential of multiple simultaneous systems in use). After a baseline is collected the application uses current and historical data form sensors to classify blocks of behaviour as normal, in need of a further look, and probably MCI. From this description the baseline data, which represents 'normal' sensor interaction, will be duplicated as long as the end-user remains cognitively in a normal range, is ser data. The tuples of sensor data that are the object of classification constitute estar data.

Why is it useful to make this discrimination in both applications? In the educational content delivery system the separation of the Device Model supports the end-user seamlessly utilizing different interface devices in differing conditions (e.g. network bandwidth). In the MCI diagnostic system the baseline ADL classified sensor signatures are conceptually easier to use to build up generic ADL signatures and *these* sets of sensor data (not just the attributes and values but also sequence of these tuples forming the classification of ADL sub-routine states) can then be used to create diagnostic systems for new individuals. As the classification model becomes more refined the generic model that instances the system always points to the latest, most accurate and representative set.

Another advantage of separating user and context/device models is the ability to have cross system reusability of the user model, speeding up the configuration and propagating the current user information across relevant applications.

3.7 Further Work

As was discussed in Sect. 3.3, further implementation of select and deliver architecture needs to be designed and used across several domains, starting with distance education and in those that rely on presentation of digital content. More challenging but in the end more important are the development of content adaptation systems, first as stand alone applications for narrow niche domains and then for generic use. Authoring tools for either the select and deliver or transform approaches need to be developed, with a focus on ease of use and adoptability. An associated problem, tied to the transformation problem is the design of meta data schemas for such a system.

In the case of the diagnostic system described in Sect. 3.4, many things can be done beyond this first approach. Our first feeling is that we could incorporate more emerging (but non-low-cost) technologies that, on the on hand, better characterize activities of daily living, for example, sounds detection and interpretation. On the other hand, the personal health condition must be widely monitored to complement the activity performance. Beyond physical condition monitoring, emotional or affective computing is another important clue to learn about the real state and health condition of the person, and not only for specific mood detection but also to know how speech expression or postural movements are degrading. New learning processes for the automatic adjusting of the model must be implemented and some other intelligent elements can also be applied to learn about real clinician interpretation.

Finally, more thought and exploration of the ser and estar approach in user modelling would be most welcome.

Acknowledgments The authors would like to thank their colleagues for their insightful comments on earlier drafts of this paper and for contributing to this paper in various ways. Stefan Carmien wishes to thank Carlos Velasco, Andy Heath, and Chris Powers and the EU4ALL project which provided the inspiration for Sect. 3.3. Alberto Martínez wishes to thank all the members of the BEDMOND Project Team, the ones close to end-users for their efficient work done while specifying requirements, the researchers highly involved in the Ambient Assisted Living environment and technologies to apply and, finally, the market oriented companies of the consortium guiding our development for the project results impact. This project is sponsored and partially funded by the European AAL JP and the National Funding Agencies from Austria (FFG), Portugal and Spain.

References

1. Abowd G, Mynatt E (2004) Designing for the human experience in smart environments. In: Cook D, Das S (eds) Smart environments: technology, protocols, and applications. Wiley, New York
2. Aztiria A, Izaguirre A, Basagoiti R, Augusto JC (2009) Learning about preferences and common behaviours of the user in an intelligent environment. In: Gottfried B, Aghajan H (eds) Behaviour monitoring and interpretation. IOS Press, Amsterdam
3. Aztiria A, Izaguirre A, Basagoiti R, Augusto JC, Cook DJ (2010) Automatic modeling of frequent user behaviours in intelligent environments. In: sixth international conference on intelligent environments (IE), Kuala-Lumpur, Malaysia, 19–21 July 2010
4. Blei DM, Ng AY, Jordan MI (2003) Latent Dirichlet allocation. J Mach Learn Res 3:993–1022
5. Carmien S (2007) Leveraging skills into independent living-distributed cognition and cognitive disability. VDM Verlag Dr. Mueller e.K, Saarbrucken
6. Codd EF (1990) The relational model for database management, 2nd edn. Addison Wesley Publishing Company, Reading
7. Deerwester S, Dumais ST, Furnas GW, Landauer TK, Harshman R (1990) Indexing by latent semantic analysis. J Am Soc Inf Sci 41(6):391–407
8. Doctor F, Hagras H, Callaghan V (2005) A fuzzy embedded agent-based approach for realizing ambient intelligence in intelligent inhabited environments. IEEE Trans Syst Man Cybern A 35(1):55–65
9. EU4ALL (European Unified Approch for Assisted Longlife Learning) (2007) Overview. http://www.eu4all-project.eu. Accessed 16 July 2012
10. Farrahi KD, Gatica-Perez D (2008) Discovering human routines from cell phone data with topic models. In: Proceedings of the 2008 12th IEEE international symposium on wearable computers (ISWC '08). IEEE Computer Society, Washington, DC
11. Fink J, Kobsa A (2000) A review and analysis of commercial user modeling servers for personalization on the World Wide Web. User Model User-Adapt Interact 10:209–249
12. Fischer G (2001) User modeling in human-computer interaction. User Model User-Adapt Interact 11(1):65–86
13. Hamid R, Johnson A, Batta S, Bobick A, Isbell C, Coleman G (2005) Detection and explanation of anomalous activities: representing activities as bags of event n-grams. In: Proceedings of the 2005 IEEE computer society conference on computer vision and pattern recognition (CVPR'05), vol 1. IEEE Computer Society, Washington, DC, pp 1031–1038

14. Hamid R, Maddi S, Bobick A, Essa I (2007) Structure from statistics – unsupervised activity analysis using suffix trees. In: Proceedings of IEEE 11th international conference on computer vision, ICCV 2007, Rio de Janeiro, Brazil, 14–20 Oct 2007

15. Helal S, Mann W, El-Zabadani H, King J, Kaddoura Y, Jansen E (2005) The Gator Tech smart house: a programmable pervasive space. IEEE Comput 38(3):50–60

16. IANA (Internet Assigned Numbers Authority), RFC 2045-RFC 2046 (1996) in Multipurpose Internet Mail Extensions IANA. http://www.ietf.org/rfc/rfc2045.txt?number=2045 Accessed Mar 2012

17. IMS Global Learning Consortium (2007) IMS learner information package accessibility for LIP information model version 1.0 final specification. http://www.imsglobal.org/accessibility/acclipv1p0/imsacclip_infov1p0.html

18. INCTS. V2 – Information Technology Access Interfaces (2007) http://www.ncits.org/tc_home/v2.htm

19. Jones KS (1989) Realism about user modeling. In: Kobsa A, Wahlster W (eds) User modeling in dialog systems. Springer, Berlin

20. Keates S, Langdon P, Clarkson PJ, Robinson P (2001) User models and user physical capability. User Model User-Adapt Interact 12:139–169

21. Knops H, Bühler C (1999) Assistive technology on the threshold of the new millennium. IOS Press, Amsterdam

22. Kobsa A (1995) Special issue on user modeling shell systems. User Model User-Adapt Interact 4(2):ii–v

23. Kobsa A (2001) Generic user modeling systems. User Model User-Adapt Interact 11:49–63

24. Kobsa A (2007) Generic user modeling systems. In: Brusilovsky P, Nejdl W (eds) The adaptive web: methods and strategies of web personalization. Springer, Berlin

25. Kobsa A, Wahlster W (eds) (1989) User models in dialog systems. Springer, New York

26. KONNEX. KONNEX (KNX) Association. http://www.knx.org Accessed Mar 2012

27. Langley P (1999) User modeling in adaptive interfaces. In: Kay J (ed) Proceedings of the seventh international conference on user modeling (UM '99). Springer, New York

28. Lassila O, Swick RR (1999) Resource description framework (RDF), model and syntax specification, W3C Recommendation 22 February 1999. World Wide Web Consortium. 1999 15 May 2007. http://www.w3.org/TR/REC-rdf-syntax/

29. Manning C, Schütze H (1999) Foundations of statistical natural language processing. MIT Press, Cambridge

30. Martínez A, Etxeberria I, Aldaz E, Roedl L, Hochgatterer A, Wöckl B, Bund J (2011) Supporting diagnostic decision for early detection of a neurodegenerative disease on a behavioural altered pattern basis. In: IADIS multi conference on computer science and information systems (e-Health Conference)

31. McKeown KR (1990) User modeling and user interfaces. In: Eighth national conference on artificial intelligence. AAAI Press/The MIT Press, Cambridge, pp 1138–1139

32. Moore D, Essa I (2002) Multitasked activities using stochastic context-free grammar, using video. In: Dechter R, Kearns M, Sutton R (eds) Eighteenth national conference on artificial intelligence, American Association for Artificial Intelligence, Menlo Park

33. Mozer MC (2004) Lessons from an adaptive home. In: Cook D, Das S (eds) Smart environments: technology, protocols, and applications. Wiley, New York City, NY

34. Oliver N, Horvitz E, Garg A (2002) Layered representations for human activity recognition. In: Proceedings of the 4th IEEE international conference on multimodal interfaces (ICMI '02). IEEE Computer Society, Washington, DC

35. Open Mobile Alliance (2007) OMA Technical Section Profile Data (UAProf). http://www.openmobilealliance.org/tech/profiles/index.html

36. Reisberg B, Ferris SH, Franssen EH, Shulman E, Monteiro I, Sclan SG, Steinberg G, Kluger A, Torossian C, de Leon MJ, Laska E (1996) Mortality and temporal course of probable Alzheimer's disease: a 5-year prospective study. Int Psychogeriatr 2:291–311

37. Salton G (1971) The SMART retrieval system – experiment in automatic document processing. Prentice-Hall, Englewood Cliffs

38. Singla G, Cook D, Schmitter-Edgecombe M (2009) Tracking activities in complex settings using smart environment technologies. Int J BioSci Psychiatry Technol 1(1):25–35
39. Singla G, Cook D, Schmitter-Edgecombe M (2008) Incorporating temporal reasoning into activity recognition for Smart Home Residents. In: AAAI workshop on spatial and temporal reasoning, pp 53–61
40. Starner T, Pentland A, Weaver J (1998) Real-time American sign language recognition using desk and wearable computer based video. IEEE Trans Pattern Anal Mach Intell 20(12): 1371–1375
41. Stauffer C, Grimson W (2000) Learning patterns of activity using real-time tracking. IEEE Trans Pattern Anal Mach Intell 22(8):747–757
42. Steinhoff U, Schiele B (2009) An exploration of daily routine modeling based on bluetooth, GSM-Data. In: International symposium on wearable computers, pp 141–142
43. Sullivan J (2004) Mobility for all project. http://www.cs.colorado.edu/l3d/clever/projects/mobility.html
44. trace.wisc.edu (2005) V2 support project at trace – toward a universal remote console standard. http://trace.wisc.edu/urc/
45. URC Consortium. The Universal Remote Console Consortium (2007) http://myurc.org/
46. Velasco CA, Mohamad Y, Carmien S (2007) Universally accessible lifelong learning by user and device profiling adaptation. In: Workshop of towards user modelling and adaptive systems for all, international conference on user modeling (UM), Corfu
47. Velasco CA, Mohamad Y (2002) Web services and user/device profiling for accessible internet services provision. In: CSUN's seventeenth annual international conference technology and persons with disabilities, Los Angeles, USA, 18–23 Mar 2002
48. Velasco A, Mohamad Y, Gilman S, Viorres N, Vlachogiannis E, Arnellos A, Darzentas S (2004) Universal access to information services – the need for user information and its relationship to device profiles. Universal Access Info Soc 3(1):88–95
49. W3C. Composite Capability/Preference Profiles (CC/PP): Structure and Vocabularies 2.0 (2007) http://www.w3.org/TR/2007/WD-CCPP-struct-vocab2-20070430/
50. W3C. The World Wide Web Consortium (W3C) (2007) http://www.w3.org/
51. W3C. WAI-ARIA Overview (2009) http://www.w3.org/WAI/intro/aria
52. Wireless Application Protocol Forum, L. WAG UAProf (2001) http://www.openmobilealliance.org/tech/affiliates/wap/wap-248-uaprof-20011020-a.pdf
53. Youngblood GM, Cook D (2007) Data mining for hierarchical model creation. IEEE Trans Syst Man Cybern C 37(4):1–12
54. Zhong H, Shi J, Visontai M (2004) Detecting unusual activity in video. In: Proceedings of the 2004 conference on computer vision and pattern recognition (CVPR'04). IEEE Computer Society, Washington, DC

Chapter 4
User Modeling in Social Interaction with a Caring Agent

Berardina De Carolis, Irene Mazzotta, Nicole Novielli, and Sebastiano Pizzutilo

Abstract Ambient Intelligence solutions may provide a great opportunity for elder people to live longer at home. When assistance and care are delegated to the intelligence embedded in the environment, besides considering task-oriented response to the user needs, it is necessary to take into account the establishment of social relations. To this aim, it becomes crucial to model both the rational and the affective components of the user state of mind. In this chapter we mainly focus on the problem of modeling the cognitive and affective variables involved in the definition of a user model suitable for this domain. After providing an overlook of the state of the art, we report about our experience in designing NICA (as the name of the project Natural Interaction with a Caring Agent), a social agent acting as a virtual caregiver able to assist elderly people in a smart environment for taking care of both the physical and mental state of the users.

4.1 Introduction

The development of Ambient Intelligence (AmI) solutions to provide assistance to elders for improving their quality of life is a very fervid research field [9, 52, 72]. In this vision, assistance and care are delegated to the intelligence embedded in the environment that should act as a virtual caregiver. Obviously, technology should not represent a further obstacle in achieving the user goals and therefore, besides providing efficient infrastructures for managing domestic automated services, it is necessary to put the emphasis on human-technology interaction. Then the environment should provide an easy and natural interface in order to make service fruition effective and adapted to the user needs. This becomes of particular importance

B. De Carolis (✉) • I. Mazzotta • N. Novielli • S. Pizzutilo
Dipartimento di Informatica, Università di Bari, Via E. Orabona, 4, 70126 Bari, Italy
e-mail: decarolis@di.uniba.it; mazzotta@di.uniba.it; novielli@di.uniba.it; pizzutilo@di.uniba.it

E. Martín et al. (eds.), *User Modeling and Adaptation for Daily Routines: Providing Assistance to People with Special Needs*, Human–Computer Interaction Series, DOI 10.1007/978-1-4471-4778-7_4, © Springer-Verlag London 2013

when the users are elderly or people with special needs. Moreover, when assistance and care of users are delegated to the intelligence embedded in the environment, besides considering task-oriented response to their needs, it is necessary to take into account the establishment of social relations, which become particularly relevant when media are not boxed in a desktop computer but are integrated pervasively in everyday life environments. In this case, according to Reeves and Nass [64] work on the media equation, in which they report how people react to media as if they were social actors, there is a growing interest in on-screen agents and robotic characters that are endowed with human-like behaviour. Embodied Conversational Agents (ECAs) and Social Robots, if properly designed and implemented, may improve the naturalness and effectiveness of the interaction between users and smart environment services [55, 56]. They have the potential to involve users in a human-like conversation using verbal and non-verbal signals for providing feedback, showing empathy and emotions in their behavior [30, 53, 59, 65]. Due to these features, embodied agents can be employed in the assisted living domain where it is important to settle long-term relations with the user.

In this chapter we describe our experience in this domain and we propose the use of a social agent that acts as virtual caregiver in a smart home, taking care of the user. After providing an overlook of the state of the art in the domain, we will report on the importance of modeling the user from both cognitive and affective points of view. As an application example we will describe our experience in designing and implementing NICA (as the name of the project Natural Interaction with a Caring Agent), a virtual caregiver able to assist elderly people in a smart environment.

4.2 Background: State of the Art and Motivation

The problem of taking care of the elderly is becoming of great importance: significant demographical and social changes affected our society in the last decades and population between 65 and 80 will increase significantly over the next decade. The aging of the population has severe consequences for both society and elderly: on one hand, there is a growing demand for caregivers; on the other hand, elderly ability to live independently becomes more difficult to achieve. Moreover, the elderly usually prefer to live at home or in an environment they feel comfortable in. In this perspective, research in Ambient Assisted Living (AAL) provides a great opportunity to improve the life quality of elderly needing special care and assistance, by providing cognitive and physical support and access to the environment services [7, 50, 72].

The use of intelligent technology to support people at home for enhancing an independent lifestyle is an issue addressed in several AAL research projects [40, 58, 60]. For instance, the *AMICA* system aims at increasing the quality of life of people suffering from Chronic Obstructive Pulmonary Disease (COPD) by monitoring their health situation using un-obtrusive sensors (e.g., small wireless sensor to track the data about the daily activity and the vital parameters of the elderly) so as to prevent diseases and provide help when needed [23]. Yet, the aim of the *SOPRANO* project [7] is to develop highly innovative, context-aware, smart services with natural and comfortable interfaces for aging people in order to significantly extend the time they can live independently in their homes. Finally, the *PERSONA* project [71] also aims to help the elders at home in the loss of skills due to the normal aging process, by providing a set of services supporting social inclusion, daily life activities, health monitoring and risk prevention. The BEDMOND project [13] aims at developing an ICT-based system for an early detection of Mild Cognitive Impairment in elderly people living at home. In this project, the model of the user's daily activities is built in order to detect signals of the disease degeneration.

The main focus of these projects is to develop technological platforms that allow on one side to monitor the health state of the user and on another side to provide natural and pleasant interfaces to the smart environment services. However, according to Nijholt et al. [54], one consequence of embedding technology in our everyday life environments is that it will be continuous in time and will involve a disparate range of devices providing support for different types of services. According to the ubiquitous computing vision, these devices will disappear in the background and the user will relate dialogically to the environment.

Since people already have a tendency to attribute human like properties to interactive systems [64], it is expected that implementing human like properties in such environment dialog systems will have an important impact on the user–system interaction. The use of embodied agents, then, could give to the users the feeling of cooperating with a human partner or having a companion rather than just using a tool [65]. However, if the social agent behavior is not properly designed and implemented there could be the risk of creating unrealistic expectations on the part of the users, and to lead to wrong mental models about the system's functionality and capacity [10]. On the other side, several studies report successful results on how expressive ECAs and robots can be employed as interaction metaphor in the assisted living domain and in other ones [6, 33, 47] where it is important to settle long-term relations with the user [4, 5, 19]. For instance, *ROBOCARE* [18], *Nursebot* [61], *Care-o-bot* [39] and *CompaniAble* [20] are projects aiming at creating assistive intelligent environments for the elderly in which robots offer support to the user at home. In some of these projects the robot, besides assisting the elderly user in daily tasks, has a companion role. Yet, several studies have been conducted to investigate the human-robot interaction and their results show how robots can be successfully employed as a good interaction metaphor when acting in the role of assistant, companions, therapeutic and socially assistive robots [25, 36, 37, 58, 77]. For example, van Ruiten et al. [75] conducted a controlled study using I-Cat, a robot developed in order to study personal robotic applications and human-robot interactions [74]. They confirmed the results, shown in [17], about the fact that elderly users like to interact with a social robot and to establish a relation with it (see [11] for a comprehensive review). The reason of the success of socially intelligent agents is probably due to the fact that interaction between human and machine has a fundamental social component [51, 64]. While not being particularly indicated in the achievement of information provision tasks (the presence of the face may cause distraction in the users and thus could prevent them from remembering the information provided), embodied agents have been particularly appreciated by users when employed in social tasks where they appear to be reliable and believable [3]. Moreover, robots have two additional properties with respect to ECAs: (1) they have a real presence that is important since it is not the user who enters in a virtual world, but the robot that participate into the real life, so that the users can interact with a physical counterpart [38, 69]; (2) they can move around, follow and observe the user in the environment, which is fundamental when designing such an interaction scenario with elderly people [67].

In the following section we discuss the issue of endowing conversational agents with user models that involve the consideration of both cognitive and affective components of the user state of mind, in order to enable the adaptation of the agents behavior to both physical and emotional user needs.

4.3 Modeling the User Cognitive and Affective State

As far as AAL is concerned, Aizpurua et al. [1] suggest that the user model should contain data about preferences, interests and cognitive characteristics. Besides these data, the modeling of the user's affective state is a key factor for the development of affect-aware systems. In particular, computer science recently began, with success, to endow user interfaces with emotions. User modeling allows socially intelligent systems to adapt to the users' behavior by constantly monitoring it and by continuously collecting their direct and indirect feedback.

Since the early Ekman and Friesen [35] classification of facial expressions according to the six basic emotions (anger, disgust, fear, happiness, sadness, and surprise), a plethora of research studies has been conducted in the domain of the affect recognition and modeling and the term *affect* is now employed to refer to a wider range of affective states.

According to Scherer's classification [69], affective states vary in their degree of stability, ranging from long-standing features (personality traits) to more transient ones (emotions), while others (such as moods or interpersonal stances are in the middle of this scale). Researchers have widely investigated the complete range of affective states by employing recognition and modeling approaches according to the main goal of their studies. In particular, middle-term affective states are usually influenced by the stable user features, such as the gender or the personality traits.

A user model is the fundamental component of an intelligent assistance system. It allows the system to capture and interpret the signals of the human users' behavior useful for inferring their goals, intentions, affective states and needs. To model the user cognitive and affective state the system has to wait to get knowledge about the user attitudes (values, interests, goals, etc.) before planning the behavior to adopt in a given situation and to observe the user feedback to the system behavior in order to revise it by correcting inappropriate choices. In the perspective of socially adaptive intelligent systems, the problem of modeling the user's state of mind commonly involves the following main types of knowledge:

(a) Stable and known subject characteristics, such as background;
(b) Gender, that may initially determine specific affective states;
(c) Dynamic context characteristics, describing the situation the user is in;
(d) Dynamically evolving cognitive and affective components of the user's state of mind, such as variables describing moods, emotions, interpersonal stances, etc.;
(e) Evidences about the user behavior in the multimodal interaction with the system: collecting evidence about the user's behavior during the interaction is fundamental to infer the cognitive and affective state components of her state of mind.

To build a user model that includes consideration of such variables means to:

• Define and test a method for recognizing the user's cognitive and affective state by means of the analysis of her behavior;
• Integrate the results of such analysis into a framework that dynamically collects these evidences and combines them with context variables and the stable user's feature in order to recognize and monitor her affective state, consistently with the task of the interaction.

Due to the uncertainty typical of emotion modeling, probabilistic approaches are very often used for user affect modeling tasks.

Klein et al. [43] propose an experimental study aimed at evaluating interfaces that implement strategies for affectively supporting users experience with negative moods and emotions by showing empathy and by actively supporting them. Results show how the affect-support settings of the experiment was effective in relieving the user negative affective states, with particular focus on frustration they experience in interacting with the computer.

Along this perspective we find the work by Prendinger et al. [62] in the scope of the Empathic Companion project. The authors developed and described an embodied agent developed in the scenario of job interviews that is able to recognize physiological data of users in real-time, to interpret this information as affective states, and to respond to affect by employing an animated agent. The emotions are represented in a two dimensional valence-arousal space and are inferred through a probabilistic decision models, which includes consideration of evidences about nodes represent the user physiological parameters collected through sensors, the agent choices and the agent's utility function.

A probabilistic model is used also by Conati [21] to monitor a user's emotions and engagement during the interaction with educational games. Conati's Dynamic Decision Network includes the consideration of dialogue related variables representing possible causes for the user's emotional state (e.g. the state of the interaction) and observable variables representing the bodily expressions caused by the emotional arousal, that is the effects of the emotions experienced by the users.

The result of the evaluation of the user affective state is used by pedagogical agents to generate the most appropriate agent's behavior to foster both user's learning and engagement in interacting with educational games. In particular, a decision-theoretic agent has been developed, that is able to select the most effective action to perform with respect to this goal.

In the learning domain, we find the work by Conati and Maclaren [22] about integrating the output of physical sensors in a more complex model based on the OCC (Ortony, Clore & Collins [57]) theory of appraisal of emotions. In the same domain, D'Mello and Graesser [31] consider the student facial expression and body posture to predict student's emotions.

Similarly, Arroyo et al. [2] combine evidences about multiple channels of physical behavior such as facial expressions, skin conductivity, posture, and pressure with contextual features in tutoring environment.

Moreover, Sabourin et al. [68] present a study about designing pedagogical empathic virtual agents in a narrative-centered learning environment. Authors adopt a cognitive model, structured as a Bayesian network, which includes personal attributes of users (i.e. personality and goals of students), environment variables (i.e. dynamic attribute capturing a snapshot of the student's situation and activity) and physiological data about the user behavior (i.e. biofeedback parameters such as heart rate or galvanic skin response).

de Rosis et al. [32] propose a way for integrating linguistic and acoustic analysis for inferring the social attitude of users while interacting with a virtual agent acting as a therapist in the diet domain. In their probabilistic framework, authors integrate evidences about lexical choices and acoustic features in order to recognize the user friendly (or unfriendly) attitude towards the agent, with the long-term goal of adapting its behavior accordingly.

De Carolis and Cozzolongo [25] describe how the prosodic analysis of the user's utterance can be successfully employed to disambiguate the meaning and the valence of user's feedback in human-robot interaction.

Multimodal analysis is also the focus of the study by Caridakis et al. [12]. They rely on a combination of facial expression detection and prosodic parameters to recognize the user emotional state in naturalistic interaction. Recognition is performed using neural networks, due to their efficacy in modeling short-term dynamic events that characterize the facial and acoustic expressivity of users. Once again, the discrete emotion labels are mapped onto a two-dimensional scheme describing valence and activation level.

Table 4.1 summarizes the main characteristics of the surveyed research. A detailed review on methods and approaches adopted in literature for performing user emotion modeling may be found in [44].

In the following section we describe our approach to modeling the user in a smart environment, by taking into account a combination of her stable features, attitudes and beliefs, as inferred by an integration of both linguistic and acoustic analysis.

Table 4.1 A summary of the surveyed research

Study	Domain and Goal	Observable features involved in the model
Prendinger et al. [62]	Developing an emotionally intelligent embodied conversational agent	*Physiological* data
Conati [21]	Monitoring a user's emotions and engagement during the interaction with educational games	*Context* related variables (e.g. the state of the interaction) combined with *physical* features (i.e. bodily expressions of arousal)
Conati and Maclaren [22]		*Physical* behavior combined with *cognitive modeling* of emotions (OCC)
D'Mello and Graesser [31]	Predicting student's emotions during learning	*Physical* behavior: facial expression and body posture
Arroyo et al. [2]	Recognizing student's emotions during learning	*Physical* behavior (such as facial expressions, skin conductivity, posture, and pressure) are combined with *contextual* features in the tutoring environment
Sabourin et al. [68]	Designing pedagogical empathic virtual agents	*Cognitive* (e.g. personality traits and goals), *contextual* (i.e. the student's situation and activity) and *physiological* (i.e. biofeedback parameters) features
de Rosis et al. [34]	Recognizing the user's social attitude towards an embodied conversational agent	Combination of *linguistic* and *acoustic* features
De Carolis and Cozzolongo [25]	Recognizing the valence of user's feedback in human-robot interaction	Combination of *linguistic* and *acoustic* features
Caridakis et al. [12]	Recognizing the user emotional state in naturalistic interaction	Combination of *facial expression* and *prosody*

4.4 NICA as An Example of a Socially Intelligent Caring Agent

In order to show how the considerations outlined in the previous sections can be successfully employed in designing and implementing a social agent able to act as an emotion-aware virtual caregiver (see [18, 42] for a review), we have developed a framework in which adaptation of the services provided by the smart environment is combined with the assistance provided by a Social Agent named NICA (Natural Interaction with a Caring Agent).

In particular, NICA combines the interpretation of the user behavior (i.e. sentences, actions, etc.) with the sensors data (i.e. room temperature, presence in a room, etc.) in order to provide proactively and reactively the needed assistance by acting as a social interface between the user and the home services. To this aim, it is crucial for the agent to maintain a user model in which several kinds of information are included: stable user characteristics, temporary user traits or attitudes, beliefs about the user preferences and interest, beliefs about the user affective states. Moreover, in order to react appropriately to the events occurring in the smart environment, the agent has to keep in its memory information about which are the antecedents of emotions for the user, that is what trigger the emotions (events, situations, thoughts, etc.) [15].

NICA's reasoning then has to be able to interleave a deliberative and a reactive behavior. To this aim NICA has been modeled as a BDI (Belief, Desire, Intention) agent [63]. In particular, the belief and goal processing cycle has been developed as a simplification of the one presented by Castelfranchi et al. [16]. This model is particularly suitable for the purpose of our study since it is based on the identification of the role of supporting beliefs on goal dynamics, showing how beliefs regulate goal processing and determine intention revision. In fact, actions of NICA are regulated by relations between beliefs about the user and the environment and goals. In particular, at each stage of the goal processing it is important to understand which beliefs about the user or the environment state support or trigger a goal and whether the fate of a goal is compromised because a specific supporting belief has been threatened. To this aim, the agent has to take care of the physical and emotional state of the user as well as to manage possible unexpected situations triggered by contextual factor or events (either desirable or not). NICA uses a meta-level reasoner to interpret the context and to understand when to interrupt the current behavior in order to handle the new situation: it monitors user's cognitive and affective state of mind during the interaction and, when necessary, it reacts properly.

For successfully achieving its goal of taking care of the user, NICA is able to do the following activities:

- To pursue the main goal of performing the tasks included in the daily schedule, preserving the user's health and comfort, trying to avoid a user's negative attitude and reacting to unexpected situations appropriately;
- To interact with humans in a natural way;

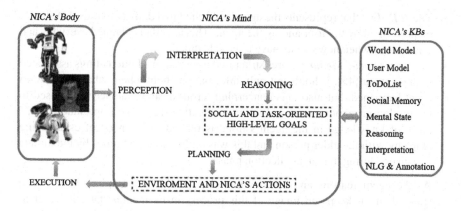

Fig. 4.1 NICA's architecture

- To behave in the appropriate way by eventually communicating and conveying social and affective signals according to the current situation.

In particular, NICA implements a life cycle based on the following steps (see Fig. 4.1):

- *Perception:* this phase allows collecting data from sensors present in the environment and to handle the user input (speech or actions in the environment).
- *Interpretation*: this module evaluates changes in the world and user state that are relevant to the agent reasoning and transforms them into a set of agent's beliefs.
- *Goal Activation*: in this phase, goals are triggered on the basis of the current beliefs.
- *Planning and Execution*: once a goal has been triggered it is achieved through the execution of a plan that is most appropriate to the situation.

In order to effectively solve the problem of adapting the robot's behavior to the user's needs and preferences, NICA's mental state reasons on and stores different types of knowledge:

- The *World Model* that represents a set of relevant beliefs about the current environment context. Example of variables included in this knowledge base are collected by diverse sensors: the environment temperature, the weather conditions, the time, the date, the list of relevant events such as birthdays, holydays, etc.
- The *User Model* that contains the representation of diverse beliefs about the users. In particular, we model long terms factors concerning stable user data (i.e. sex, age, chronic diseases, allergies, main personality traits, interests, etc.) and short-term factors concerning belief about the current user context [see 1 in this book for more details], physical and affective state, health conditions, etc.

- The *ToDoList* that represents the agenda of scheduled daily activities that should be performed by the user and by the agent. This agenda is planned everyday and it is revised when new events have to be scheduled.
- The *Agent Social Memory* stores structured information about feelings associated with an event [45]. It holds not only information about when, what and how an event happened, but also tags concerning 'arousal' and 'valence'. It is used to learn relations about events and the user affective state. The importance of this piece of knowledge in the agent's mind is related to the need of establishing empathy with the elder person and this was outlined several times by the human caregivers during the data collection phase.

As the agent reasons and updates its beliefs, infers goals, plans actions and executes them, it keeps an image of this process in its mental state. In order to deal with the uncertainty typical of this domain (e.g. dealing with exceptional situation or with the smooth evolution of the user's affective state over time), we employ probabilistic approaches in the formal representation of beliefs, intentions and goals their probability to be true. Using probabilistic models, NICA decides which behavior to adopt, that is the most appropriate set of actions to perform for achieving the inferred user's goal. These actions may be either activation of services in the environment or execution of communicative goals. In the following, we describe in detail how we collected the information for building the knowledge bases used by NICA.

At the moment we simulate and test the behaviors of NICA in different situations using a toy house equipped with a robot (Lego MindStorm with sensors for detecting its position in the house), light, temperature and presence sensors. We simulate the interaction with the user using a vocal interface. Moreover, we developed an interface for setting some parameters concerning the world state and some other user data that are the moment we are not capturing in real time (i.e. facial expressions, hands movements, physical parameters such as fever, blood pressure, etc.). We do not consider this a strong limitation of our approach since a lot or wearable and wireless devices are coming out on the market and therefore in a real setting we will be able to receive these data. We are aware that in real settings a the appearance of Lego Mindstorm could provoke a negative effects in the user, but before testing the system in smart home environment we wanted to be sure that the agent's mind was reasoning in a reliable and consistent way and therefore we employed the toy house scenario. Our research group has used the AIBO robot [25] or the ECA Valentina [27] in other projects and they could be used also in this case in future experiment with elderly users. From the implementation point of view changing the embodiment of our agent is not a problem since we adopt the mind-body architecture developed in a previous project [28]. Therefore the plan computed by the "mind" module contains the meaning to express and the "body" has to convey these meaning according to its communicative capabilities. In order to decouple meanings from signals we use the APML mark-up language [28].

4.4.1   Data Sets: Collecting Data from Human Caregivers

To define and implement feasible behaviors of NICA, we adopted a mixed approach in collecting data from which to extract the information to formalize and model in NICA's knowledge bases.

To this aim, we integrated data collected from human caregivers with the guidelines that they follow in assistance of elderly people. To collect data relevant for building the NICA's knowledge bases and behavior model, we asked two human caregivers to record their experience during the assistance of two elder women, both affected by chronic diseases during a period of 1 month. These women lived alone and had a son/daughter who could intervene only in case of need and for solving relevant medical and logistic problems.

Data have been collected using a paper-diary. Everyday the caregiver had to annotate her paper-diary with two kinds of entries: (1) the schedule of the daily tasks and (2) the relevant events of the day, using a schema like the one reported in Table 4.2.

In particular, each row of the Table 4.2 represents a relevant event with the attributes for describing it and the action performed by the caregiver when this event occurred.

For example, let's consider the second row: at 10.45 (*time*) Maria is worried (*event*). The caregiver inferred Maria's state since she is moaning, saying "Oh my, oh my" and tapping fingers on the table (*signs*) because she had to go to the doctor (*reason*). The caregiver recognized Maria's anxiety (*recognized affective state*). Hence, she went toward Maria (*action*) trying to encourage her by saying "Come on, don't worry! You will not have any problem for sure." (*communicative action*). After this action she noticed that Maria was less anxious (*effect*).

From the collected data, we extracted the knowledge needed to build the reasoning strategies of the agent, so as to make its behavior believable.

Overall, we collected a corpus of about 900 entries, which we used for: (1) understanding which are the events and context conditions relevant to goal and action triggering; (2) understanding when considering affective and social factors is important during the interaction in real-life scenarios; (3) defining situation-oriented action plans and dialogue strategies; (4) collecting example dialogues between elderly people and human caregivers useful for testing NICA behavior.

4.4.2   Representing Goals and Beliefs

In order to guide NICA's behavior, according to a set of supergoals representing its mission, we explicitly formalized, in the agent's mental state, the relation between beliefs about the user and the environment and goals.

As far as goals are concerned, the agent's *mental state* stores Persistent and Contingent Goals. The Persistent Goals (P-GOALs) never change because denote

Table 4.2 Some entries from the caregivers' paper-diary

Time	Event	Signs	Reason	Action	Communicative action	Recognized affect	Effect
10.00	…	…	Medical visit	I remind Maria about the appointment at the doctor at 11.00	Remind *"Maria, I would like to remind you that today you have an appointment at the doctor at 11.00 in the morning."*	…	…
10.30	…	…	Medical visit	I ask and help Maria to dress up according to the weather condition	Ask_for *"Today is a wonderful summer day. You can put on your beautiful dress that you like so much."*	…	Maria is dressed
10.40	…	…	medical visit	I send a reminder to Maria's daughter about the medical visit of her mother	…	…	The daughter answered that she is coming
10.45	Maria is worried	Sit down, Moaning "Oh my … Oh my" Tapping fingers	medical visit	I go toward Maria and try to encourage her	Encourage *"Come on, don't worry! You will not have any problem for sure."*	anxious	Maria is less anxious

the agent's nature, its mission, and guide its reasoning (i.e. keep the wellness of the user). Their achievement is then interleaved with the fulfillment of *contingent goals* that are triggered by the situation (i.e. call the doctor because the user is sick). The current goals to achieve are saved into the Goal Stack that is updated according to the evolution of the situation.

Goals are related to Beliefs that, in order to handle goal processing and dynamics, are classified into the agent mental state as:

- **Maintenance Beliefs**, a set of beliefs supporting P-GOALs. These beliefs must be kept true with a high level of certainty in order to support the mission and motivations of the agent. For instance, believing that the user is in a comfortable situation supports the P-GOAL of keeping the wellness of the user.
- **Triggering Beliefs** that are used to denote changes in the world that may trigger new contingent goals or may be related to maintenance beliefs. For instance, the fact that the user has high fever triggers the contingent goal of calling the doctor.

4.4.3   Reasoning on Beliefs About the User

Due to the uncertainty in the interpretation of data coming from sensors, typical of this domain, we denote with (BEL $A\,f\,p$) a belief of an agent A about f, denoting a fact about the world, that is true with a probability p.

In our application scenario, let's denote with N NICA and with U the User. Let's indicate variables in small letters and constants in capitals. Predicates, initiating with a capital, denotes a fact about the user or the world. In particular, the followings maintenance beliefs have been identified as being relevant for the mission of NICA:

- (BEL N (Feel(U, comfort)) 0.75): "NICA has to believe, with a good degree of certainty, that the user is in a quite comfortable situation".
- (BEL N (Has(U, Normal(health_state))) 0.75): "NICA has to belief with a good degree of certainty that the user is in a normal health condition", i.e. the value of the diabetes, blood pressure and heart beats are in a normal range.
- (BEL N NOT (Is(U, Negative(affective_state))) 0.75): "NICA has to belief that the user is not in a negative affective state".

The probability values of these beliefs can be inferred starting from a set of perceptions about the user and context state, or trough a dialog with the user.

Beliefs may be either elementary or complex structures. The former are derived simply by data collected by the sensors. For instance, the belief that the (BEL N (Has(Maria, fever)) 1) can be derived directly by the body temperature sensor.

The complex ones require an inference process that starts from a set of data perceived by the agent through the sensors. For example, if we consider the belief about the user's affective state, the information that may be used to infer it, with a certain degree of uncertainty, are measures about:

- the user's behavior and situation (i.e. emotional actions, physical situation, etc.),
- the fact that the current event already caused a positive/negative affective state in the past;
- information extracted from the linguistic and acoustic analysis of the user's spoken input during the dialog with NICA.

To deal with the uncertainty typical of the modeling of such subjective phenomena, as well as to cope with the problem of incompleteness of data, we decided to implement a probabilistic approach to reasoning. In particular, we adopted the formalism of Dynamic Belief Networks (DBNs) to calculate the probabilities of the inferred NICA's beliefs. DBNs [41], also called time-stamped models, are local belief networks (called time slices) expanded over time; time slices are connected through temporal links to constitute a full model. Belief Networks are a well-known formalism to simulate probabilistic reasoning in directed acyclic graphs whose nodes represent random variables and whose oriented arcs represent any kind of relationship among variables [41]. A probability distribution is assigned to the variables associated with the 'root nodes' of the network (those which have no parents) and a conditional probability table to the other nodes. The method allows dealing with uncertainty in the relationships among the variables involved in inference process.

When dealing with modeling of affective phenomena we have to take into account the fact that affective state smoothly evolve during the interaction, from one step to the subsequent one [14]. As a consequence, the affective state should be monitored and modeled as a temporal phenomenon, whose value at every time of the interaction depends on the value it assumes in the previous dialogue turn. For this reason, the DBN formalism is particularly suitable for representing situations that gradually evolve from a dialog step to the next one.

At this stage of the project there is a DBN for each complex maintenance belief of the agent. Figure 4.2 shows an example of DBN in which low level beliefs, deriving from perceptions, can be used to infer beliefs about the affective state of the user. In particular this network can be used to infer the probability that the user is in a negative, neutral or positive affective state or the probability that the user feels a particular emotion. In this model we consider only sadness, anxiety, anger and happiness that are relevant for the purpose of the system since were reported in the diary of the human caregivers.

This dynamic model allows us to take into account the influence of the user's state at the previous step. For instance, in the DBN in Fig. 4.2 this is expressed by a temporal link between the Bel(AffectiveState)Prev variable and the Bel(AffectiveState). Analogously, the evidences and the probability values of the root nodes of the BN may be extracted from other modules. This allows to manage the complexity of the network and to integrate in the model evidences deriving from different modules performing different and independent analysis.

For example, the Voice node in Fig. 4.2 is evaluated according to the results of the acoustic analysis of the users' utterances. Research in emotional speech has shown that acoustic and prosodic features can be extracted from the speech signal and used

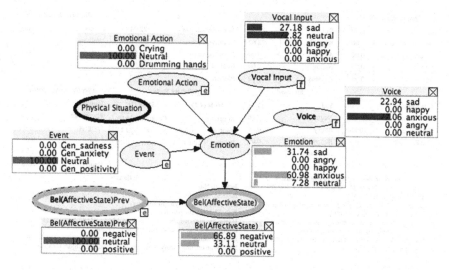

Fig. 4.2 Inferring low-level beliefs from perceptions'

to develop models for recognizing emotions and attitudes [46] In fact, the effects of emotion in speech tend to alter the pitch, timing, voice quality, and articulation of the speech signal [76] and reliable acoustic features can be extracted from speech that vary with the speaker's affective state [73]. We used Praat functions [8] in order to perform a macro-prosodic or global analysis and to extract from the audio file of each move features related to:

- The variation of the fundamental frequency (f0): pitch minimum, mean, maximum and standard deviation, slope;
- The variation of energy (RMS): min, max and standard deviation.
- The variation of harmonicity: min, max and standard deviation.
- The central spectral moment, standard deviation, gravity center, skewness and kurtosis.
- The speech rate.

The sensors responsible for capturing the speech classify the user's affective state and attitude towards the system, adopting an approach analogous to the one described in De Carolis and Cozzolongo [25]. At present, our classifier exploits the Nearest Neighbor with generalization (NNge) algorithm [48] and recognizes the valence with an accuracy of 89 %, evaluated on a dataset of 4 speakers and 748 user moves overall. The accuracy of the classifier has been validated with the *ten-fold Cross Validation technique.*

The aim of the model described in Fig. 4.2 is twofold: on one hand the model is employed to guess which specific emotional state the user is experiencing at every step of the interaction; on the other hand it is used to monitor the overall evolution of the user's affective state (i.e. the belief of the agent about the positive or negative

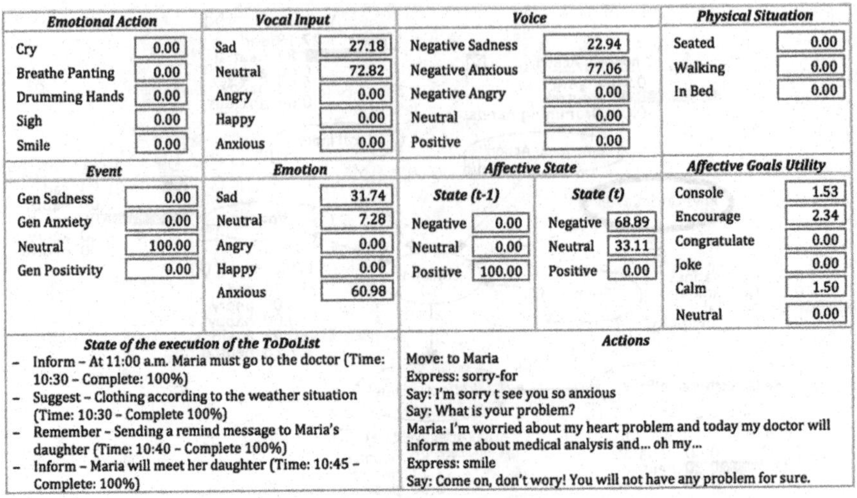

Emotional Action		Vocal Input		Voice		Physical Situation	
Cry	0.00	Sad	27.18	Negative Sadness	22.94	Seated	0.00
Breathe Panting	0.00	Neutral	72.82	Negative Anxious	77.06	Walking	0.00
Drumming Hands	0.00	Angry	0.00	Negative Angry	0.00	In Bed	0.00
Sigh	0.00	Happy	0.00	Neutral	0.00		
Smile	0.00	Anxious	0.00	Positive	0.00		

Event		Emotion		Affective State				Affective Goals Utility	
Gen Sadness	0.00	Sad	31.74	State (t-1)		State (t)		Console	1.53
Gen Anxiety	0.00	Neutral	7.28	Negative	0.00	Negative	68.89	Encourage	2.34
Neutral	100.00	Angry	0.00	Neutral	0.00	Neutral	33.11	Congratulate	0.00
Gen Positivity	0.00	Happy	0.00	Positive	100.00	Positive	0.00	Joke	0.00
		Anxious	60.98					Calm	1.50
								Neutral	0.00

State of the execution of the ToDoList	Actions
– Inform – At 11:00 a.m. Maria must go to the doctor (Time: 10:30 – Complete: 100%) – Suggest – Clothing according to the weather situation (Time: 10:30 – Complete 100%) – Remember – Sending a remind message to Maria's daughter (Time: 10:40 – Complete 100%) – Inform – Maria will meet her daughter (Time: 10:45 – Complete: 100%)	Move: to Maria Express: sorry-for Say: I'm sorry t see you so anxious Say: What is your problem? Maria: I'm worried about my heart problem and today my doctor will inform me about medical analysis and... oh my... Express: smile Say: Come on, don't wory! You will not have any problem for sure.

Fig. 4.3 A screenshot of NICA monitor window

affective state of the user). In particular, every time a new user move is entered, its linguistic and acoustic features are analyzed with respect to the context variable and the resulting evidence are introduced and propagated in the network to recognize the user's emotion and the overall polarity of her affective state. The new probabilities of individual emotions are read and contribute to formulate the next move of the agent; the probability of the dynamic variable (Bel(AffectiveState)) representing the valence of user's affective state is employed by the agent to check the consistency between its persistent goal of maintaining the user in a positive affective state and the actual emotional state the user is in at the time t, thus causing the activation or the revision of high-level planning of the agent's behavior. Then, the values of the node Vocal Input derive from a module that integrate the linguistic content of the user move with the recognition of its acoustic feature to recognize the actual user's communicative goal [25].

At present we concentrated on spoken interaction and we are not working at the recognition of facial expressions, gestures, postures and so on. For this reason the initial probability values of the other nodes Event, Physical Situation and Emotional Action, of the network in Fig. 4.2, are simulated using the framework shown in Fig. 4.3. For instance, it is possible to set parameters for running a scenario simulation like the one that will be described later on.

4.4.4 Reasoning on Goals

As mentioned previously, the mission of NICA is guided by P-GOALs. Accordingly, every day NICA plans the ToDoList and executes the scheduled actions concerning

Table 4.3 NICA's persistent goals

Persistent goal	Maintenance beliefs supporting goals
keep the wellness of the user	`(P-GOAL N (BEL N (Feel(U,comfort))))`
	`(P-GOAL N (BEL N`
	`(Has(U,normal(health_state)))))`
	`(P-GOAL N (BEL N`
	`NOT(Is(U,Negative(affective_state)))))`
schedule daily ToDoList	`(P-GOAL N (Int-To-Do N Plan(N ToDoList)))`
execute actions in ToDoList	`FORALL z element of ToDoList: (P-GOAL N`
	`(Intend-To_Do N z))`

the tasks and social actions. The agent, at each stage of its life cycle, evaluates whether there have been changes in the environment or in the user's state that may cause a change in the planned behavior by triggering new goals and/or by modifying the schedule of the planned actions.

Table 4.3 shows the set of persistent goals valid in the considered scenario. These goals are the ones that human caregivers indicated as the most important ones in their daily assistance. In our case, the goal revision process is triggered whenever a change in the environment causes the need for the activation of new contingent goal 'on demand'. For example, when a too high value is detected by the sensor that monitors the house temperature, the contingent goal of restoring a comfortable temperature is activated on-demand.

In order to decide what goal to activate, the agent reasons on the utility of an action in a certain situation. For this reason, starting from the beliefs about the current state and taking into account the agent's persistent goals using a set of reasoning rules the model selects the influence diagrams describing the possible utility of pursuing possible contingent goals in the current context. Influence Diagrams (ID) [41] have been selected as modeling formalism since the agent has to reason on the utility of pursuing a goal in the current context. In particular it models the relation between goals, random uncertain quantities (e.g. context situation) and values (e.g. utility of the goal). In an ID, the **square box** denotes a decision, the **round nodes** are chance variables, like in a BN, and the **rhombus nodes** represents the expected utility of a decision threatens one of the persistent goals of the agent (e.g. a negative attitude of the user is detected).

Among the several aspect of the goal triggering implemented by NICA, in this paper we decided to focus on the reactive revisions of the agent's socio-emotional goals. Therefore, in the next section we will show an example of how the activation of a goal is performed, with respect to a socially intelligent reaction of our agent to a negative affective state of the user.

Figure 4.4 shows an example of ID for deciding the utility of pursuing one of the goals listed in the decision node of the diagram in order to change the affective state of the user. In this figure, the square box denotes the decision about selecting a goal G_k at time t_i given the current affective state of the user. This decision influence the affective state at time t_{i+1}; the utility value is computed considering the probability

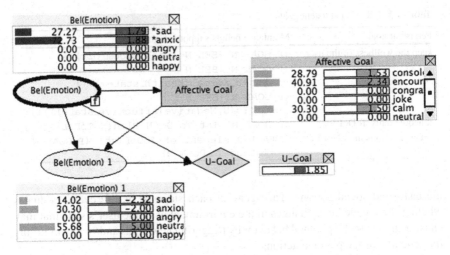

Fig. 4.4 An example of goal activation

of an improvement in the user affective state when one state value of G_k is selected and the correspondent plan will be executed. Each goal will have a utility, which defines how much it is worth to be pursued. The Evaluation Phase then decides whether or not active goals can in principle be pursued, according to the beliefs in the mental state of the user. After this checking, goals with the maximum utility are selected. In this stage of the project we did not implement a complex goal prioritization and conflict resolution mechanism. When there active goals of the same type, we use a priority function $P: G\text{-}> N$, where G is the set of active goals and N is a number expressing the priority level. The priority is computed as follows: initially each goal has a static priority that is assigned in the agent knowledge based according to the goal importance, this priority can be changed according to contextual factors and therefore according to the utility of pursuing that goal in that context. For a classification of goals according to their importance we considered the priority level indicated by human caregivers during the data gathering phase. For instance, let's suppose that there are two social goals G_1 and G_2 with the same utility in the same context C (say 1,85) but two different static priorities $p_1 = 1$ and $p_2 = 2$ then $P(G_i) = u(G_i,C)*p_i$. Then, in this case G_2 will be pursued.

In this example, since the most probable emotion, recognized from the user behavior, is anxiety, the *encourage* goal should be triggered. In fact, looking at Fig. 4.4, it should be the most effective one since it has the highest utility.

At present the agent has a limited set of IDs that correspond to the monitoring of the maintenance beliefs supporting NICA's P-Goals.

4.4.5   Representing Plans

Plans may concern the execution of tasks, actually related to the ToDoList, or dialog moves including social and affective actions, driving in this way the communicative behavior of the agent. In both cases a plan is represented as context-adapted recipe described by a set of *preconditions*, the conditions that have to be true to select the plan, the *effect* that the plan achieves and the *body*, the conditional actions that constitute the plan. After the execution of each action in the plan the correspondent effect is used to update beliefs in the agent's mental state. The following is an example of a portion of plan for scheduled actions in the ToDoList:

```
<Plan name = "SendSMSToSomeone">
    <SelectCond > <Cond var = "goal" value= "send_message"/></SelectCond>
    <Body>
        <Act name = "Request" to="PhoneAgent" var="SendRemind(X, fact)"/>
    </Body>
</Plan>
```

In particular this plan is used to achieve the goal to send a message to someone ('X') about 'fact' by requesting this action for instance to the agent controlling the telephone device. In the < SelectCond > tag, precondition for selecting the plan are specified. The following is an example of a portion of instantiated communicative plan:

```
<Plan name = "Encourage">
<SelectCond> <Cond var ="affective_goal" value="encourage"/></SelectCond>
<Body>
        <Act name = "Move" to="U"/>
        <Cond var="Feel(U,Anxious)">
        <Act name = "Express" to="U" var=" Sorry-for(NICA,U))"/>
        </Cond>
        <Cond var="know_reason" p-down="0" p-up="0,49">
        <Act name = "Ask" to="U" var="Why(U,Is(U,Anxious))"/>
        </Cond>
        <Cond var="know_reason" p-down="0,5" p-up="1">
        <Act name = "Inform" to="U" var="Understand(NICA,U)"/>
        </Cond>
        <Act name = "Express" to="U" var="Encourage(NICA,U)"/>
        ... ... ...
</Body>
</Plan>
```

The tag < Cond > allows selecting actions on the basis of the current situation. For instance, the action < Act name = "Express" to="U" var=" Sorry-for(NICA,U)/> expressing the sorry attitude of the agent, will be performed only if the user is in a negative affective state. In the same way, the action "Ask" about "Why Maria is anxious" will be performed only if the agent does not know with a certainty higher than 0.5 why the user is in the current state. Moreover, if the action is complex, then it is specified in a subplan describing elementary agent behaviors. Each communicative act in the plan is then rendered using simple template-based surface generation technique [66]. These templates are selected on the basis of the type of communicative act and its content and are expressed in APML [28] that is then interpreted and executed by the agent's body. Plans and surface generation templates have been created and optimized combining actions on the basis of pragmatic rules that were derived from the corpus dataset.

4.5   An Example Scenario

In this section we show an example of socially intelligent behavior of NICA in a typical interaction scenario. From the analysis of collected data we depicted the following scenario, which was present, with slight differences, in the diaries and that we envisaged as a suitable one for testing our agent framework:

> Maria is an old woman living alone in her smart house equipped with smart sensors and devices typical of an AmI system. She suffers of diabetes and a mild form of heart disease. Her daughter lives in another town and she is quite busy. NICA is a social robot that has the role of taking care of Maria. NICA, in order to perform its tasks, can take advantage of the AmI system capabilities. For instance, NICA may detect and communicate an alarming state of affairs. NICA, for instance, can ask the AmI system to call immediately a medical specialist, or the daughter according to the urgency of the situation.

We work on a simulation of this scenario that allows us to abstract from many technological issues, raised by the use of devices that are outside the main scope of this paper. Hence, for our purposes, all the AmI devices are embedded in software agents that are integrated in a multi-agent system, as discussed in De Carolis et al. [26]. In fact, in this scenario we want to outline the importance of integrating the social aspects of taking care of a person with task-oriented assistance.

As a running example for our simulation scenario we will consider the following:

> Maria has to go to the doctor in order to discuss the results of blood tests. NICA's selected plan is made up of the following actions correspondent to the daily ToDoList: to remember Maria about the appointment, to suggest about the dressing according to the weather situation, and to send a reminder to Maria's daughter about the medical visit of her mother. For performing the last action NICA has to ask to the agent controlling the telephone device to send a remind message to the daughter. Suddenly Maria, sitting on a chair waiting for her daughter, starts whispering and moaning and says: "Oh My... oh my...".

This utterance is recognized as having the meaning *expressing an affective state* and its prosody identifies a *negative state* and, in particular, the recognized emotion is anxiety. NICA does not know that the event *medical visit* causes anxiety in Maria, since it is the first time that this happens.

The values of the initial probability of the nodes *Voice* and *Vocal Input* are derived automatically by the speech recognition module of NICA, while the setting of the other values of the root nodes in the DBN is done through the framework interface (Fig. 4.3). These evidences are propagated in the DBN and the belief about the affective state of the user has a negative valence with a high probability (66, 89), as shown in Fig. 4.2. This fact threatens one of the maintenance beliefs for the persistent goal: P-GOAL N (BEL N NOT(Is(U,Negative(affective_state)))), then the agent decides whether a reaction is needed to restore the belief. To this aim, according to the category of the threaten maintenance belief, the appropriate influence diagram is applied. As it is possible to observe in Fig. 4.4, the most convenient goal to pursue in this situation, since it is the one with the highest priority, is the "encourage" one. Then, the most appropriate plan is selected according to its precondition (in this case the plan named "Encourage" in the previous section) and the execution of its actions begins. The plan includes the following actions since NICA does not know why the user is anxious and it will ask the user about it:

```
MoveTo(N,MARIA)
Express(N,Sorry-for(N,MARIA))
Ask(N,MARIA,Why(MARIA,Anxious))
Express(N,MARIA,Encourage(N,MARIA))
```

Figure 4.5 shows the simulation of this scenario in the toy house. Maria starts moaning and NICA shows empathy toward Maria's behavior. Then, there are different action sequences that NICA may take. If NICA does not know why Maria is anxious, then the agent decides to ask the reason of this affective state. The user answer is evaluated and, if the active goal keeps its validity than the current plan execution proceeds, otherwise the goal is dropped, actions in the list are cancelled and a new goal is triggered. The new beliefs related to the affective sphere that are acquired by the agent during the interaction with the user are stored in the Social Memory. NICA will remember that the event "medical visit" is associated to the affective state "being anxious". An example of how this information is stored in NICA's KB is reported in Table 4.4. This information can be used by NICA in the dialogue with the user for preventing this state. As a consequence, from now on NICA knows that 'medical visit' is an event that has a negative valence and generates 'anxiety' in Maria.

4.6   Evaluation

A preliminary evaluation of the system behavior in testing and refining the reasoning strategies of the agent in order to improve its performance has been performed. In this phase of the project we decided to perform a quantitative evaluation of

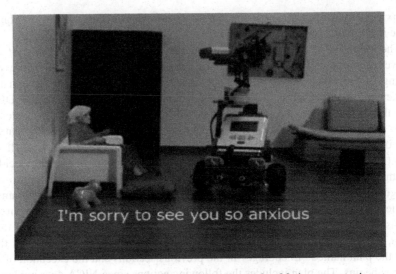

I'm sorry to see you so anxious

Fig. 4.5 A simulation of NICA's behaviors in the toy house when Maria starts moaning

Table 4.4 An entry in NICA's Social Memory

Subject	Event/action	Target	Feeling	Where	When
Maria	Medical_visit	–	Anxiety	Home	–
Maria	Visit	Lucia	Joy	Home	Sunday

the decisions and plans executed by the agent, compared to the behaviors of the human caregivers. In particular, we conducted an experimental evaluation to test whether NICA's behavior properly reflects the behavior of the human caregivers as described in the diary. Using the toy house to test the system performance allowed us to evaluate also the real-time behavior of the agent.

To this aim we randomly split our corpus into 70/30 training/test partitions. For each item of the test set, we formalized the corresponding scenario in order to set the evidence on the simulation interface graphically described in Fig. 4.3. Then, we observed NICA's behavior in terms of the physical and communicative action selected: the behavior of NICA is classified as 'correct' if it matches the choice of the human caregiver, as 'incorrect' vice versa.

Results of the evaluation are encouraging and indicate that the system performance is quite good since the choices of the agent match the human actions in the dataset in the 79% of cases.

Using the toy house to test the system performance allowed us to evaluate also the real-time behavior of the robot, which answers in a timely fashion.

4.7 Final Remarks and Conclusions

This chapter presented issues concerning the importance of taking into account both cognitive and affective factors when modeling the user in social interaction with a caring agent. In our opinion, besides assisting the elderly user in performing tasks, the agent has to establish a social long-term relationship with the user so as to enforce trust and confidence. The underlying idea of our work, in fact, is that endowing the agent with a socially intelligent behavior is fundamental when the devices of a smart home are integrated pervasively in everyday life environments. As an example, we illustrated the design and implementation of NICA, a social agent acting as a caring assistant for elderly people living in a smart home. NICA's behavior has being modeled according to the analysis of a corpus collected by human caregivers that contains the description of their experience during the assistance of two elder women. The annotation has been organized in form of a diary in which we collected 900 items describing daily tasks and the relevant events of the day.

Though, there is still room for improvement and we have to be cautious. We are aware of the main limitations in the use of a robot as the one described in the present study. First of all, the use of anthropomorphism might have negative effects in the interaction with the system. So far, we have not performed any experiment on the effect of NICA's embodiment on elderly users, since we evaluated the agent's behavior using Lego Mindstorm in a toy house. We adopt this Therefore, until now we could not evaluate the effectiveness of the non-verbal communication because it considerably limits the agent's expressivity (e.g. possibility to show a human-like face expressing an 'Happy-for' or a 'Sorry-for', and so on). In the next future, we plan to perform shortly an experiment aiming at assessing the impact of the use of a social robot vs. seamless interaction with the environment services. In this way we could also evaluate the effects agent's behavior on the affective state of the user.

Moreover, NICA's behavior is modeled according to the assumption that NICA is an empathic agent. Though, while studying the behavior of human caregivers in the early stage of the project, we observed that they play an 'educational' role and therefore, they do not always reciprocate the user's attitude. For example, if the user keeps on moaning without a clear reason then NICA should try to adopt a more assertive behavior, instead of keeping on expressing that she is sorry-for the user, trying in this way to spur the user to react the situation. In this perspective, we will include in NICA a more sophisticated reasoning on the triggering of the agent's affective state, as described in Carofiglio et al. [14] as well as a persuasion module [49] to strengthen NICA's actions in supporting and motivating the user.

Another important issue to be addressed in our future work is the interpretation of multimodal human communicative actions. For instance, understanding the user attitude from facial expressions, postures and gestures can be important in order to understand properly the semantics of the communicative act. In De Carolis et al. [29], we describe our preliminary steps towards the recognition of the user social attitude from a combination of spoken and gestural communication using a probabilistic approach that allows accommodating for the uncertainty typical of this domain.

References

1. Aizpurua A, Cearreta I, Gamecho B, Miñón R, Garay-Vitoria N, Gardeazabal L, Abascal J (2013) Extending in-home user and context models to provide ubiquitous adaptive support outside the home. In: Martín E, Haya PA, Carro RM (eds) User modeling and adaptation for daily routines. Springer, London, pp 25–59
2. Arroyo I, Cooper D, Burleson W, Woolf B, Muldner K, Christopherson R (2009) Emotion sensors go to school. In: Proceedings of the 14th International conference on artificial intelligence in education, Amsterdam, pp 17–24
3. Berry DC, Butler LT, de Rosis F (2005) Evaluating a realistic agent in an advice-giving task. Int J Hum-Comput Stud 63:304–327
4. Bickmore T, Picard RW (2005) Establishing and maintaining long-term human-computer relationships. ACM Trans Comput Hum Interact 12(2):293–327
5. Bickmore T, Cassell J (2005) Social dialogue with embodied conversational agents. In: van Kuppevelt J, Dybkjaer L, Bernsen N (eds) Advances in natural, multimodal dialogue systems. Kluwer, New York
6. Bickmore T (2003) Relational agents: effecting change through human-computer relationships. Dissertation, Massachusetts Institute of Technology
7. Bierhoff I, van Berlo A (2008) More intelligent smart houses for better care and health. In: Jordanova M, Lievens F (eds) Global telemedicine and eHealth updates: knowledge resources, vol 1. Luxexpo, Luxembourg. ISSN 1998-5509
8. Boersma P, Weenink D (2007) Praat: doing phonetics by computer (version 4.5.15) [computer program]. http://www.praat.org/. Retrieved 24 Feb 2007
9. Bomarius F, Becker M, Kleinberger T (2006) Embedded intelligence for ambient assisted living. In ERCIM special edition 67:19–20
10. Brahnam S, De Angeli A (2008) Special issue on the abuse and misuse of social agents. Interact Comput 20(3):287–291
11. Broekens J, Heerink M, Rosendal H (2009) Assistive social robots in elderly care: a review. Gerontechnology 8(2):94–103
12. Caridakis G, Karpouzis K, Wallace M, Kessous L, Amir N (2009) Multimodal user's affective state analysis in naturalistic interaction. J Multimodal User Interfaces 3(1–2):49–66
13. Carmien SP, Martínez Cantera A (2013) Diagnostic and accessibility based user modelling. In: Martín E, Haya PA, Carro RM (eds) User modeling and adaptation for daily routines. Springer, London, pp 61–88
14. Carofiglio V, de Rosis F, Grassano R (2008) Dynamic models of mixed emotion activation. In: Canamero L, Aylett R (eds) Animating expressive characters for social interactions. John Benjamins, Amsterdam
15. Carofiglio V, de Rosis F, Novielli N (2009) Cognitive emotion modeling in natural language communication. In: Tao J, Tan T (eds) Affective information processing. Springer, London. doi: 10.1007/978-1-84800-306-4
16. Castelfranchi C, Paglieri F (2007) The role of beliefs in goal dynamics: prolegomena to a constructive theory of intentions. Synthese 155:237–263. doi:10.1007/s11229-006-9156-3
17. Cearreta JM, López K, López De Ipiña C, Hernandez N, Garay M, Graña A, Álvarez (2007) Affective computing as a component of ambient intelligence. In: Information sciences 2007, Proceedings of the 10th joint conference, Salt Lake City, UT, pp 1580–1586
18. Cesta A, Cortellessa G, Giuliani MV, Iocchi L, Leone GR, Nardi D, Pecora F, Rasconi R, Scopelliti M, Tiberio L (2006) The roboCare assistive home robot: environment, features and evaluation. The roboCare technical report, RC-TR-0906-6
19. Cesta A, Cortellessa G, Pecora F, Rasconi R (2007) Supporting interaction in the roboCare intelligent assistive environment, AAAI 2007 spring symposium, interaction challenges for intelligent assistants, 26–28 Mar 2007, Stanford University, CA
20. CompanionAble project (2011) http://www.companionable.net/. Retrieved 15 Mar 2012
21. Conati C (2002) Probabilistic assessment of user's emotions in educational games. Appl Artif Intell 16:555–575

22. Conati C, Maclaren H (2010) Empirically building and evaluating a probabilistic model of user affect. User Model User-Adapt Interact 19(3):267–303
23. Crespo M, Sánchez D, Crespo Foix LF, Astorga S, León A (2010) Collaborative dialogue agent for COPD self-management in AMICA: a first insight. In: Demazeau Y, Dignum F, Corchado JM, Bajo J (eds) Advances in practical applications of agents and multiagent systems, 8th international conference on practical applications of agents and multiagent systems (PAAMS 2010), advances in intelligent and soft computing, vol 70. Springer, Heidelberg, pp 75–80
24. Dautenhahn K (1998) The art of designing socially intelligent agents – science, fiction and the human in the loop. Appl Artif Intell 12:573–617
25. De Carolis B, Cozzolongo G (2009) Interpretation of user's feedback in human-robot interaction. J Phys Agents 3(2):47–58
26. De Carolis B, Cozzolongo G, Pizzutilo S (2006) A Butler agent for personalized house control. In: Esposito F, Ras ZW, Malerba D, Semeraro G (eds) Foundations of intelligent systems, 16th international symposium, ISMIS 2006, Bari, Italy, 27–29 Sept 2006. Lecture notes in computer science, vol 4203. Springer, Heidelberg, pp 157–166
27. De Carolis B, Mazzotta I, Novielli N (2010) Enhancing conversational access to information through a socially intelligent agent. In: Armano G, de Gemmis M, Semeraro G Vargiu E (eds) Intelligent information access, studies in computational intelligence, 2010, vol 301. Springer, Heidelberg, pp 1–20, doi:10.1007/978-3-642-14000-6
28. De Carolis B, Pelachaud C, Poggi I, Steedman M (2004) APML, a mark-up language for believable behavior generation. In: Prendinger H (ed) Life-like characters, tools, affective functions and applications. Springer, Berlin
29. De Carolis B, Ferilli S, Novielli N (2012) Towards a model for recognising the social attitude in natural interaction with embodied agents. In: Proceedings IHCI-2012: the 5th international workshop on intelligent interfaces for human-computer interaction, Palermo, Italy, 4–6 July 2012
30. Dehn M, Mulken SV (2000) The impact of animated interface agents: a review of empirical research. Int J Hum-Comput Stud 52:1–22
31. D'Mello S, Graesser A (2010) Multimodal semi-automated affect detection from conversational cues, gross body language, and facial features. User Model User- Adapt Interact 20(2):147–187
32. de Rosis F, De Carolis B, Carofiglio V, Pizzutilo S (2003) Shallow and inner forms of emotional intelligence in advisory dialog simulation. In: Prendinger H, Ishizuka M (eds) Life-like characters. Tools, affective functions and applications. Springer, Berlin
33. de Rosis F, Novielli N, Carofiglio V, Cavalluzzi A, De Carolis B (2006) User modeling and adaptation in health promotion dialogs with an animated character. Int J Biomed Inform 39(5):514–531
34. de Rosis F, Batliner A, Novielli N, Steidl S (2007) You are sooo cool, valentina! Recognizing social attitude in speech-based dialogues with an ECA. In: Paiva A, Picard R, Prada R (eds) Affective computing and intelligent interaction. Lecture notes in computer science, vol 4738. Springer, Heidelberg, pp 179–190
35. Ekman P, Friesen W (1978) Facial action coding system: a technique for the measurement of facial movement. Consulting Psychologists Press, Palo Alto
36. Eriksson J, Mataric' MJ, Winstein CJ (2005) Hands-off assistive robotics for post-stroke arm rehabilitation. In: IEEE 9th international conference on rehabilitation robotics: Frontiers of the Human-Machine Interface, Chicago, Illinois, June 28-July 1 2005
37. Feil-Seifer D, Mataric' MJ (2005) Defining socially assistive robotics. IEEE 9th international conference on rehabilitation robotics: Frontiers of the Human-Machine Interface, Chicago, Illinois, June 28-July 1 2005
38. Fong T, Nourbakhsh I, Dautenhahn K (2003) A survey of socially interactive robots. Robot Autonomous Syst 42:143–166
39. Graf B, Hans M, Schraft RD (2004) Care-O-bot II – development of a next generation robotics home assistant. Auton Robots 16:193–205

40. Haigh Z, Kiff LM, Myers J, Guralnik V, Kirschbaum K, Phelps J, Plocher T, Toms D (2003) The independent lifestyle assistant (ILSA): lessons learned, technical report, technical report ACSPO3023. Honeywell Laboratories, Minneapolis
41. Jensen FV (2001) Bayesian networks and decision graphs, statistics for engineering and information science. Springer, New York
42. Jungum NV, Laurent E (2009) Emotions in pervasive computing environments. Int J Comput Sci Issues 6(1):8–22
43. Klein J, Moon Y, Picard R (2002) This computer responds to user frustration: theory, design, and results. Interact Comput 14:119–140
44. Li X (2008) Integrating user affective state assessment in enhancing HCI: review and proposition. Open Cybern Systemics J 2:192–205
45. Lim MY, Aylett R, Ho WC, Vargas P, Enz S (2009) A Socially-aware memory for companion agents. In: Ruttkay Z, Kipp M, Nijholt A, Vilhjálmsson HH (eds) Intelligent virtual agents, 9th international conference, IVA 2009, Amsterdam, The Netherlands, 14–16 Sept 2009, Lecture notes in computer science, vol 5773. Springer, Heidelberg, pp 20–26
46. Litman D, Forbes K, Silliman S (2003) Towards emotion prediction in spoken tutoring dialogues. In: Proceedings of the 2003 conference of the North American chapter of the association for computational linguistics on human language technology: companion volume of the proceedings of HLT-NAACL 2003 – short papers – Volume 2 (NAACL-Short '03), vol 2. Association for Computational Linguistics, Stroudsburg, pp 52–54
47. Marsella SC, Johnson WL, LaBore CM (2003) Interactive pedagogical drama for health interventions. In: Hoppe U et al (eds) Artificial intelligence in education: shaping the future of learning through intelligent technologies. Ios Press, Amsterdam
48. Martin B (1995) Instance-based learning: nearest neighbor with generalization. Dissertation, University of Waikato, New Zealand
49. Mazzotta I, Silvestri V, de Rosis F (2008) Emotional and non emotional persuasion strength. In: Proceedings of the AISB 2008 symposium on persuasive technology, vol 3, The Society for the Study of Artificial Intelligence and Simulation of Behaviour, London, pp 14–21
50. McFadden T, Indulska J (2004) Context-aware environments for independent living. In: Underwood M, Suridge K (eds) Contibuting to an ageing agenda: abstracts and proceedings of ERA 2004: the 3rd national conference for emerging researchers in ageing, Brisbane, Australia, 2 Dec 2004, Australasian Centre on Ageing, The University of Queensland
51. Nass C, Steuer J, Tauber ER (1994) Computers are social actors. In: Adelson B, Dumais S, Olson J (eds) Proceedings of the SIGCHI conference on human factors in computing systems: celebrating interdependence (CHI '94), ACM Press, New York
52. Nehmer J, Becker M, Karshmer A, Lamm R (2006) Living assistance systems: an ambient intelligence approach. In: Proceedings of the 28th international conference on software engineering (ICSE '06). ACM, New York
53. Niewiadomski R, Ochs M, Pelachaud C (2008) In: Prendinger H, Lester J, Ishizuka M (eds) Intelligent virtual agents, 8th international conference, IVA 2008, Tokyo, Japan, 1–3 Sept 2008. Lecture notes in computer science, vol 5208. Springer, Heidelberg, pp 37–44
54. Nijholt A, de Ruyter B, Heylen D, Privender S (2006) Social interfaces for ambient intelligence environments. In: Aarts E, Encarnaçao J (eds) True visions: the emergence of ambient intelligence. Springer, New York
55. Nijholt A (2003) Disappearing computers, social actors and embodied agents. In: Kunii T, Hock SS, Sourin A, (eds) Proceedings of the 2003 international conference on cyberworlds (CW '03). IEEE Computer Society, Washington, DC
56. Ortiz A, Del Puy Carretero M, Oyarzun D, Yanguas JJ, Buiza C, Gonzalez MF, Etxeberria I (2006) Elderly users in ambient intelligence: does an avatar improve the interaction? In: Stephanidis C, Pieper M (eds) Universal access in ambient intelligence environments, 9th ERCIM workshop on user interfaces for all, Königswinter, Germany, 27–28 Sept 2006. Lecture notes in computer science, vol 4397. Springer, Heidelberg, pp 99–114

57. Ortony A, Clore GL, Collins A (1998) The cognitive structure of emotions. University Press, Cambridge
58. Pineau J, Montemerlo M, Pollack M, Roy N, Thrun S (2003) Towards robotic assistants in nursing homes: challenges and results. Robot Auton Syst 42(3–4):271–281
59. Poggi I, Pelachaud C, de Rosis F, Carofiglio V, De Carolis B (2004) GRETA. A believable embodied conversational agent. In: Stock O, Zancanaro M (eds) Multimodal intelligent information presentation. Kluwer, New York
60. Pollack ME (2005) Intelligent technology for an aging population: the use of AI to assist elders with cognitive impairment. AI Mag 26(2):9–24
61. Pollack ME, Engberg S, Matthews LT, Thrun S, Brown L et al. (2002) Pearl: a mobile robotic assistant for the elderly. In: Proceedings of workshop on Automation as Caregiver: the Role of Intelligent Technology in Elder Care, AAAI, Edmonton, Alberta, Canada
62. Prendinger H, Mori J, Ishizuka M (2005) Recognizing, modeling, and responding to users affective states. In: Ardissono L, Brna P, Mitrovic A (eds) User modeling 2005, 10th international conference, UM 2005, Edinburgh, Scotland, UK, 24–29 July 2005. Lecture notes in computer science, vol 3538. Springer, Heidelberg, pp 60–69
63. Rao M, Georgeff M (1995) BDI agents from theory to practice. Technical note 56, AAII
64. Reeves B, Nass C (1996) The media equation: how people treat computers, television, and new media like real people and places. Cambridge University Press, New York
65. Reilly WSN (1996) Believable social and emotional agents. Dissertation, Carnegie Mellon University
66. Reiter E, Dale R (2000) Building natural language generation systems. Studies in natural language processing. Cambridge University Press, Cambridge
67. Thrun S (2004) Towards a framework for human-robot interaction. Hum Comput Interact 19(1&2):9–24
68. Sabourin J, Mott B, Lester J (2011) Computational models of affect and empathy for. Pedagogical virtual agents. Standards in emotion modeling, Lorentz Center International Center for workshops in the Sciences
69. Sakamoto D, Ono T (2006) Sociality of robots: do robots construct or collapse human relations? In: Proceedings of the 1st ACM SIGCHI/SIGART conference on Human-robot interaction (HRI '06). ACM, New York
70. Scherer KR, Wranik T, Sangsue J, Tran V, Scherer U (2004) Emotions in everyday life: probability of occurrence, risk factors, appraisal and reaction patterns. Soc Sci Info 43(4): 499–570
71. Soler V, Peñalver A, Zuffanelli S, Roig J, Aguiló J (2010) Domotic hardware infrastructure in PERSONA project. In: Augusto JC, Corchado JM, Novais P, Analide C (eds) Ambient intelligence and future trends-international symposium on ambient intelligence (ISAmI 2010), Advances in intelligent and soft computing, vol 72. Springer, Heidelberg, pp 149–155
72. Stephanidis C (2011) Ambient assisted living and ambient intelligence: improving the quality of life for European Citizens. ERCIM News, Keynote for the Special Theme: Ambient Assisted Living 87:2–3
73. Sundberg J, Patel S, Björkner E, Scherer KR (2011) Interdependencies among voice source parameters in emotional speech. IEEE Trans Affect Comput 2(3):162–174
74. van Breemen JN (2004) iCat: a generic platform for studying personal robot applications. In: Proceedings of IEEE-SMC 2004 conference 10–13 Oct, Den Haag, The Netherlands
75. van Ruiten AM, Haitas D, Bingley P, Hoonhout HCM, Meerbeek BW, Terken JMB (2007) Attitude of elderly towards a robotic game-and-train- buddy: evaluation of empathy and objective control. In: Cowie R, de Rosis F (eds) Proceedings of the doctoral consortium, in the scope of the second international conference on affective computing and intelligent interaction (ACII2007), Lisbon, 13 and 14 Sept 2007

76. Vogt T, Andre' E, Bee N (2008) EmoVoice – a framework for online recognition of emotions from voice. In: André E, Dybkjær L, Minker W, Neumann H, Pieraccini R, Weber M (eds) Perception in multimodal dialogue systems, 4th IEEE tutorial and research workshop on perception and interactive technologies for speech-based systems, PIT 2008, Kloster Irsee, Germany, 16–18 June 2008. LNAI, vol 5078. Springer, Heidelberg, pp 188–199
77. Wada T, Shibata T, Saito T, Tanie K (2002) Analysis of factors that bring mental effects to elderly people in robot assisted activity. In: Proceedings of the IEEE international conference on intelligent robots and system, vol 2. IEEE Computer Society, Washington, DC, pp 1152–1157

Part II
Design, Prototyping and Implementation

Part II
Design, Prototyping and Implementation

Chapter 5
AGILE Interface for 'No-Learning Nor Experience Required' Interaction

Santiago Martinez, Antonio L. Carrillo, Kenneth C. Scott-Brown, and Juan Falgueras

Abstract The wide variety of technological devices is a barrier to satisfactory usage and learning over all. Different types of interface element distribution and dissimilarities of their functionalities, even in the same category of products under the same brand, can steepen the learning curve to effective device operation. Interface design can be understood as a mechanism for the adequacy of the technological environment to substantially improve performance, satisfaction and life of the user with special requirements. Based on an inclusive paradigm, we aim to improve the usability, accessibility and satisfiability of the interface for a specific group of users, such as *novice elderly*, to benefit all types of users in their daily lives. The requirements derived from a holistic analysis of user, goals and context lead to the introduction of the AGILE Interface (Assisted Guided Interaction with no Learning nor Experience required). This interface is the pillar of a new interaction style designed to assist and guide users with specific needs owing to age and non-Information and Technology experience. In the context of present-day technology interactions, the ultimate goal of this work is to move beyond out of date user stereotypes to tailor appropriate interface design adapted to realistic and specific user demands.

S. Martinez (✉) • K.C. Scott-Brown
Centre for Psychology, School of Social and Health Sciences, University of Abertay Dundee, Bell Street, Dundee DD1 1HG, UK
e-mail: s.martinez@abertay.ac.uk; k.scott-brown@abertay.ac.uk

A.L. Carrillo
Lenguajes y Ciencias de la Computación, Escuela Técnica Superior de Ingeniería Industrial de Málaga, Universidad de Málaga, Edificio de Ingenierías, C/Doctor Ortiz Ramos s/n. Campus de Teatinos, Málaga 29071, Spain
e-mail: carrillo@lcc.uma.es

J. Falgueras
Lenguajes y Ciencias de la Computación, Escuela Técnica Superior de Ingeniería de Telecomunicación, Universidad de Málaga, Campus de Teatinos s/n, Málaga 29071, Spain
e-mail: juanfc@uma.es

E. Martín et al. (eds.), *User Modeling and Adaptation for Daily Routines: Providing Assistance to People with Special Needs*, Human–Computer Interaction Series, DOI 10.1007/978-1-4471-4778-7_5, © Springer-Verlag London 2013

5.1 Introduction

5.1.1 What Is AGILE

AGILE (Assisted Guided Interaction with no Learning nor Experience required) is an assistive interaction style for optimal performance of a digital transaction without requiring previous learning of how to use the interface, and designed for users with no technological experience. AGILE is the acronym of Assistive Guided Interaction with no Learning nor Experience required. The name is similar to the AGILE Software Engineering methodology [10]. They have in common the iterative design typical of any user-centred interface design. Beyond that feature, there is no inspiration or relationship between the two terms. The benefits of the AGILE type of interaction is reflected in its interface, designed to improve the performance, satisfaction and life of users with distinctive requirements, with special mention to the novice elderly. The interaction style is designed to assist and guide inexperienced user throughout the interaction process of a regular digital transaction. Its ultimate goal is to tailor appropriate interface design adapted to realistic and diverse user demands.

A clear classification and representation of the target user is necessary to effectively design for their needs. First, we will visit a concept presents on user classifications related with interface design. Second, we will look the traditional interaction styles over to select what relevant features could be useful to be incorporated to the new interaction style. At the end of this section we will describe in depth our intended target users, elderly users with no technological experience, described as novice elderly users.

5.1.2 The Misleading Concept of the 'Average User'

Our starting point in this chapter is to discuss whether the stereotype of an average user is convenient to fairly represent the heterogeneous spectrum of users in general, and any special type of user in particular. In the case of users with no Information and Communication Technology (ICT) experience, it does not seem to be the case.

5.1.2.1 Research Question: Is the Average Able-Bodied User a Useful and Fair Concept for Interface Design?

It is common to find that system interface requests are generally constructed on the assimilated concept of an average user (Norman alludes to it as "the representative user" [42]). This representation is meant to illustrate a prototype of the intended user of the application interface. As a result of that, the design cycle of technology

interaction has been predominantly evaluated from the perspective of a homogeneous user stereotype. However, continuous introduction of new technologies alter
and extend prevalent scenarios of use, increasing the number of target users and,
more importantly, diversifying those prevailing user types. This means that, at
present, traditional user profiles do not entirely reflect a spectrum of users constantly
growing in variability, requiring a fairer analysis of user needs and their context
where technology use occurs. Whilst it is true that the incorporation of Accessibility
[1, 34, 61, 63] and Usability [16, 17, 44] principles of design have increased
heterogeneity in design for users in mainstream technology, in comparison, there is
still a reduced number of effective applications developed for specific target users,
such as elderly, children, disabled, or any with special needs [29, 31]. Quoting
Langdon and Thimbleby [27]:

> Much of the accepted research [on usability work], is likely to be inadequate for informing
> user interface design in the future, and certainly inadequate for informing inclusive design
> of user interfaces.

On the other hand, fields such as Universal Design [12] and Inclusive Design [52]
deservedly attempt to equilibrate the User Interface (UI) research scene, increasing
the quality and number of designs for those special types of users, laying aside the
traditional marginal approach of supposed user uniformity.

Different categories of software, hardware and context of use may easily derive
a different average user representation for each one; because what average user
definition means in one context may differ in another. For instance, an average
user of an old typewriter with an analog and mechanical interface does not exactly
fit into the same parameters as an average user on a daily shopping trip to the
supermarket, using a Self-Service Checkout with a touch interface. The experience
of the user in the first scenario, may or may not translate to the context of the
second, but both users could be the same. In addition, rapid changes in device
technology make it difficult to say if the traditional computer model based on the
average user is applicable for other devices, or other types of users, or different
contexts of use. Besides, device technology evolution also requires developments
in the accessibility, ubiquity and interaction techniques of such devices, and always
considering a realistic target set of users. This leads the authors to have doubts about
the utility of the average user concept in UI design. These issues clearly suggest that
a relationship between the cognitive and physical human aptitudes, in conjunction
with new types of devices and their scenarios of use have to be devised.

5.1.3   A Fairer Approach: Understanding Users
and Their Limitations

The variety in type and number of the range of different disabilities makes it difficult
to use the term average disabled user. In this work, we pursue the Inclusive Design
[52] paradigm, which implies that it is the diversification not the homogeneity

that should lead research decisions in the context of specific types of users to therefore apply the results to the widest number of users with or without the same characteristics. Awareness of user needs in unison with capabilities and limitations are necessary for a correct interface design. However, the reasons for such importance are rarely described. Intrinsic advantages are: more usable systems, more appropriate interfaces, less trial and error in use and design, and reduced user training [48]. The study of the user limitations with their context of use has to be done considering the technology interaction as a cognitive process, involving multitude of different actions such as perception, attention, recognition, reasoning, thinking, use of memory, etc. It is important to know their mechanisms and intrinsic limits of operation to properly adapt design methodologies. Thus, the Cognitive Psychology discipline is becoming more important in the identification of problems users have when they use technology, based on their profile and context. Along the same line of thought, the mentioned discipline's approach, Inclusive Design, tackles problems found when 'less-able' users face technology. It pursues two goals: to reduce the exclusion on target users and the frustration able-bodied users find using the same products. This work applies the intersection of both disciplines, Cognitive Psychology and Inclusive Design, to contribute with guidance and methods that lead the design of optimal interactive products.

5.1.4 Our Target User Group: Novice Elderly Users

HCI user models have not traditionally considered the user with specific requirements in the same classification where able-bodied users were commonly described [55]. Whether these users are described, they belong to differentiated and separated set. While it is true that they do not share the same characteristics of able-bodied users (i.e., they would not probably present the same tendency of knowledge progression, as it will be described in Fig. 5.1), usage may coincide in terms of goals. From an Inclusive Design perspective, we accept that all users have needs. The issue is to find those needs that can be covered and solved by the design of an effective interface. We argue that a true usability and accessibility approach for a specific subset of users is thus transferable to all users. The improvement can be appreciated by target users but also for those outside the scope originally considered (i.e., able-bodied with no experience nor time to learn, cognitive mild impairments, etc). Quoting Newell [37],

> Designing interfaces that benefit users with special needs can benefit all users.

In this work our target users are the novice elderly users, those users above 55-years old and with not enough ICT experience to undertake a digital transaction with a sufficient threshold of knowledge and confidence. These users have further special requirements due to deteriorated cognitive processes created by age, which are essential to be considered in the UI design. The following list shows the senses and

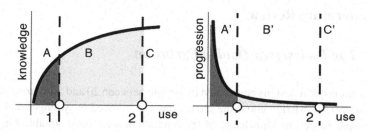

Fig. 5.1 Knowledge progression of the able-bodied user of a system: x-axis denotes accumulated experience of use; y-axis learning about application domain and functionality of the system. The *region A* (*left-hand side on both graphs*) represents where the knowledge is rising with the use and the highest progression tendency. The *region B* (*middle on both graphs*) represents where the knowledge rate is reduced, resulting in a digressive progression. The *region C* (*right-hand side on both graphs*), where the progression tends to disappear and the knowledge remain constant. Point 1 is where the knowledge reaches the peak. Point 2, where the knowledge progression ends

cognitive skills typically affected by the involutional process of aging [15, 60, 61] and examples of their associated limitations:

- Vision, i.e., low vision, blindness
- Sound, i.e., hearing impairment, deafness
- Touch, i.e., haptic disruption, paraplegia
- Reading, i.e., illiteracy, dyslexia
- Attention, i.e., attention deficit disorder
- Emotion, i.e., anxiety, depression, autism

AGILE is focused on enhancing the interaction on vision, touch and sound channels. Age introduces sense deficits affecting not only the sensory data, but also the cognitive processes associated with them. For instance, response time and cognition processes are gradually and negatively affected with the age progression. Attentional focus and shifts are difficult to maintain, operate and equally to learn. Previously learned skills, together with long term memory and reason are still well exercised. However, capabilities likely to be involved in unfamiliar or first time tasks, are more impaired with increasing age: instantaneous reasoning, working memory and executive control (adapted from [27]).

In the following sections we will thoroughly introduce a new guided interaction style for users with no ICT experience, and with no learning required for its first use, with novice elderly as target users. In Sect. 5.2, we will describe the literature relating to elderly users, focused on inclusive methodologies. In Sect. 5.3 we will describe the AGILE fundamentals, selecting relevant information to conform new experimental variables. In Sect. 5.4 the new interaction paradigm, AGILE, will be presented. We will describe the evaluation of the AGILE interface in Sect. 5.5. Finally, in Sect. 5.6, we will discuss the overall conclusions in the context of interface design, user models and future work.

5.2   Literature Review

5.2.1   The Undeserved Double Exclusion

Many technological designs are created by people between 20 and 50 years old, who lack practical knowledge about the challenges experienced by younger and older user groups, as well as knowledge of the interaction style most suitable for them [7]. Thus, historically, designers have ignored users who do not fit the intended target, such as those who have physical disabilities or are functionally illiterate [37]. In response to that marginal approach, differences created by age have been reported by studies on interaction styles for user groups with different age [26, 65]. Furthermore, styles of interaction widely accepted [68] and seen as revolutionary paradigms for interface design, such as WIMP (windows, icons, menus, pointer) (WIMP GUIs were popularized by the Macintosh in 1984 [64]), were putting aside the consideration of possible exclusion. For instance, blind users *had to see the items* to effectively interact with them (i.e., for interactions such as item selection, drag and drop, etc) [37].

Taking into account the fact that young people have a natural tendency to use technologies and can easily adopt new ones, most marketing investments are driven to engage those users with high expectations of using new devices and services related. However, elderly users do not usually have easy access to and usage of technology. It was well stated by Pieper in 2002, on his concept of the *Digital Divide* about the divergence between those users who can access the technology and those people, potential users, who do not or cannot [14, 46]. For instance, in 2008, there were more people over 60 years old than fewer than 16 in the U.K. [26]. Demographics of aging anticipate research near future direction, showing a 7% of population older than 65 years old in 2008, with expectations to be doubled in the next 30 years [26].

5.2.2   Validity of Inclusion

Research on universal technology access has been mainly focused on user groups with special needs (SN users). Usually, these special needs are represented by different factors such as speech, motor, hearing, and vision impairments; cognitive limitations; emotional and learning disabilities; as well as aging and environmental factors [41]. Fields that addressed computer access for the disabled started in the early 1970s, where methods for keystroke reduction were of interest to rehabilitation engineers. There have been many designs for older or disabled people, which led to mainstream products. For instance, in 1985, anticipating the direction of Inclusion Design, a predictive interface to reduce typing effort was demonstrated to be beneficial for people with no obvious disability other than problems with spelling [62]; talking calculators designed for blind were useful for eyes-busy tasks and low luminance conditions; less 'wordy' or 'verbose' interfaces with mostly visual content designed for people with language dysfunction were valuable for multilingual environments [37]; the first cassette tape recorder was designed specifically for blind people, and because of the poor sound quality, there were no expectations for it to be a universal product as it eventually became [38]; the large button telephone produced by British Telecom, was an example of a commercially successful product with both visually-impaired and mainstream customers; etc (see [49] for an extended list).

5.2.3 *Inclusive, Task and Cognitive Models Examples*

Inclusive models are the newest across the user models existing in the literature. Generally speaking, they consider the user as a wide set of features categorized in several levels, such as cognitive, perceptual and physical. Their goals pursue adaptation for user with special requirements and inclusivity projection for the wider spectrum of users. For instance, Jacko and Vitense made reference to specific cognitive, perceptual and physical abilities to draw a capability classification. They were interested in age related degeneration of the retina and constructed a user profile based on the information of loss of central vision. Importantly they stated some guidelines in order to overcome and bring an adaptation to the new state of user vision. Those guidelines involved font size, colour background and input and output speech [23]. Newell and Gregor broke the traditional UI design and gave priority to cognitive and physical needs of non standard user to later accommodate mainstream design in that process, understanding non-standard user as that one with requirements beyond the user profile erroneously considered average (adapted from [40]). Langdon et al. analyzed processes of cognition from the information processing models perspective. Their empirical studies pointed the high levels of adaptation that a user model will have to gather, and for that the user had to be necessarily studied based in a holistic awareness of their capabilities [28]. Hanson revisited the digital divide situation, describing the interconnectivity between older adults, network services and technology on computers and mobile platforms [13]. Another interesting approach is the Universal Access Reference Model (UARM) focuses on the accessibility of the interaction between users and systems. It is aimed to discover the common knowledge and abilities shared between users and systems reducing their handicaps. It used the Common Accessibility Profile (CAP) to describe user profile disabilities [9].

Tasks models are valuable for synthesizing the transactions into stages that can be built and analyzed. For instance, ConcurTaskTrees (CTT) [36] is a notation for model specification. It has a hierarchical structure of tasks, graphical syntax, concurrent notation and is task-centred. However, it is a notation mainly focused on the analyst's work, which will use it to design a solution based on tasks. Unfortunately, the user is not taking part on that solution building. The specification and interaction type result of that process is plain, without distinguishing between user types or their requirements. So, a novel user will have been alienated at the same level as an expert user. This can bring some problems into the overall performance and experience not on the model, otherwise in the satisfaction and effectiveness of the interaction built.

Regarding cognitive models, the work of GOMS (Goals, Operators, Methods, Selection) [5] has had great influence in this work. From there is taken the concept that the main goal is to guide and drive user, step by step, in a progressive fashion over a hierarchical predefined goal structure. To accomplish these goals in a satisfactory way, tasks and actions have to be conducted in the same way they were described. Consecution mechanisms should be simple and coherent in all moments and using the user interface. In fact, parallel works are being carried out by authors to develop specification tools that extend and improve the NGOMSL (Natural GOMS Language) notation [25].

Other main standard with influences in this work has been ISO 9241-171, including some guidelines used in the AGILE interactions style, such as suitability for the widest range of use, provide text label display option for icons or provide user-preference profiles [21].

5.2.4 Why the Mainstream Misfits Novice Elderly User Needs

UI Design has traditionally used two key factors to shape the able-bodied user: experience and learning. These factors are commonly assumed in a sufficient level to not consider explanations of how to use the interface, which can consume time and disturb the experienced user in prospective use of the interface. Nowadays, some applications include tutorials and demonstrations (which visualization can be voluntary or obliged) to show how to use the interface. The number of such applications is still reduced, particularly in the case of non-experienced users or those with special requirements, such as elderly.

To build a successful interaction style, it is important to understand the relationship between user, their experience and learning about technology. For this, we need to study why traditional models do not reflect these special users. Under normal conditions of cognition and no physical limitations, we analyze how experience of the same or analogue technology affects the knowledge a user acquires. Figure 5.1 shows this influence in a graph where the x-axis represents the accumulated experience of use, while the y-axis sets up the learning about the application domain and functionality of the system. It can be observed how the knowledge-progression about the system starts from a maximum and decreases as the use of the system grows (Fig. 5.1, region A). This situation remains until a specific point is achieved (Fig. 5.1, point 1), after which the knowledge progression is digressive. This point represents the moment where the user has reached sufficient knowledge about the application, and subsequent use of the same system will provide little knowledge compared with previous sessions (Fig. 5.1, region B). This fashion will end up at the point where no more sessions will provide any new knowledge about the system (Fig. 5.1, point 2).

The previously discussed average user (previously seen in Sect. 5.1, second paragraph) would be hypothetically placed in the centre of the curve (region B), representing the set of users with an average experience of the system. The region B described delimits other two different sets of users outside the central region of the distribution (region A and region C). Unfortunately, novice elderly users or any other user with special needs do not fit into the latter regions (B or C). The dynamic diversity of elderly users makes the traditional user-centred paradigm incomplete [67], based on homogeneous groups of user testing [45]. The key point is how to lead a user in the correct use of an interface, increasing motivation through a didactical approach to demonstrate its use from the very first and ensuing times (region A).

This idea of knowledge associated with previous experience and expected future uses of the same interface, explains the lack of success on the one-time user interface, or any of those where the user is unfamiliar with them. Their design is many times based on the assumption of the future sessions with the same interface that will provide the sufficient knowledge to improve the interaction. This trial and error exploration process, apart from non-optimal, fails when we talk about users with no experience or users unfamiliar with the interface faced. This is why there is a clear misfit between the models applied to average users and those applied to elderly or special needs users. The result is that misfit users perceive the inadequacy of interaction, and many times feel fear of technology use or see themselves as incompetent users.

5.3   AGILE Fundamentals

5.3.1   The Importance of the Environment

In this work, we are focused on users with specific limitations occasioned by age, which result in their subsequent needs, presented too when they interact with technology on their daily lives. These interactions occur in specific scenarios, and they matter at least as much as the technology itself. The environment has to be accounted as another key element in the equation of design. Citing J.A. Whiteside [65]:

> [. . .] There is nothing absolute about user characteristics; they are only meaningful within a context. Removing individuals from the context destroys the meaning of the characteristics used to classify them.

To illustrate the consequence of the mismatch between the user's needs and abilities regard the environment, we introduce here the definition of "handicap" (The International Classification of Functioning, Disability and Health (ICF), 1983), which expressed disadvantage for a given individual due to impairment or disability, but from the perspective of the interaction with and adaptation to the person's surroundings [30]. For instance, a person could have impairment and a disability but at the same time avoid the handicap: a wheelchair user could avoid the handicap issue whether the environment propitiates inclusion for such impediment, for instance, through the use of dropped kerbs to allow easy access from sidewalk to street (adapted from [42]). Thus, a strong correlation is found between the extent of how the environment accommodates to user's needs and the resulting avoidance of a handicap.

In addition, it is important to work towards how the environment fits the users' needs in a given situation to compensate so user's deficits in relation with such environment. There is a translation of responsibility from the user with specific needs to the environment and its designers, acknowledging the necessity of adaptation. We do not refer to limitations or capacities in isolation; it is a holistic approach to focus on how the environment can help to achieve user requests, including the dependency between their condition and the environment. Thus, it is the environment, not the person, which is seen as the *disabler*, noting the importance of the interaction between the individual and the environment [47].

5.3.2   User Participation

One problem a user usually confronts on everyday interactions is that their success is depending of how well (or bad) designed is the interface they have to face. To more finely describe this situation, we use some qualifiers created by the World Health Organisation's International Classification of Impairment, Disability and Handicap, ICIDH [66], and are the following:

- *Capacity*, describes an individual's ability to execute a task or action, without personal assistance or use of assistive devices;
- *Performance*, describes what an individual does in their current environment in a life situation, including personal assistance or use of assistive devices;
- *Environmental Factors* establishes the distinction between environmental 'barriers' and 'facilitators', as well as the extent to which an environmental factor acts in one way or another [24].

Thereby, we could say there could be different performance for same capacity, depending on the adaptation of each environment the user develops in. In Fig. 5.2, we can observe a common situation on interface use. In the figure on the left (Fig. 5.2a), the user performance is depending on each interface design, which is not homogeneous and together with other environmental factors involved may provoke the same transaction be successful in one case and fails in another. In contrast, AGILE methodology pursues the goal of augmenting user performance across a guided and self-explained interface, using consistency and permanency on the interface style and designed elements across the different types of interfaces in consonance with the environment (see Fig. 5.2).

5.3.3   Process of Adaptation for Novice Elderly Users

Traditionally, adaptive interfaces have been focused on a series of selected elements to build up the adjustment of the interface during their usage. Brusilovsky and

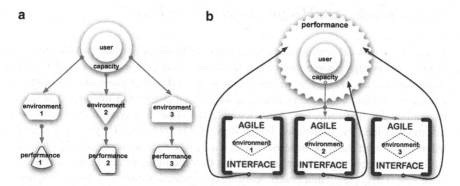

Fig. 5.2 (**a**) The graph shows the traditional approach of User Interface design ignoring enviro-mental factors that result into different performance for the same user's capacity. (**b**) The other graph shows the new AGILE interface approach, which encapsulates the environmental factor to offer a unified and augmented performance for the same user and their capacity

Millán [4] reviewed the five most popular features to be considered in adaptive web systems as well as how to model the context of user's work. Following, we will describe those features that appertain with some considerations to novice elderly users. In that article, the authors presented the *Knowledge* as the understanding of the subject being taught or the domain represented by the system. It was a changeable feature by learning (increased) or forgetfulness (decreased), from session to session or even in the same session. This last particular feature of variance of the knowledge depending on the learning process involved in the interface use and on the memory functioning applies straightforwardly to elderly users. *Goals* represented what the user wants to achieve, and they were catalogued to let the system recognize them. Goal and task hierarchy follow this line of research and are a central part of the AGILE interface. *Background* constituted a set of features related to the user's previous experience outside the core domain of a specific web system. In our particular case of novice elderly users, only the minimum information necessary to be understood and used across the variability of possible backgrounds is shown. Inside the *Individual Traits* they included *Cognitive* and *Learning styles* [4]. The former affected the way information was organized and presented, the latter the way people preferred to learn. Both components are used in the new style presented, but conveniently modified for the specific target users. That is, the presentation and organization of the information is simplified as much as possible and the learning requirements are minimal. Regarding the *Context of work*, it also applies to the new style in the form of the *environment* and *human dimensions*. About the *environment dimension*, the physical context around the user plays a vital role during the whole interaction process, becoming another part of the interaction. The *human dimension* contained the important feature of cognitive load, taken into account in the design of the interface. In conclusion, all these features presented above are a starting point for the construction of a new interaction style suitable for novice elderly users and then presented.

5.3.4 Specific Variables for Novice Elderly User

The proliferation of new contexts of use and technologies require a redefinition of the relationships between users and machines. Transactions are no longer only about data extraction, they are often interactions for different goals such as buying a ticket in a train station ticket machine, scanning a passport at the airport, a web transaction for first time, etc. A novice elderly person is a type of user with no Information and Communication Technology (ICT) experience. They have even less incentive to learn than one-time users (i.e., a user who uses an interface only once in a lifetime). Anecdotal evidence suggests that they are likely to say: "I am too old to learn new skills" [38]. Their cost of learning is increased because the time to acquire new skills is higher compared with younger population with undegraded cognitive skills. Consequently for elderly users, the cost and motivation of learning is the first serious obstacle to successful use of same technology in the near future, an easier task and common incentive for younger users. We argue that assistive information and communication technologies can play a vital role in the issue of traditional exclusion to elderly users from the mainstream.

Hence, they may not have interest in any fine details of software or hardware, and so their motivation for such use can be only increased by didactical and guided methods. Guidance during the process, assistance in case of error and demonstration of goal achievement are the core of the interaction for this type of users. Even if successful learning of the use of the interface is achieved, the future use, if any, should be considered as 'first' in terms of memory and functionality recalling. A set of relevant variables related with such technology use is described below:

1. Motivation: reason that triggers the use of the system.
2. Familiarity: user's acquaintance of the interface and analogous systems.
3. Skill level: the capability that the user has regarding employing of technology in general or computer related systems in particular.
4. Cost of learning use: the effort necessary to achieve a sufficient level of knowledge to use the interface.
5. Learning procedural aspects: the requests for the user to learn methodical aspects in order to satisfactorily use the system.

Two additional variables associated with time are critical in understanding the novice elderly user: *experience on the interface* and *frequency of prospective use*. The former identifies the prior experience the user has with the interface. In case of occasional use, such as the one of novice elderly, the value is near zero. This means that whether the user has had an encounter with the same or analogous technology, the difficulties they experience on learning and, in many cases, their absence of motivation, make it unwise to rely on user memory recall as the sole mechanism to recognize how to use the interface. It is recommended to consider that the user, then, faces an unknown interface. The latter variable, frequency of prospective use, is an explicit reference to the probability or guarantee about the use of the same system by the same user in the near future. Because the likelihood of use in the future of the same interface cannot be inferred with fair level of probability, this constrains the probability to be always less than 1, and in terms of implications to design for learning, very near to zero. In conclusion, the ranges of values for the two factors (variables associated with time) are characteristically defined for novice elderly users: experience on the interface ($\approx$ nil) and the probability of prospective use ($0 \approx$ P(prospective use of same interface) <1).

5.3.5   *Design Variable Values for Novice Elderly Users*

Once described the user variables involved in design of the AGILE interface, we need to specify their values. Considering all said until now, for the novice elderly user those values are:

- motivation: very low or none
- familiarity: very low or none
- skill level: very low
- cost of learning use: high or very high
- learning procedural aspects = f(AGILE interface implementation)
- experience on the interface: none
- capacity: inherent to the user
- performance = f(capacity, environmental factors)
- environmental factors = f(AGILE interface implementation) + others_not_considered

We explain the values selected for the target users. In the first instance, the motivation value has been already argued that it is *very low* or *none*, a distinctive feature of elderly users. Motivation to use new technology is not present unless it is well explained the purpose, benefits and eased the attached learning of how to use it. Familiarity with the interface or analogous systems and skill level values are also *very low*, also *or none* in the former variable, typical of novice users. About the cost of learning value of *high* or *very high* it has been also described as a characteristic of elderly users, due to their cognitive limitations or deteriorations by age. The value of the learning procedural aspects, that means the request of the interface for the user to learn methodical aspects of use, it is in dependency of the AGILE interface implementation. Experience on the same interface is *none* due to the challenge of first time users we want to face; capacity value is inherent and intrinsically determined by the specific user; and performance's value is a function of the capacity of the user together with the environmental factors. In the evaluation shown later, the only environmental factor studied is the implementation and effectiveness of the AGILE interface.

5.3.6 Implications of the Variables and Their Values on Designing for Novice Elderly Users

The previous selection of the variables and their values has several important implications in the interface design and interaction.

(a) *Learnability*: the interface should be developed taking into account the fact that the number of sessions the same user is going to perform is limited to 1. This means that possible future interactions are not accounted for. Mechanisms of learning functionalities of the interface, by retention, or by repetition, are extremely limited. Better than expecting the user to acquire how to use the system, it is recommended to spend time and effort in showing the user how to achieve their required goals. A recommendation would be the correct use of the metaphor to establish intuitive links with the real world elements (see Carroll's work on the metaphor [6]).

(b) *Guidance*: where possible, efficient mechanisms of guidance through the interaction should be provided. This aspect is addressed to compensate the deficiency of the learnability. For instance, in each stage of the process a clear map of steps achieved and possibilities of the interaction flow would be valuable for inexperienced user in general.

(c) *Assistance*: there should be an effective help system, valuable to demonstrate critical points in the interaction in terms of complexity or novelty. This system should also be useful in any case of error or impossibility to achieve a goal. This aspect is related straight away with user's feedback, and will have an influence on the notion user takes from the interaction process and the system.

The adaptation process is therefore applied in the design stage. Firstly, there is an adaptation of contents, where only elements relevant for the user interaction are shown in the interface. The purpose is to reduce at minimum distractions that can induce time waste during irrelevant inspection or meaningless interpretation of such elements. Secondly, the adaptation occurs in the guidance system employed. There will be an appreciable area dedicated for the guidance system, responsible of directing user's attention to the interactive interface elements in each transaction's step. Finally, mechanisms of assistance will provide user with procedures to be helped and amend information in an effortless way. This approach could be seen as a cross-adaptation process in terms of the adaptive presentation and adaptive navigation support that Brusilovsky [3] used in the taxonomy of adaptive hypermedia methods and techniques, but placed in a static fashion in the interface design stage.

5.3.7 Goals as Determinants of User Behaviour

Newell and Simon [39] described user's goals as the determinants of user behaviour. User interaction is motivated and driven by goals, applying their knowledge and limited by the task architecture and their cognitive capacity:

> He [the user] attempts to accomplish his goal as effortlessly as possible, within the constraints imposed upon him by the structure of the task, by what he knows, and by his own information-processing limits.

For Moran [35], all the actions a user performs are impelled to accomplish a goal. He enumerated four different factors that determine and help to predict user behaviour. These determinants can be altered to improve user performance in a given situation (and presumably, to increase user satisfaction and reduce user frustration): altering user interface → changing the task structure; instructing the user → teaching to increase their knowledge; assistance for user's limitations → efficient error recovery; automation of subtasks → to ease the accomplishment of major tasks.

He gave an example describing two common issues on the human user:

> Two examples of processing limits are the human's limited short-term memory capacity and his tendency to make errors occasionally (for a variety of reasons). These limits covertly manifest themselves in the human propensity to break larger tasks down into smaller tasks, which puts fewer demands on memory and which tends to limit the scope of errors.

5.3.8 The Immediacy of the Goal in the Occasional Use

Occasional interactions with technology have defined characteristics, which should be taken into account during their design. Among others, the unfamiliar environment where they take place; whether the interaction occurs outdoors introducing external factors such as noise, distractions or weather conditions; etc. Above all, in this work we highlight goal achievement as a determinant factor to shape and underpin the interaction with technology in our everyday lives. The importance of achieving the goal in every interaction imposes restrictions at all levels. In the case of an occasional use, such as buying a ticket in a train station in a ticket machine, or scanning a passport at the airport, learning how to perform the transaction correctly cannot rely on future uses of the interface as seen on desktop programs (i.e., next day or session). Novice elderly users should be considered in this aspect of occasional use, because even whether they learn how to use the system in a diary repetitive task, it can be easily forgotten.

The case of a user travelling everyday by train could be considered as an example. Would a user who has to take occasionally a train and thus use a ticket machine be considered as an occasional user? What about the first time they use the ticket machine? In this particular situation, the probability of prospective use could be inferred to be greater than zero. However, in the first use of the machine the user has no previous knowledge accumulated through the experience, and the learning in future uses cannot be helpful in the actual transaction, maybe only in the future ones. The same circumstances occur in the subsequent transactions. In every transaction with a ticket machine, getting a ticket from the machine is an immediate goal, which cannot rely on the future use of the interface in the next session. So, every user of these types of machines should be catalogued as occasional, no matter the number of future sessions, which are interpreted as none during a specific transaction. Desktop applications can rely on the difficulty of finding the specific option hidden in some menu in a finite, but greater than one, number of sessions. There, error is assumed and expected to be improved in next try. Goal achievement is as important as learning the best ways to perform functions, and in case of error, solution cannot be relied on learning in future uses. Performance on every interaction should be maximized. In the case of an everyday user of a self-service ticket machine, the transaction's goal and time are critical, more than to learn how to do it in the best way.

In this chapter we argue that novice elderly users in transactions succeed the premises of an occasional user, with learning, memory and interactivity issues accentuated by the elder state of such users.

5.4 AGILE Model: Assisted Interaction with No Learning Nor Experience Required

5.4.1 Philosophy

In this work, a new interaction style is proposed, based in the hierarchical task analysis and namely AGILE Interaction. It pursues the ease of use, but taking into account the lack of traditional mechanisms of learning by repetition or retention. This style sacrifices the possibility of developing the execution of processes in parallel and other typical advantages of WIMP interfaces [64]. It works towards simplifying, ideally, the syntax of knowledge to optimize the use of the system and its semantics. The user should be able to interact without a previous intensive study of them. Semantics should be sufficiently intuitive to allow the user to correctly interpret the interface structure with a minimum effort. Thus, the interface contains essentially short but meaningful descriptions and an overall clear language and content. An effective approach to develop this concept is the correct and effective use of the metaphor. The metaphor is a pillar of any current interface design. It is, in essence, a vehicle to transfer a concept, knowledge or idea to the user. In the context of users with no experience and reduced cognitive function, such as elderly, this transference becomes critical to effectively transmit, interpret, and reorient if necessary, the meaning that the metaphor represents. As a consequence, it is crucial to include a new dimension of literality into the metaphor to achieve a correct use of the AGILE interface. This literality will be introduced by two elements: a virtual agent will represent the assistant part of the interface, explaining and indicating the options in each step. The second element will be, wherever possible, a representative icon of the option accompanying the text. These two elements represent the faithful connection between the explanations and decisions making inside the interface with the reality outside the interface.

5.4.2 Learning from Traditional Interaction Styles

Traditional interaction styles may bring some useful characteristics to put up a suitable interaction style for the elderly user. For instance, *direct manipulation* [18, 54] is already placed in almost any interface in greater or lesser extent. The immediate handling of objects is primarily connected with how we see and use object in the world and it becomes a critical feature of this new interaction style. In addition, the active component of *questions and answers* [43, 51] and the tutored approach of the *wizards* [8] make them very recommendable for elderly users. Other features from other styles like form filling should be used only when absolutely necessary (i.e., authentication with introduction of password), and even in those cases any alternative with the same effectiveness and minimum text input should be examined. For instance, the interface should offer best ways to deal with the information than the traditional typing, where the environment allows to it (i.e., if the source of target destinations for a trip is publicly available, a predictive search considering the default location where the user currently is, will save time and effort). Command language is manifestly discarded for lack of experience and the complexity and time required learning how to use it.

5.4.3 Methodology

To overcome the habitual short sightedness of information and communication technology (ICT) designers [11], this work is oriented to prevail over functional limitations [19] of users. This perspective incorporates into the interface design what really matters for user with specific requirements: the capacity of doing an assisted and guided definite task. Based on the variables previously described (in Sect. 5.3, second paragraph) and taking on board their implications for designing, the specific aims of this methodology are:

(1) Simplifying the decision making on every transaction step.
(2) Guiding the user in all the steps of the interaction process.
(3) Assisting and demonstrating the use of interactive components on the interface.

To simplify the decision making, there is a transformation of the task tree structure, flattening its depth to transform the transaction in a process with greater number of decision steps but with much lower complexity in each decision. The number of steps has been increased reducing the complexity of each. Many times in digital transactions the steps are overloaded of multiple decisions and information, which often overwhelmed the senses of the user, especially during the first-time uses.

To achieve aims ii and iii, innovative ways of assistance and guidance are proposed. First, a virtual agent implements the personification of the assistance concept. Using animation principles, quick and effective demonstrations of 'what to do?' and 'how to do it?' are shown by the virtual agent. In addition, user's attention

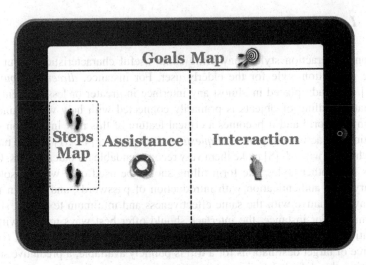

Fig. 5.3 First schematic prototype of AGILE interface, shown in a tablet. It consists, from *left to right* and *top to bottom*, on a map of goals, a map of steps, an assistive area and an interaction area

is directed to relevant items or areas on the interface by head, gaze cues and gestures of the agent. This paradigm is based on multi-frame animated physical cues used to orient attention of the user [32] on digital and touch interfaces [33] in combination with animation principles to predict perception on the observer [57]. In the following list, focused on overcoming any of the deficits (stated on the left), principles are stated on the right as resources for the design of the interface and will be used with discretion over the iteration of the interface design:

- Attention → simple layout; Physical Cues [32, 33]; Animation Principles [56].
- Touch → touch screen, customizable size of items, input redundancy: mouse, track pad, keys, phone.
- Reading → avoid meaningless text buttons, use icons, speakers.
- Vision → animation principles: Exaggeration, Silhouette [57].
- Sound → text and sound, indications, flashes.
- Emotion → simple, exaggerated characters.

Having identified these principles, we discuss how some of these are employed in the AGILE interface design.

5.4.4 AGILE Initial Prototype Description

The initial prototype divided the screen into four different areas of interest in a landscape screen mode (see Fig. 5.3).

Goals Area: this area is placed in the top of the screen. Its purpose is to show the hierarchy of active goals in each moment. It starts showing the immediate goal to achieve (i.e., goal A), and a sequence of sub goals (i.e., goal B, goal C, etc) necessary to accomplish the former (goal A). Each time a goal needs other subgoals to be accomplished, the goals' list would be updated, showing the subsequent subgoals. This area is not intended to allow any type of interaction. Thus, its role is merely informative.

Assistance Area: it shows the sequence of steps necessary to accomplish the actual goal. Steps are ordered, sequenced, and numbered. However, there is only one step activated at any time (noted by bold font type), rest of the steps appears deactivated (noted by a non-bold font type). In addition, a virtual agent (a female assistant character was chosen for this prototype) who would be in charge to point out which is the current step. The virtual assistant's main aim is to assist in the use of the interactive components of the interface. It is also a vehicle to orient the attention of the user to the relevant areas of the interface, where the demonstration or posterior interactivity will occur. This area is intended to receive interaction from the user in order to confirm the finalization of the step (all the interactions inside that step are accomplished and finished by the user).

Interaction Area: the area designed to receive most of the interaction from the user. It also shows the information relative for the interaction flow (physical layouts, measures, etc). Item selection, form filling and direct manipulation will occur in this area.

5.5   AGILE Prototype Evaluation

5.5.1   AGILE Prototype Evaluation Methodology

The evaluation of the prototype was distributed in three different parts. First, the developing of a prototype with the aims previously exposed in the Methodology: simplification of decision making, guiding the user, and assisting and demonstrating the use of the elements of the interface. Second, the prototype was tested on a digital transaction that users occasionally perform. The device chosen is a portable device (tablet) and the input channel was the touch. Target users were novice elderly users, with little or no experience on touch devices and little or none with other technological devices such as computers. Third, the iterative design and test of such prototype based on the analysis and conclusions obtained from the evaluation.

5.5.2   Iteration 1: AGILE Prototype in MS Power Point with Human Assistance

The first iteration of the prototype consisted in a preliminary evaluation of a MS Power Point (MS Power Point 2008 for Mac, v. 12.1) presentation, shown on a PC,

Fig. 5.4 First prototype of AGILE interface, shown in a PC with MS Power Point. It can be appreciated, from *left to right* and *top to bottom*, clouds with name of goals (map of goals); speech bubbles (map of steps); a virtual agent (assistive area); a confirmation task (interaction area)

about a Kitchen Design application (see Fig. 5.4), inspired by the IKEA kitchen planning tool [20]. Controls were set up to advance to the next slide whenever the user selected an option available. The total number of steps (slides) presented was eight (8). When the user got 'stuck' in any step, the researcher helped, carefully explaining how to perform the corresponding action. Typically the most common problem was how to do a selection (press a specific button), when there was more than one element active on the screen.

The number of participants was four (4) with an average age of 74 years. They gave informed consent from the Computer Science Languages and Systems department from the University of Malaga, Spain. Participants were not disabled and their cognitive abilities were typical of that age, with no special impairments described. They were given instructions of building their own kitchen using the application. The researcher would assist the participant only if they were stuck for certain time in the same step, or operation.

Conclusions of this iteration showed that the map of goals was not seen or useful at all. Instead, it was disturbing normal interaction because when participants were asked if they perceived it, only two of them did, and they did not find it meaningful. The same happened with the step map, which was getting in the way when users thought they had to click on the speech bubbles, disrupting the interaction instead of informing it. The trend from the user was to think that every thing appearing on the screen was clickable and relevant for the current task, instead of distinguishing what was informative and what interactive.

Fig. 5.5 The second iteration of the prototype of AGILE interface for the train ticket transaction, shown in an iPad2. Note the absence of Goals and Steps maps. There still remain the virtual agent (assistive area) and the region with buttons (interactive area)

5.5.3 Iteration 2: AGILE Prototype in iPAD2

Based on the previous iteration, an evaluation was carried out on the evolved AGILE prototype. The prototype was tested in a portable device, a tablet device (iPad2) and it was implemented in iOS (see Fig. 5.5).

5.5.3.1 Evaluation Process for Comparison with Other Digital Transaction

A post event evaluation was done in order to refine the early prototype. The evaluation was carried out comparing the transaction in the AGILE interface versus another train ticket purchase in a rail website (see Fig. 5.6), using the same tablet device. Each user made two transactions, one on each different application, with a counterbalanced design. This evaluation was carried out in Scotland (UK) at elderly users home and in Malaga (Spain), at a health centre and adult learning centre. In total, the number of participants tested was 11. The age range was between of 58 and 83 years (average age in Scotland was 77 years, in Spain was 69.58 years, overall was 70.93 years) with no disability described, and with cognitive and physical impairments typical of those ages. All participants gave informed consent under the regulations of the School of Health and Social Sciences of the University of Abertay Dundee in English, translated into Spanish where necessary. To make the test more suitable, the absence of Spanish translation for the rail website lead to the selection

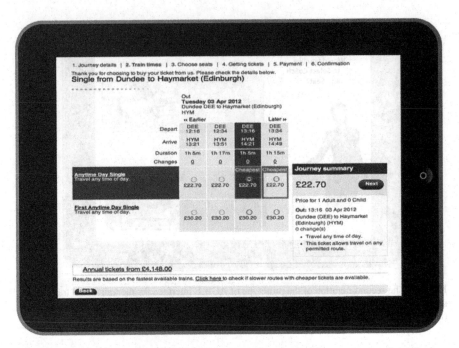

Fig. 5.6 The rail website that participants had to use to buy a train ticket transaction. In particular, when the user had to select the service time, type of ticket and price

of other website, a common web store (see Fig. 5.7) and the transaction changed to a book purchase. The adjusting in the AGILE version was done minimizing the differences with the AGILE version previously developed for the train ticket. This resulted in the same characteristic screens and tasks, but a reduction in the number of steps due to the book purchase transaction properties.

There were a camera recording (Panasonic SDR-H85 with tripod) and Eyetracking (SMI Eye Tracking Glasses [58, 59]: non-invasive video based glasses-type eye tracker, 30 HZ binocular, spatial resolution 0.1°, gaze position accuracy 0.5° over all distances, 3-point calibration, HD scene camera and audio recording) during the test. All transactions were performed on the same tablet device (iPad2 with iOS version 4.3.5 and the interface designed using Objective-C language in XCODE 4.2, SDK 5.0), in a controlled room with absence of noise, disturbance and any other potential disruptions. Instructions of the transactions were the same (distinguishing between train ticket layout and data and book purchase layout and data, respectively) and provided in a sheet of paper, constantly visible for the participant in all trials. AGILE interface versus rail / book buying website tests were counterbalanced across participants.

The evaluation methodology worked toward adding quantitative and qualitative data to enrich evaluation results and refine the prototype as much as possible. First, the whole interaction process was recorded in a video camera, pointing to the

Fig. 5.7 Detail of the website used for the book purchase transaction. In particular, when the book title had been found and the Quantity had to be introduced (on the *right side* of the screen above the rectangular button *Añadir Cesta* (in English "add to the basket"))

tablet device to record users' touch interaction. All the operations, questions and answers during and after the interaction were recorded. Second, some participants were eye tracked to facilitate the analysis of the performance with the tablet. After both transactions, participant were asked a qualitative questionnaire about their experience overall, particular issues and recommendations about both applications.

5.5.4 Results of the Test of Train Ticket Transaction on Rail Website on iPad2

Analysis of the camera recordings showed that the transaction time was almost double on a rail website. Comparatively, the number of comments and assistance provided by the human helper was four times less than the one provide using the AGILE prototype. Furthermore, the content of the assistance was more loaded on the rail website, while in the AGILE comments were merely short confirmations or reminders to follow the instructions provided.

In addition to this quantitative difference, the major findings were qualitative. Comments and answers to the questionnaire described the problems the users faced during the use of the rail website. Mainly, problems were found in how to use the controls for inserting text (some participants missed the physical keyboard and it took them some time to realize there was the possibility to have one displayed on the screen when a text box was selected), for selecting time and dates (very little space for their fingers) and how to scroll down or up the page to find the button to carry out the next step on the transaction. In addition, there was a screen where the button to go to the next step was not initially displayed and it only appeared when a train service was selected, increasing the confusion of "what to do next" in that specific step.

5.5.5 Results of the Test of Book Purchase on Website on iPad2

Similar results were obtained from the book purchase test transaction using a book buying website in Spanish. Despite there were only three screens to go through, the time elapsed was again so much longer (an average of 10.1 min (SD = 0.68) compared with an average of 3 min (SD = 0.5) in the AGILE interface). The complaints were about the overloaded interface, with too many unnecessary elements no relevant for the current task. Publicity, and the display of elements not required were all major distractions for participants. They argued that they had to spend much time reading messages and inspecting elements, with the high risk of clicking on them and moving into undesired screens. Also only one participant could find the search bar without help. The rest of the participants had to be guided by the researcher to successfully introduce the title of the book.

5.5.6 Discussion

The evaluation of the AGILE prototype (see Fig. 5.8) has brought different and important findings. The early prototype has shown how the goals map is irrelevant for users when they face an unknown transaction. At first glance, it was relevant to know where the user is in the transaction flow, but when there are too many new elements on the screen, so the priority of that knowledge does not seem to be the most important aspect of layout. Furthermore showing the goals map seems to be completely irrelevant for the current operation the user is performing.

A similar situation occurs with the Steps map. Many users were distracted with the steps, and semantically, they did not bring any useful meaning for the current operation. It was a distraction more than a help. This early prototype gave us the opportunity to refine the interface for the next iteration, removing the Goals and Steps maps from the interface on the next interface design iteration.

In the evaluations on the tablet device, the comparison with a website to do a similar train ticket or book purchase transaction was very helpful. The problem of small screen space or using controls can be partially solved whether the website

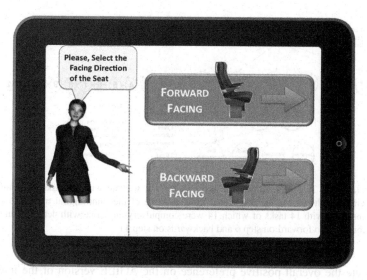

Fig. 5.8 One of the screens of the second iteration of the AGILE interface for the train ticket transaction. In particular, the *Facing Direction* choice

implements the best controls available for such operations, such as the ones that Apple Corporation provides for time and dates (scroll wheels) on iOS devices. However, again how to use these controls are not publicly known for every user who faces the interface, for example, novice elderly users. Such is the case, that when participants were asked whether they knew the existence of accessibility features such as the 'Zoom in or out' using two fingers to do the pinch gesture on the screen, they were surprised and argued that "I was not born knowing that, nobody taught it to me. Now it is too late". The concept of the virtual agent is to overcome this problem. In the prototype shown the agent is explaining clearly, and with good manners, the instructions in every step. In addition, prospective implementations of the AGILE interface will include the animation of such agent, presenting it in coordination and in sequence with the relevant items on the interactive screen. Tutorials before each screen could be provided to explain how to perform it.

Another conclusion from the evaluation test is the performance of the transaction. At first instance, the transformation into AGILE interface of the train ticket transaction has increased the number of steps (from 7 compulsory, to 14) (see Fig. 5.9). However, the questionnaire answers brought the conclusion that in fact the AGILE interface was preferred in case of having to choose one application to purchase. It seems that despite the fact that the number of steps was increased, the approach of the AGILE interface in general and the simplicity of the decision making in particular have had a positive direct influence on user satisfaction. In addition, the way that users could amend the decisions made (on step 11), or quickly go to last screen whether user was in a hurry and wanted the default values on all the subsequent screens to not waste time (step 6), were learned and used intuitively with no effort.

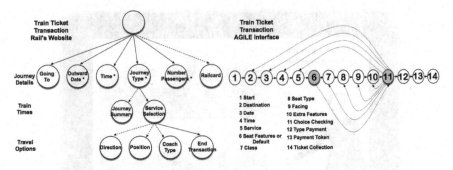

Fig. 5.9 (a) Task Tree representing the tasks in the rail website with 12 tasks: 7 compulsory with 5 with default values, and 5 optional. (b) Task tree of the same digital transaction in the AGILE interface with 14 tasks of which 14 were compulsory and none with default value. Note the possibility to go forward on step 6 and backwards on step 11

Despite the overall positive preference on the AGILE version of the interface (11 participants preferred the AGILE version, 0 the other), some critical reflections must be mentioned about AGILE interface. First, the AGILE version did not have a text input option. Instead, the search was predefined and elements showed were already known (destination city in the train ticket and book title in the book purchase). Second, there was a step in the AGILE interface that distinctly took more time for participants to perform and learn how to use. It was the clock in the train ticket application or counter of number of same items in the book purchase application (see Fig. 5.10). Some participants were 'stuck' until they found how to change the value, which was deliberately set up on zero. At the beginning, evaluators thought that the problem came from the digital numbers, which could be improved using other type of numbers. However, eyetracker data showed that for instance one participant was stuck in that step, looking to the numbers, then look at the speech bubble and the agent, and back to the numbers again. It was a clear cycle of not knowing what to do next (see Fig. 5.11).

The participant touched the numbers trying to change their value, and for a long time after he did not realize that the green triangles above and below the numbers increased and decreased the value respectively. In addition, the most pressed arrow was the bottom one, probably for their proximity to the 'OK' button. Another issue with the arrows was that some users simply pressed or held their finger down on the arrow waiting to see the value increased automatically when the button was held down. That option was deliberately discarded on the design process, thinking that maybe it was found only in recent technology and thus too advanced for novice elderly users. However, the questionnaire brought the reason for such behaviour: some videos and microwaves counters have the option of keeping the button hold to increase the value automatically and faster, as do many digital alarm clocks. All these differences would have influence in user preferences.

It could be argued that better than using a website run on a tablet, the test should have run a specific mobile versions of the same website. Clearly this would have

Fig. 5.10 One of the screens of the second iteration of the AGILE interface for the train ticket transaction. In particular, the *Time to Travel* choice

Fig. 5.11 Detail of the AGILE interface for book purchase. In particular, the number of books to be purchased. The *line* represents the scanpath of the participant (74-years old), this is, the trajectory the participant's gaze draws on the scene recording. The *circles* represent the fixations of the participant, and the size of such circles means the fixation duration. On the *left* it can be seen how, from the number of items, the gaze goes to the speech bubble and agent. On the *right* hand side, the cycle is clearly visible going switching between counter of items and speech bubble, with very few lines directed to the 'OK' button. The participant touched the number, instead of the *arrows* above and below, trying to increase the number of items. Without a doubt, the lack of information to show the participant how to operate the control is a design error

increased the performance and suitability of such application on portable devices. However, many retail and transport companies do not have separate applications, and many first time users may not seek to download specific apps even if they are available. Thus, we still considered the comparison fair for the following reasons.

In the case of a specific application developed for mobile platform, the differences would be on the suitability of controls and maybe some differences in the number and size of the elements shown. In that hypothetical situation, it would still be far from optimal because the main problems found will remain: there will still be a lack of knowledge on the users of how to use such controls, like the accessibility issues, which are normally unknown for many users, because nobody would have taught the users how to use them, such as scrolling wheels for time and date, or pinch gesture to zoom in and out, etc. In this case, user performance would increase in line with their intuition. Thus, the necessity of assistance, clear explanations and concise messages are essential for the correct use of the interface for first time users, and particularly for those with no technological experience. These problems were overcome as far as possible in the second iteration of the AGILE interface. The virtual agent expressed a polite and clear message in the speech bubble and pointed to the relevant area where interaction occurs. The size of the buttons, look and feel of the interface, and the few options for selection (2 option in most of the cases, 4 options in two cases and only once with 8 options; not counting the calendar where technically the number of options would be around 30 depending of the month), are also part of the approach.

To overcome these issues and generally improved the performance, a third iteration would introduce animation on the virtual agent and its extremities, and on-the-fly quick tutorial for explaining the use of complex controls. In tablet devices, an 'incorrect' tap of the numbers rather than the increment or decrement should generate an advisory message politely suggesting that the arrows can be used to dial up the required number. In addition, an order on the sequence of interface's elements presentation should be introduced. First, the agent would appear and then its speech bubble would appear, and after that, the elements on the interactive area. So, the prominence of the agent and the message with instructions would be increased. Finally, the introduction of the sound would be carefully implemented.

5.6   Conclusions and Future Work

In this paper we have described the ordinary model of user that many Graphical User Interface (GUI) designers have in mind, the average user. Particularly, each situation provides an intuitive cataloguing of the conceived average user in its own context. Then we have questioned whether this stereotype truly reflects the wide spectrum of users and whether it is ultimately useful for the design of any interactive system.

Subsequently, a review of the traditional approaches in design was made to explore the variables, in which users with special needs, such as elderly, were based, to ascertain whether they covered the whole spectrum of actual users. Because of the permanent change on the context where the technology is used and the constant evolution of user stereotypes, those commonly accepted procedures were revisited with a target update, to accommodate new trends and user profiles.

Fig. 5.12 One of the screens of the second iteration of the AGILE interface for the train ticket transaction. In particular, the *Type of Seat Extra Features* choice

Without asserting what sort of the approach is better for HCI interface design ((1) designing for one uniform user group; (2) designing different interfaces for different user groups; (3) designing an adaptive interface [2]), the interface adaptation has been done in the design stage. We have placed the user and their needs as an essential component of user interface design. A new interaction style has been described, ideally conceived for users with no IT experience nor time to learn, the AGILE interaction style (see Fig. 5.12), focused to adapt to the idiosyncrasy of a non-archetypical user, in this case the novice elderly user. This type of user meets some peculiarities, such as no motivation to learn; or absence of memory even in the same session, exacerbated by the lack of didactical approach commonly found in many GUI. We have covered this issue by the use of an effective guidance and assistance system for every step of the interaction process. The assistance has been implemented in a virtual agent, in charge of guiding the user in the current goal achievement, and in lecturing how to perform operations on the interface by simple and effective animations. Physical cues and gestures orient the user's attention to relevant areas of the interface to enhance interactivity. The simplicity of the interface layout becomes essential, as well as the effectiveness of the assistance and concise use of the metaphor. Reducing the number of items on any one screen has the benefit of minimizing the risk of change blindness from the observer of the interface (e.g. [50]). Even simultaneously presented items can be difficult to segment and parse appropriately when there are too many items [53]. By minimizing comparisons and items, decisions and detections have been maximally facilitated. For instance, to enhance touch [60] and visual experience, clear and large sized icons have been selected, accompanied by text descriptions (as recommended in [21]).

This work has carried out transnational novice elderly user testing using touch interface on tablet devices, with video camera recording, eye tracking recording where possible, and qualitative questionnaires. The evaluation process has brought helpful findings as the suitability of the AGILE interface for occasional digital transactions, such as buying a train ticket or purchasing a book. A clear validity of the style presented has been successfully evaluated on our target users, the novice elderly. Among the most valuable features demonstrating their suitability, we highlight the simplicity and clarity, guidance and error-minimized that the AGILE interface presented during the whole interaction process. Simplicity in the effortless of decision making exhibited in each step, with a minimum cognitive load attached. Clarity in the display of only indispensable number of elements necessary to accomplish the transaction, with large buttons, legible font and overall concise messages. Guidance in the succinct instructions given by an agent in each step, placed in a wide and visible region inside the interaction area. Error-minimization by restricting the possible options user has in each step, without affecting the effectiveness of the goal accomplishment and therefore satisfaction involved. All these features could be adapted in the design process whether the target user group varies, for instance, maximizing the use of the sound channel for a blind user, or the assistance method to show how-to do a gesture in the case of not knowing how to do it, etc. However, these revisions of the interface should always be part of the design process, carefully tested and iterated. It is the ultimate goal of this style to present a consistent interface among users with no technology experience, lessening unpredicted changes during its use to maximize stability and productivity of the interface.

A third iteration of the interface would be needed to avoid problems on design and effectiveness, with certain elements such as the clock/counter and the increase operation associated. Animations of the virtual agent, quick tutorials of such controls and order of the sequence of elements revealed are to be included in it.

The content of this work is the corner stone of a new approach on interface design. Furthermore, development will explore different types of tasks, widening in variety and complexity to present new challenges for designers, modifying or updating any of the principles exposed here. Finally, testing the interaction paradigm with users with other cognitive limitations, such as dementia or Parkinson's, and finding exemplary interactive elements for their interface is on the agenda of the authors.

Acknowledgments Martinez is grateful for support from the Alison Armstrong Studentship at Abertay University. We are grateful to Sensomotric Instruments (Teltow, Germany) SMI [58] for assistance with the use of eye-tracking equipment (especially to Stefanie Gehrke and Jose Barreiros); also, for extensive training received by Richard Lilley from Tracksys Ltd. (Nottingham, UK). Special thanks to María Ángeles López at the Centro de Salud Nueva Málaga (Málaga, SPAIN) and to Purificación Roldán at the Educación Permanente SEPER (Málaga, SPAIN) for their effective collaboration in the elderly user testing. Besides, thank to Dr Paula Forbes and all the members of the User Centre Group of the University of Dundee (Dundee, UK), who were a profound motivation for the development of this work. This research has been inspired by the European Project FP7 iAGE, in which authors from Abertay University contribute.

References

1. Americans with Disabilities (1990) Act of 1990 incorporating the changes made by the ADA Amendments Act of 2008. http://www.ada.gov/pubs/adastatute08.pdf. Accessed 1 Aug 2011
2. Aykin NM, Aykin T (1991) Individual differences in human-computer interaction. Comp Ind Eng 20(3):373–379. doi:http://dx.doi.org/10.1016/0360-8352(91)90009-U
3. Brusilovsky P (2001) Adaptive hypermedia. User Model User-Adap Inter 11(1):87–110, doi:http://dx.doi.org/10.1023/A:1011143116306
4. Brusilovsky P, Millán E (2007) User models for adaptive hypermedia and adaptive educational systems. In: Brusilovsky P, Kobsa A, Nejdl W (eds) The adaptive web, methods and strategies of web personalization. Lecture notes in computer science, vol 4321. Springer, Heidelberg, pp 3–53
5. Card SK, Moran TP, Newell A (1983) The psychology of human-computer interaction. CRC, Boca Raton
6. Carroll JM, Thomas JC (1982) Metaphor and the cognitive representation of computing systems. IEEE Trans Syst Man Cybern 12(2):107–116
7. Chisnell D (2007) Where technology meets green bananas. Interactions 14(2):10–11, doi:http://dx.doi.org/10.1145/1229863.1229876
8. de Jesus Stoll MT, Wickham DP et al (2005) Use of conceptual diagrams to support relationships between launchpads and its wizards. US Patent 6,968,505
9. Fourney DW, Carter JA (2006) A standard method of profiling the accessibility needs of computer users with vision and hearing impairments. In: Hersh MA (ed) Proceedings of conference and workshop on assistive technologies for people with vision and hearing impairments. Technology for Inclusion CVHI, Kufstein
10. Fowler M, Highsmith J (2001) The AGILE manifesto. Softw Dev 9(8):28–35
11. Glinert EP, York BW (1992) Computers and people with disabilities. Commun ACM 35(5):32–35, doi:http://dx.doi.org/10.1145/129875.129876
12. Goldsmith S (1976) Design for the disabled. Royal Institute of British Architects, London
13. Hanson VL (2010) Influencing technology adoption by older adults. Interact Comput 22(6):502–509, doi:http://dx.doi.org/10.1016/j.intcom.2010.09.001
14. Hargittai E (2010) Digital Na(t)ives? Variation in internet skills and uses among members of the "Net Generation". Sociol Inquiry 80(1):92–113, doi:http://dx.doi.org/10.1111/j.1475-682X.2009.00317.x
15. Hawthorn D (2000) Possible implications of aging for interface designers. Interact Comput 12(5):507–528, doi:http://dx.doi.org/10.1016/S0953-5438(99)00021-1
16. Hewett TT (1986) The role of iterative evaluation in designing systems for usability. In: Harrison MD, Monk AF (eds) Proceedings of the 2nd conference of the British Computer Society, human computer interaction specialist group on people and computers: designing for usability. Cambridge University Press, New York, pp 196–214
17. Hix D, Hartson H (1993) Developing user interfaces: ensuring usability through product and process. John Wiley & Sons, New York
18. Hutchins EL, Hollan JD, Norman DA (1986) Direct manipulation interfaces. In: Norman DA, Draper SW (eds) User-centered system design. Erlbaum, Hillsdale, pp 87–124
19. Hyppönen H (2001) Industry awareness and transfer in Europe and the USA. In: Roe PRW (ed) Bridging the gap? Access to telecommunications for all people. Commission of European Communities, Brussels
20. IKEA (2012) Kitchen planner. http://www.ikea.com/ms/en_US/rooms_ideas/splashplanners.html. Accessed 16 Dec 2012
21. ISO 9241-171 (2008) Ergonomics of human-system interaction – part 171: guidance on software accessibility. http://www.iso.org/iso/iso_catalogue/catalogue_tc/catalogue_detail.htm?csnumber=39080. Accessed 1 April 2012
22. ISO 9241-210 (2010) Ergonomics of human-system interaction – part 210: human-centred design for interactive systems. http://www.iso.org/iso/catalogue_detail.htm?csnumber=52075. Accessed 1 Aug 2011

23. Jacko JA, Vitense H (2001) A review and reappraisal of information technologies within a conceptual framework for individuals with disabilities. Universal Access Inform Soc 1(1): 56–76
24. Jette AM (2006) Toward a common language for function, disability, and health. Phys Ther 86(5):726–734
25. John BE, Kieras DE (1996) The GOMS family of user interface analysis techniques: comparison and contrast. ACM Transact Comput Hum Interact 3(4):320–351, doi:http://dx.doi.org/10.1145/235833.236054
26. Kinsella K, He W (2009) An aging world: 2008. US census bureau, international population 1017 reports, PS95/09-1. US Government Printing Office, Washington DC
27. Langdon P, Thimbleby H (2010) Inclusion and interaction: designing interaction for inclusive populations. Interact Comput 22(6):439–448, doi:http://dx.doi.org/10.1016/j.intcom.2010.08.007
28. Langdon P, Persad U, John Clarkson P (2010) Developing a model of cognitive interaction for analytical inclusive design evaluation. Interact Comput 22(6):510–529, doi:http://dx.doi.org/10.1016/j.intcom.2010.08.008
29. Ling R (2008) Exclusion or self-isolation? Texting and the elderly users. Inform Soc 24(5)
30. Madden R, Hogan T (1997) The definition of disability in Australia: moving towards national consistency. AIHW, Canberra
31. Marschollek M et al (2007) ICT-based health information services for elderly people: past experiences, current trends, and future strategies. Inform Health Soc Care 32(4):251–261, doi:http://dx.doi.org/10.1080/14639230701692736
32. Martinez S, Sloan R, Szymkowiak A, Scott-Brown K (2010) Using virtual agents to cue observer attention: assessment of the impact of agent animation. In: The second international conference on creative content technologies. CONTENT, Lisbon, 21–26 Nov 2010, pp 7–12
33. Martinez S et al (2012) Animated virtual agents to cue user attention. Int J Adv Intell Sys 4(3&4):299–308
34. McDonough FA, Ladner RE, Roth W, Scadden LA and Vanderheiden GC (1988) Public law 99-506, "Section 508" Electronic equipment accessibility for disabled workers. In: O'Hare JJ (ed) Proceedings of the SIGCHI conference on human factors in computing systems (CHI '88), ACM, New York, pp 219–222. doi:10.1145/57167.57204 http://doi.acm.org/10.1145/57167.57204
35. Moran TP (1981) Guest editor's introduction: an applied psychology of the user. ACM Comput Surv 13:1–11, doi:http://dx.doi.org/10.1145/356835.356836
36. Mori G, Paternò F, Santoro C (2002) CTTE: support for developing and analyzing task models for interactive system design. IEEE Trans Soft Eng 28(8):797–813
37. Newell A (1993) Interfaces for the ordinary and beyond. IEEE Soft 10(5):76–78, doi:http://dx.doi.org/10.1109/52.232406
38. Newell AF (2006) Older people as a focus for inclusive design. Gerontechnology 4(4):190–199, doi:http://dx.doi.org/10.4017/gt.2006.04.04.003.00
39. Newell A, Simon HA et al (1972) Human problem solving. Prentice-Hall, Englewood Cliffs
40. Newell AF (2008) Accessible computing–past trends and future suggestions: commentary on "computers and people with disabilities." ACM Trans Access Comput 1(2): Article 9
41. Nicolle C, Abascal J (2001) Inclusive design guidelines for HCI. In: Proceedings of INCLUDE 2001, London, 18–20 April
42. Nicolle C, Peters B (1999) Elderly and disabled travelers: intelligent transp. Systems designed for the 3rd millennium. Transp Hum Fact 1(2):121–134, doi:http://dx.doi.org/10.1207/sthf0102_1
43. Nielsen J (1993) Iterative user-interface design. Comp 26(11):32–41, Academic, San Diego, doi:http://dx.doi.org/10.1109/2.241424
44. Nielsen J (1993) Usability engineering. Academic Press, San Diego
45. Nielsen J (1995) Usability engineering. Morgan Kaufmann, Burlington
46. Pieper M, Morasch H, Piéla G (2003) Bridging the educational divide. Univ Acc Inf Soc 2(3):243–254, doi:http://dx.doi.org/10.1007/s10209-003-0061-y

47. Porrero IP (1998) Improving the quality of life for the European citizen: technology for inclusive design and equality. IOS Press, Amsterdam
48. Potosnak K et al (1986) Classifying users: a hard look at some controversial issues. ACM SIGCHI Bull 17(4):84–88, doi:http://dx.doi.org/10.1145/22339.22353
49. Pullin G, Newell AF (2007) Focussing on extra-ordinary users. In: Proceedings of HCiI 2007, coping with diversity, 4th international conference on universal access in human-computer interaction, UAHCI 2007, Beijing, China, 22–27 July 2007, Proceedings, part I lecture notes in computer science, vol 4554, Springer, ISBN:978 3 540 73278-5
50. Rensink RA et al (2010) To see or not to see: the need for attention to perceive changes in scenes. Psych Sci 8(5):368–373
51. Rogers Y, Sharp H, Preece J (2011) Interaction design: beyond human-computer interaction. Wiley, New Jersey
52. Savidis A, Stephanidis C (2004) Unified user interface design: designing universally accessible interactions. Interact Comp 16(2): 243–270. http://linkinghub.elsevier.com/retrieve/pii/S0953543804000025. Accessed 18 Nov 2011
53. Scott-Brown KC, Baker MR, Orbach HS (2000) Comparison blindness. Vis Cogn 7(1–3): 253–267
54. Shneiderman B (1983) Direct manipulation: a step beyond programming languages. IEEE Comp 16(8):57–69, doi:http://dx.doi.org/10.1109/MC.1983.1654471
55. Shneiderman B, Plaisant C (2005) Designing the user interface: strategies for effective human-computer interaction, 4th edn. Addison-Wesley, Boston
56. Sloan RJS (2011) Emotional avatars: choreographing emotional facial expression animation. Dissertation, University of Abertay, Dundee
57. Sloan RJS, Martinez S, Scott-Brown K (2012) Using the principles of animation to predict allocation of attention. In: Predicting Perceptions 2012, Edinburgh, 17–19 April 2012
58. SensoMotric Instruments (2012) Eye & Gaze Tracking Systems. http://www.smivision.com/. Accessed 16 Dec 2012
59. SensoMotric Instruments (2012) SMI Eye Tracking Glasses. http://eyetracking-glasses.com/. Accessed 16 Dec 2012
60. Stevens JC (1992) Aging and spatial acuity of touch. J Gerontol 47(1):35–40
61. Stevens JC et al (1998) A multimodal assessment of sensory thresholds in aging. J Gerontol 53(4):263
62. Swiffin AL, Pickering JA, Arnott JL, Newell AF (1985) Pal: an effort efficient portable communication aid and keyboard emulator. In: Proceedings of the 8th annual conference on rehabilitation techonology, RESNA 8th Annual Conference, Memphis, Tennessee, pp 197–199
63. United States Department of Education Questions & Answers Title IV–Rehabilitation Act Amendments of 1998 section 508. Electronic and information technology. http://www.justice.gov/crt/508/archive/deptofed.pdf. Accessed 1 Aug 2011
64. Van Dam A (1997) Post-WIMP user interfaces. Commun ACM 40(2):63–67, doi:http://dx.doi.org/10.1145/253671.253708
65. Whiteside J, Bennett J, Holzblatt K (1988) Usability engineering: our experience and evolution. In: Helander M (ed) Handbook of human-computer interaction. North Holland, Amsterdam, pp 791–817
66. WHO (2001) ICF international classification of functioning, disability and health. World Health Organization, Geneva
67. Zajicek M (2006) Aspects of HCI research for older people. Univ Acc Inf Soc 5(3):279–286, doi:http://dx.doi.org/10.1007/s10209-006-0046-8
68. Ziegler J (1996) Interactive techniques. ACM Comput Surv 28(1):185–187. doi:10.1145/234313.234392 http://doi.acm.org/10.1145/234313.234392

Chapter 6
Context-Aware Recommender Systems Influenced by the Users' Health-Related Data

Martín López-Nores, Yolanda Blanco-Fernández, José J. Pazos-Arias, and Manuela I. Martín-Vicente

Abstract This chapter provides an overview of past and current developments in the area of recommender systems, paying special attention to two concepts that we view as cornerstones to provide effective assistance to people during their daily lives: *context awareness* and *health awareness*. We will enumerate different dimensions of *context* that are handled nowadays to maximize the value of the information delivered to the users, and then explain the existing approaches to take health-related data into consideration. Finally, we will describe the main features of a mobile application we are developing that interacts with *electronic health record* repositories and manages location information to recommend commercial products to the users.

6.1 Introduction

During the last decade, the growth in the amount of information available through the Internet and broadcast networks has fostered the development of *recommender systems,* which are tools intended to proactively deliver information according to the interests, preferences and needs of each individual at any time. These systems can be seen as an evolution of the classical *search engines* of the Internet (e.g. Google and Yahoo), that would retrieve relevant web pages in response to user-entered queries. Search engines proved effective, with millions of people using them to find pieces of information and services, but the growing presence of information technologies in society has rendered this paradigm insufficient. It is no longer realistic to think that users will bother to visit a site, enter queries describing what they want, and

M. López-Nores (✉) • Y. Blanco-Fernández • J.J. Pazos-Arias • M.I. Martín-Vicente
Department of Telematics Engineering, University of Vigo, EE Telecomunicación,
Campus Universitario s/n, Vigo 36310, Spain
e-mail: mlnores@det.uvigo.es; yolanda@det.uvigo.es; jose@det.uvigo.es;
mvicente@det.uvigo.es

E. Martín et al. (eds.), *User Modeling and Adaptation for Daily Routines: Providing Assistance to People with Special Needs,* Human–Computer Interaction Series, DOI 10.1007/978-1-4471-4778-7_6, © Springer-Verlag London 2013

select certain items from among those in a list. The reasons may have to do with the users adopting a predominantly passive role (e.g. while driving or watching TV), with the absence of bidirectional communication (as in broadcasting environments), with the users feeling uneasy with the interfaces provided or, simply, with the fact that the users may not know what they need or what would be advisable for them. Recommender systems are intended to address these problems, which are the focus of a large body of research nowadays.

The point we address in this chapter is that there is much work to do in the area of recommender systems regarding two concepts that we view as cornerstones to provide effective assistance to people during their daily lives: *context awareness* and *health awareness*. On the one hand, while it is true that several authors have made experiments with many different dimensions of context (e.g. to consider where the users are or what they are doing), their approaches are most often ad hoc for one only dimension, and there are no systematic approaches to deal with several ones in a uniform way. On the other hand, it is noticeable that most of the research efforts in recommender systems have left health-related aspects aside, even though they are a non-negligible matter of interest and driver of decisions for many people. This is particularly true of people with special needs and/or disabilities. Some authors have come up with expert systems that process information from the healthcare domain, but the management of health-related data remains practically unexplored in the realm of personalized information services.

We will first take a look at the functionalities provided by recommender systems nowadays, with special attention to their context awareness features and also to the few existing proposals in the e-health domain (Sect. 6.2). Next, in Sect. 6.3, we will briefly describe the different ways to gather information about the users and their context. In Sect. 6.4, we will survey the main techniques used to match the information available about the users with the items that may be offered to them, which lead to different recommendation strategies. We will see how those strategies have been used in context-aware systems, and pay special attention to their relative strengths and weaknesses when it comes to handling health-related data and making recommendations to people with special needs and/or disabilities. In Sect. 6.5, we will describe the features of a recommender system we are developing ourselves, named HARE (*Health-Aware Recommender*), that manages health-related data and location information to proactively select potentially interesting products for the users. A summary of conclusions will be given in Sect. 6.6.

6.2   Evolution and State-of-the-Art in Recommender Systems

The first studies on personalized services arose in the realm of **adaptive hyper-media**, aimed at improving the usability of the World Wide Web. There have been countless approaches to web page recommenders [3, 4], relying on navigation histories as the main source of information about the users' interests. Some authors (e.g. [1]) introduced a notion of *informational context*, in the sense of computing recommendations live, looking for web pages related by topic to the ones being displayed at the moment on the users' web browsers. A few recommenders would also tailor the selection and presentation of contents to the time the user will have to read or watch material, the size of the screens where they will be presented or the input mechanisms available [65,66].

Personalized learning over the Internet developed hand-in-hand with adaptive hypermedia, with many authors developing and making experiments with recommender systems (e.g. [2, 56]) grounded on a number of standards for student profiling, content description, etc. These standards have been adopted in personalized TV-based learning (*t-learning*), with recommenders delivering selected pieces of educational material through simple interactions with audiovisual contents (see [46, 54]). Also, many authors are working to provide personalized learning through mobile devices (*m-learning*), with recommender systems aimed at delivering the (potentially) most interesting pieces of information following the users' movements in indoor environments (e.g. museums) or outdoors (e.g. in guided city tours) [12, 23, 39]. Other systems were presented that took into consideration features of infrastructure (e.g. surrounding communication resources) and physical conditions (noise, light, etc).

Actually, the first application area for personalization beyond the PC was that of **personalized programming guides**, to help TV viewers find interesting programs among the growing number of channels available. This is now a relatively mature field of research in what concerns TV watching at home, with various recommenders featuring semantic reasoning capabilities [15, 18]. Some systems (e.g. [55, 85]) can even adapt the recommendations depending on whether the user is watching TV alone or in groups, which is another dimension of context awareness. As for the delivery of audiovisual contents over mobile devices, there have been several approaches to build music recommenders and personalized video channels [43, 44, 48]. Research in this area has been recently boosted by promising works on *affective computing* [77,79,80], which —coupled with theories on emotion and cognition— make it possible to take the user's feelings (mood, stress, etc) into consideration as well.

Personalized e-commerce has been around on the Internet for some years [45, 70], but it was absent until very recently in other platforms. Again, the first developments arose in digital TV, with approaches to pick specific advertisements from the broadcast emissions [14]. Going one step beyond, some authors focused on the automatic composition of interactive services, developing approaches to automatically assemble applications that would provide personalized commercial functionalities [10, 17, 72]. Also, systems have been demonstrated that deliver personalized and location-aware advertisements over devices like car radios, PDAs and smartphones [78].

Some authors have worked on **personalization in e-government**, too. The need arises from the fact that users often get lost in the information space of e-government portals, needing specific hints that are easily obtained in administrative buildings (e.g. finding the office responsible for a given service or asking for assistance to fill out certain fields of a form). Approaches to address this problem include strategies to help discover administrative proceedings one has to fulfill [71] and solutions to identify contexts in which a given proceeding is applicable [31].

Recommender systems are progressively gaining other new areas of application. Just to enhance the picture of the preceding paragraphs, we can cite research works in location-aware restaurant recommenders [84], bibliography recommenders [38] and personalized friend making [88]. Indeed, recommenders are already working behind the scenes in numerous well-known sites and applications, like Amazon, Netflix, Movielens, Last.fm, Facebook, MySpace, LinkedIn, Foursquare, etc.

6.2.1 Recommenders in the e-Health Domain

Personalized healthcare remains an area with very few specific solutions, notwithstanding the fact that health-related data are undoubtedly a wealthy source of knowledge about the interests, preferences and needs of many users. Mainstream research in e-health ranges from the design of wearable/implantable devices (see [32, 57]) that sense physiological parameters to expert systems for information processing and diagnosis [68, 73, 87]. Yet, there are a number of personalization systems that are worth describing, because they may be paving the road for further research in the area.

Several authors have focused on providing useful information to people with chronic diseases, such as diabetes, chronic obstructive pulmonary disease (COPD), coeliac disease or obesity. For instance, the system of [22, 25] aims to deliver health-related educational material (both video- and text-based) from any knowledge available about the users' health conditions, including real-time monitoring of vital signs (heart rate, oxygen saturation, and blood glucose values, etc). In the same line, the authors of [33] presented a lifestyle recommender for people touched by diabetes, which can suggest meals and physical activities by managing information entered by the users or by doctors, real-time vital signs and a record of previous recommendations to keep track of the particular culinary preferences of each individual. The system of [40] went a little bit further for people with coronary heart disease, delivering diet recommendations by also looking at the history of diseases of the users' relatives. Other interesting pieces of work about personalized diets can be found in [28, 82].

Among the works that did not focus on chronic diseases, we can highlight the framework for health-aware recommender systems presented in [83], which aimed to deliver educational material and medical advice by processing the knowledge gathered in semantic networks like Wikipedia. A similar goal was pursued in the system presented in [42], which would also guide the users in hospital to reach locations where they would get certain medical cares. Likewise, in [49], we presented a smart medicine manager that would also monitor the users' intake of prescribed medicines and issue reminders and warnings through whichever means were available (mobile phones, computers, TV screens, relatives, etc). In [59], another recommender system was proposed to suggest clinical examinations for patients or physicians from patients' self-reported data, with an expert system processing information behind the scenes. In [26], the idea was to process medical histories to find the most relevant ones for physicians, researchers and students.

Finally, the authors of [35] developed a recommender system to assist patients confronted with a medical condition to decide which physician to trust.

The authors of [35] put the emphasis on the privacy aspects related to the management of health-related data, presenting two different architectures to address those concerns: the *Secure Processing Architecture* (SPA) and the *Anonymous Contributions Architecture* (ACA). In SPA, patients submit their data to the recommender systems in a protected form without revealing any information about themselves, and the computation of recommendations proceeds over the protected data using secure multi-party computation techniques. In ACA, patients submit data in the clear, but no link between a submission and patient data can be made. These architectures can be seen as greatest common factors for other authors' approaches to privacy.

Although the number and the quality of proposals in the area of health-aware recommender systems is growing noticeably, the truth is that they are still a comparatively minority topic in conferences and journals focused on personalization in general and/or recommender systems in particular. The reason could be related to the privacy concerns, since it is generally not easy to engage in collaborations with hospitals, to gain access to repositories of clinical documents or to gather a sufficient number of users with specific profiles to run statistically-significant experiments. It is also noticeable that the management of context in the aforementioned personalization systems is too reliant on ad hoc solutions, since there are no systematic approaches to exploiting location or physiological information, let alone other dimensions of context. Here, it should be possible to borrow solutions from the burgeoning area of technologies for *ambient-assisted living* [9, 36, 47], which make extensive use of ubiquitous computing concepts to assist the elderly and other people with special needs at home and outside. In any case, we can say that personalization in e-health remains too linked to pure, classical e-health scenarios, which limits the potential benefits of the research efforts to those people who are really concerned about their health conditions, probably due to chronic or long-lasting problems. With not much to say to a general user, the odds are that health-aware personalization systems will go unnoticed for a vast majority, unless they are properly integrated to provide general advice in casual or daily activities. Then, it would be necessary to find the right level of presence, halfway between a system that is not at all influenced by health-related data and one that appears as an annoying, mother-like conscience. This question about intrusiveness (which could be seen as an alter-ego of privacy) is yet to be addressed, too.

6.3   Gathering Information About the Users and Their Context

There have been numerous proposals on how to build and maintain user profiles for a personalization system. As explained in the survey of [56], this diversity stems from the many types of data structures that may be employed to capture the knowledge available about a user, e.g. in the form of purchase histories (the most common in e-commerce), web navigation or e-mail registries, feature vectors, semantic networks, associative networks, decision trees, inducted rules, matrices of ratings or simply sets of demographic features (i.e. data like age, gender or marital status).

Since a recommender system cannot work until the user profiles have been created, these tools must know as much as possible about the personal interests of each individual. There exist a wide diversity of approaches for modeling initial profiles, ranging from user-driven manual input (i.e. having the users enter an explicit description of their interests) to semi-automatic procedures based on training sets (i.e. asking the users to rate a representative set of items) [8] and *stereotyping* (i.e. categorizing the users into one from among various *stereotypes* that characterize the average preferences or demographic features of different groups of people) [41]. Recently, some authors have proposed solutions to initialize profiles by applying data mining techniques on information extracted from the users' interactions in social networks, most commonly Facebook [5]. The majority approach in health-aware recommender systems is to have the users enter their relevant information manually, even though some authors have supplemented that information with data retrieved automatically from existing *personal health records* (stored in the users' devices) and repositories of *electronic health records* (in the hands of governments or health institutions) [33,40,49,83].

Most recommender systems implement *relevance feedback* techniques to continuously gather information about each individual. The feedback can be either given explicitly by the users themselves (e.g. periodically asking the user to evaluate new items through ratings or textual comments) [61], or implicitly inferred by the recommender system from their actions and previous interactions (e.g. observing the time spent on a web page, menu choices or actions such as scrolling or enlarging windows) [19]. Likewise, contextual information can be obtained explicitly as in [24] or implicitly, for example, by retrieving information from GPS, by having a telephony company inform of a user's position in the cellular network [6] or by exchanging data over networks present in smart homes or museums to get annotations like *"in the kitchen"* or *"in front of Guernica"* [67, 86]). Additionally, since recommender systems interact with the users over long periods of time, mechanisms are needed to adapt profiles to their evolving interests and needs, discarding information that may have become obsolete. Approaches to this question range from time windows to gradual forgetting functions and even natural selection for ecosystems of agents (see [2] for an in-depth study). Noticeably, all the previous works in health-aware recommenders have relied on explicit feedback and, as far as we know, they have not specifically addressed the question of updating user profiles over time (apart from refreshing the information retrieved automatically from external sources, of course).

6.4   Reasoning and Recommendation Techniques

Given a set of items, the goal of a personalization system is to identify the most suitable ones according to the information stored in the users' profiles. In this section, we will review the main *filtering strategies* that have been proposed to do so.

The first systems were based on **demographic filtering**, recommending items that had been appealing to other users with similar data. The recommendations produced in this way tend to be imprecise and fail to reflect changes of the user preferences over time, because personal data are often stable for long periods.

A more sophisticated approach —an early one, but still present in literature and in commercial use anyway— was that of **content-based filtering** or *case-based filtering* (which we shall denote by CBF). This strategy consists in suggesting items similar to others that gained the user's interest in the past [20], which is quite simple to implement. However, the recommendations tend to be repetitive for considering that a user will always appreciate the same kind of stuff. This *overspecialization* may not pose a problem with users who want to remain informed on specific topics (e.g. people with chronic diseases), but it does so in general. Furthermore, the minimal data available about new users makes the first results highly inaccurate. Notwithstanding these shortcomings, CBF has been the predominant strategy in health-aware recommender systems (e.g. in [33, 40, 59]), most probably because it is easier to comply with privacy regulations when managing only information about one user at each time, instead of processing and matching the profiles of several ones.

In response to the problem of overspecialization, researchers came up with **user-based collaborative filtering** (UBCF), to consider the success of the recommendations previously made to users with similar interests [60]. Conceptually, UBCF is driven by the definition of clusters of users (*neighborhoods*) as per the items they have rated positively or negatively. This approach is depicted in Fig. 6.1, where solid arrows denote a positive rating given by a user to an item, and dashed arrows link items to the properties or features that characterize them. Most of the times, UBCF relies on direct links between specific users and specific items, meaning, for example, that *"Jane has liked ItemA"* or *"John has disliked ItemB"*. Thus, users *Alice* and *Carol* are put in the same neighborhood in Fig. 6.1 (UBCF) because they have given similar ratings to items i_1 and i_3. In some cases, however, the relationships that define the clusters may be identified also through the item properties. For example, *Bob* and *Carol* are put into the same cluster (the same neighborhood) because there are common properties among items they have rated positively (i_2 and i_3 share the property ip_2, whereas i_1 and i_5 share the property ip_5). This way, having the ability to manage item properties, an UBCF-based system like that of [16] can treat two users as neighbors if they are fond viewers of nature documentaries, even if they have watched different ones on different TV channels.

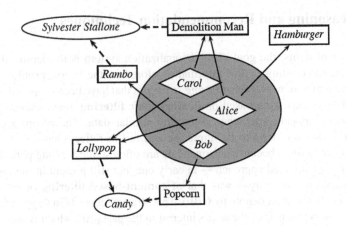

Fig. 6.1 Conceptual representation of UBCF (diamonds → users; rectangles → items; ellipses → item properties)

UBCF solves the lack of diversity of CBF, but works poorly with users (the *gray sheep*) whose preferences or needs are dissimilar to those of the majority. This is a very important issue for health-aware recommenders, inasmuch as health conditions are always a source of uniqueness. From the details available in literature, it seems that the system of [35] delivers recommendations by UBCF.

A more recent strategy is **item-based collaborative filtering** (IBCF), that consists in recommending items related to others that the target user liked in the past, considering two items related when users who like the one tend to like the other as well [69]. As depicted in Fig. 6.2, IBCF can be seen as clustering together items that have been successfully or unsuccessfully recommended to certain users. In Fig. 6.2, items *"Bologna Tour"* and *"Leather jacker"* are put into the same cluster because they have been appealing to two users, namely *Agnes* and *Brais*. Likewise, by dealing with the item properties, IBCF-based systems can detect that people who like *"Formula 1"* races tend to like *"Superbikes"* too, because both involve motor sports.

IBCF still faces several problems that were also apparent with UBCF. One of those problems is *sparsity*, implying that when the number of items available to recommend is high (as it happens in many domains of recommender systems application nowadays), it is difficult to find users with similar valuations for common subsets. Another important drawback is that of *latency*, related to the inability to recommend recently-added items, as long as there are no user ratings available for them.

Not surprisingly, there exist **hybrid approaches** that attempt to neutralize the weaknesses and combine the strengths of demographic, content-based and the different flavours of collaborative filtering, e.g. recommending items similar to the ones listed in the user's profile, but considering two items similar if the individuals who show interest in the one tend to be interested in the other [21].

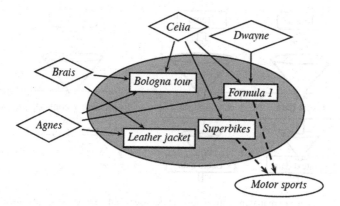

Fig. 6.2 Conceptual representation of IBCF (diamonds → users; rectangles → items; ellipses → item properties)

6.4.1 About the Management of Context

The outcome of a filtering strategy is always a list of items for each user, in decreasing order of (potential) appeal. Then, the user may be faced with only the first item, the top *n* ones or the whole list, depending on the domain of application of the recommender system. Or there may be a second round of filtering, this time considering any information available about the user's context. This is the most typical approach, even though there exist a few recommender systems that process contextual information first. To the best of our knowledge, represented in Fig. 6.3, there are no systems that process both user information and contextual information altogether, in one only round. In line with the arguments posed in [58], we believe this is important because many items may become particularly interesting for one user in very specific contexts, even though he/she would not find them relevant in other scenarios; likewise, some items may not be interesting to most of the people in a given context, but a *gray sheep* could greatly appreciate them anyway. Apparently, it is common to all forms of UBCF and IBCF that the links exploited to match items and users are characterized *statically* by the ratings that the latter have given to the former, so there is no trace of context embedded in these procedures.

6.4.2 About the Internal Reasoning Capabilities

Regardless of the filtering strategy, the first recommender systems used *heuristics* or *syntactic* matching techniques, which relate items by looking for common words in their attached metadata. Even though there exist plenty of different techniques (see [11, 13, 37, 60, 74, 89]), they all miss a lot of knowledge during the personalization process, because they are unable to reason about the meaning of the metadata. For instance, it is not possible for them to observe a relationship between

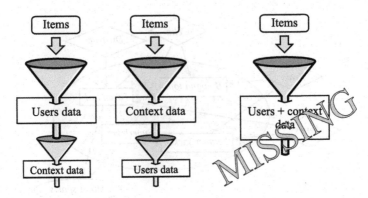

Fig. 6.3 Approaches to managing information about users and context in recommender systems

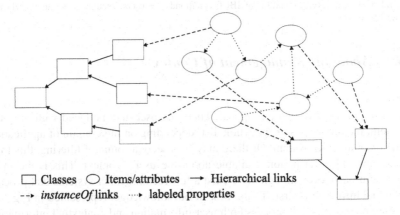

☐ Classes   ○ Items/attributes   → Hierarchical links
--→ *instanceOf* links   ·····▸ labeled properties

Fig. 6.4 The structure of an ontology

"*measles*" and "*rubella*", because the two words are dissimilar. In many areas of application, this limitation may just appear as a source of *overspecialization*, since the recommendations can only include items very similar to those the users already know [7]. When reasoning about health-related information, moreover, it entails a plethora of potential risks that would make a recommender system undependable for its little wisdom. it is possible to apply techniques from the *Semantic Web*, which enable reasoning processes that gain insight into the meaning of words —so that, for example, "*measles*" and "*rubella*" can be automatically recognized as two eruptive infectious diseases. The key here lies within the use of *ontologies* to describe and interrelate items and their attributes by means of class hierarchies and labeled properties (see Fig. 6.4). These constructs can be used to model different features of context, and to enable reasoning about them in a more sophisticated manner than the classical approaches enabled by tagging contexts with a few words [76].

6.5   HARE: A Time-Aware, Location-Aware and Health-Aware Recommender

After 8 years of research in recommender systems (see [15, 18, 50, 51] for the most relevant publications), we have been recently working to develop a semantics-based mobile application that manages health-related data and time/location information to recommend different kinds of items to the users. This application, named HARE (*Health-Aware Recommender*), relies on a broad notion of *item* that embraces web pages, TV programs, pieces of learning material, advertisements, cooking recipes, and so on. Its functionalities are not only available through a mobile web browser, but also through voice calls and SMS messaging, which makes it accessible even for people who are not much familiar with computers and smartphones.

Next, we will explain the way we obtain and manage information about items, users and contexts. Then, we will describe in some detail the new filtering strategy we have devised to reckon the distinguishing and decision-driving nature of health-related data when making recommendations. This strategy manages user and context information at the same time, and extends the ideas of collaborative filtering in a way that is compatible with the architectures for privacy put forward in [35].

6.5.1   The System's Knowledge Bases

HARE brings together a number of metadata standards to characterize items, users and contexts. To begin with, the items are characterized by the semantic properties and attributes defined in an ontology that borrows metadata from TV-Anytime [81] (for TV programs) and eCl@ss [34] (for commercial products). Other resources in general are annotated following the MPEG-7 standard [53].

As regards the users, we manage various types of data:

- Demographic features like age, gender or marital status.
- Conditions directly bound to consumption patterns, such as what can be inferred from web navigation histories (e.g. fondness for science blogs) and TV watching records (e.g. fondness for sports shows).
- Conditions not directly bound to consumption patterns, namely those retrieved from electronic health records, related to current or past conditions (e.g. pregnancy) or diseases (e.g. a broken leg), and to medical prescriptions in force.
- The representativeness of certain stereotypes, which can be easily related to the properties and attributes modeled in the aforementioned ontology—for instance, by applying classical metrics of CBF-based systems, it is easy to classify one user within the stereotypes of *"people worried about cholesterol"* or *"people concerned about weight"*.

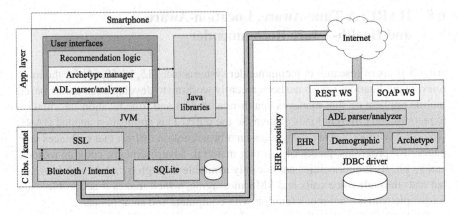

Fig. 6.5 An architecture to access openEHR electronic health records from an Android device

The users' mobile devices can retrieve information from electronic health records compliant to the openEHR[1] standard. The architecture in this regard is shown in Fig. 6.5. On the client side, we consider mobile devices running the Android operating system, which provides an object-oriented application layer on top of a Java virtual machine. Below, there are libraries written in C for graphics, web browsing, and other computationally-demanding tasks. The key element of Fig. 6.5 is the '*Archetype manager*' module, which is in charge of retrieving and processing the datatypes used in openEHR electronic health records. It relies on a parser/analyzer tool that is actually an adaptation of the one included in the Java reference implementation of the openEHR framework. On the server side, the EHR repositories can be accessed through two different approaches, namely REST [64] and SOAP [75] web services. All communications flow through SSL tunnels, secured by the cryptographic functions of the standard *java.security* and *javax.security* libraries. Local storage is managed in simple relational databases using SQLite.

As noted above, HARE handles three dimensions of context: time, location and informational context.

- Time is measured in the obvious way, and contexts are identified and labelled according to the OWL-Time[2] ontology.
- We obtain location information from geolocation methods based on either mobile telephony networks or GPS; then, we characterize context using an ontology of locations, built according to the guidelines put forward in [27].
- Finally, informational context refers to music the user is listening to using his/her mobile device, videos he/she is watching or web pages he/she is visiting.

---

[1]http://www.openehr.org

[2]http://www.w3.org/TR/owl-time/

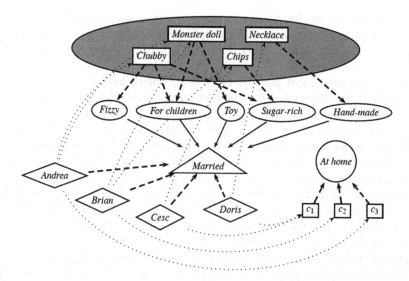

Fig. 6.6 Conceptual representation of PBCF (diamonds → users; triangle → user property; rectangles → items//contexts; ellipses → item properties; circle → context property)

6.5.2 A New Filtering Strategy: Property-Based Collaborative Filtering (PBCF)

As noted in Sect. 6.4, the classical filtering strategies may have significant drawbacks related to the management of context and health-related data. To address these problems, we have devised a new strategy called *property-based collaborative filtering* (PBCF), that maintains links between the semantic properties that characterize items, users and contexts. The aim is to capture knowledge that may be put down in rules like "*diabetic users tend not to like candy, unless they are sugar-free*", "*pregnant women usually purchase baby clothes*" or "*hot chocolate is most often sold during winter*". To do so, as shown in Fig. 6.6, we end up defining clusters of items as per the likelihood that they will be appealing to users who match certain properties in contexts that have certain properties. In the picture, for example, we see dotted lines indicating that user *Andrea* has liked items "*Chubby*" and "*Monster doll*" in context c_3, while user *Brian* has liked "*Monster doll*" and "*Chips*" in context c_2. Both contexts, c_2 and c_3, share the property "*At home*".

Internally, PBCF maintains one three-dimensional matrix: the value of cell (i,j,k) of the PBCF matrix is an indication of how good an item characterized by the item property ip_i should be for a user characterized by the user property up_j in a context characterized by up_k. For convenience, we keep these values in the range $[-1, 1]$. In contrast with the static links handled by UBCF and IBCF (see Sect. 6.4), the numbers in the PBCF matrix evolve over time, driven by the relevance feedback gathered after recommending items. Intuitively, the facts that a user characterized by properties up_2 and up_3 has given a very positive rating to an item characterized by properties ip_1 and ip_5 in a context characterized by cp_4 contributes to increasing the values of cells $(1, 2, 4)$, $(5, 2, 4)$, $(1, 3, 4)$ and $(5, 3, 4)$ —obviously, negative ratings work in the opposite way.

It is worth noting that previous filtering algorithms have been always driven by *semantic similarity* metrics of a cumulative nature, that, in essence, come down to counting the number of attributes shared between the items that may be recommended to a user and the items recorded in his/her profile [30, 62, 63]. With such metrics, item properties that do not align with the users' profile (e.g. sugar-richness in the case of a diabetic person) dilute as a negative contribution to a summation of many addends, so the items can end up appearing in the recommendations if the overall sum exceeds a given threshold. This implies, for example, that it is not possible to prevent certain recommendations depending on health-related conditions—and, conversely, to boost the value of items that might have a beneficial effect. This shortcoming disappears in PBCF, because its matrix captures explicitly what is good and bad for every single user property, which is the key to giving an appropriate treatment to the gray sheep (remember, the users whose preferences and needs are dissimilar to those of the majority): we can proceed with each one of the users' features *separately*, no matter how uncommon their combination might be.

For the same reason, PBCF allows to explain *why* the items are recommended, indicating the most decisive features when presenting the recommendations (e.g. emphasizing the words "*popular among diabetics*" or "*gluten free*"), which may serve to reduce dubiousness/distrust among users with very specific needs. Finally, it is noticeable that, by relying only on properties, PBCF can compute levels of appeal for newly-added items even if there are no user ratings available for them: it suffices to have values in the PBCF matrix for items that share properties with the new one. This way, we avoid the sparsity and latency problems of the other collaborative strategies.

6.5.3 A Quick Example

To illustrate the reasoning and the functionalities enabled by HARE, consider the case of a male user whose profile and EHR indicate, among other facts, that he is diabetic, fond of traveling and a frequent viewer of documentaries. It is Christmas season, and the user is currently watching a video about polar fauna and flora. Therefore, the filtering strategy will be traversing the rows and columns of the PBCF matrix corresponding to four user properties ("*Male*", "*Diabetic*", "*Likes traveling*" and "*Likes documentaries*") and three context properties: one about time ("*Christmas*"), another about what he is doing ("*Watching TV*") and the final one—a piece of informational context—in the characterization of the documentary ("*Nature*").

Fig. 6.7 Advertising herbal remedies in the context of a nature documentary

The user's fondness for traveling, the nature-related topic of the video and the fact that many people are on holidays during Christmas (this fact is captured in the time ontology) can yield a high relevance value for some rural tourism establishments. Likewise, Christmas is found to be a propitious season for candy and nougat bars, but the fact that they are classified as *"Candy"* in the ontology of items leads to a very low relevance value after examining the row corresponding to the user property *"Diabetes"*. This is ensured by applying a ponderation formula that grants greater weight in the computations to the features with the highest and the lowest values in the different rows and columns (see [52] for details about the computations). On the contrary, some of the herbal remedies that claim benefits for diabetic people gain increased relevance, even though they are not particularly bound to any specific context. Assuming that this suffices to exceed the value computed for the rural establishments, we can end up advertising a garlic-derived preparation as shown in Fig. 6.7.

With the advertisement on screen, as explained in [50], the user could tap on the advertisement to launch an interactive application that allows the user to learn more about the recommended item and to purchase online.

6.5.4 Current Status and Development Plan

Our implementation of HARE is practically finished, and our aim is to start evaluation by taking advantage of the deployment of the AVATAR system [18], a recommender of TV programs developed by our research group. Initially, we will have to do without access to electronic health records, because they are not yet available in the local public health system. To fill in this gap, we are resorting to explicit profile initialization mechanisms through forms and questionnaires, and we are also developing mechanisms to implicitly mine health-related data from the users' interactions on social networks. The evaluation will be driven by classical metrics used in the recommender systems literature, which are analyzed in Chap. 9 of this book [29].

6.6 Conclusions

In this chapter, we have taken a look at the state-of-the-art in the area of recommender systems, which are becoming increasingly important tools for many providers of communication and information services. We have argued that context awareness and health awareness are two important features for these systems to provide effective assistance to people during their daily lives, especially thinking of people with special needs and/or disabilities. Context-aware recommenders have been a hot research topic for some years now, but there is yet a long way to go before having systems that manage multiple dimensions of context in an integrated and coherent fashion, possibly intertwined with the reasoning about items and users. As regards personalized healthcare, there have been a few proposals with very different goals, and our impression is that we are still missing a global approach to the problem of supporting the users' well-being and medical treatments, considering the individuals' unique biological, social and cultural characteristics. We believe there is a huge potential to be exploited, since this is probably the area in which personalization may report the greatest benefits in social and economical terms.

References

1. Adomavicius G, Mobasher B, Ricci F, Tuzhilin A (2011) Context-aware recommender systems. AI Mag 32(3):117–142
2. Adomavicius G, Tuzhilin A (2005) Towards the next generation of recommender systems: a survey of the state-of-the-art and possible extensions. IEEE Trans Knowl Data Eng 17(6): 739–749
3. Aghabozorgi SR, Wah TY (2009) Recommender systems: incremental clustering on web log data. In: Proceedings of the 2nd international conference on interaction sciences: information technology, culture and human, Seoul. ACM, New York, pp 812–818
4. Alam S (2011) Intelligent web usage clustering based recommender system. In: Proceedings of the 5th ACM conference on recommender systems. ACM, New York, Chicago, pp 367–370
5. Amatriain X, Jaimes A, Oliver N, Pujol JM (2011) Data mining methods for recommender systems. In: Mathematik für Ingenieure. Springer, Berlin
6. Anand SS, Mobasher B (2007) Contextual recommendation. Lect Notes Artif Intell 4737: 142–160

7. Ardissono L, Gena C, Torasso P, Bellifemine F, Chiarotto A, Difino A, Negro B (2004) User modeling and recommendation techniques for personalized electronic program guides. In: Personalized digital television. Targeting programs to individual users. Kluwer Academic Publishers, Dordrecht

8. Asnicar F, Tasso C (1997) IfWeb: a prototype of user-models-based intelligent agent for document filtering and navigation in the World Wide Web. In: Proceedings of the 6th international conference on user modeling, Chia Laguna. http://www.dfki.de/~jameson/UM97/proceedings-overview.htm

9. Baek SH, Choi EC, Huh JD (2007) Design of information management model for sensor based context-aware service in ubiquitous home. In: Proceedings of the international conference on convergence information technology, Gyeongju. IEEE, Piscataway, pp 1040–1047

10. Bakalov F, König-Ries B, Nauerz A, Welsch M (2008) Ontology-based multidimensional personalization modeling for the automatic generation of mashups in next-generation portals. In: Proceedings of the 1st international workshop on ontologies in interactive systems, Liverpool. IEEE, Piscataway, pp 75–82

11. Balabanović M, Shoham Y (1997) Fab: content-based collaborative recommender. Commun ACM 40(3):66–72

12. Baldauf M, Dustdar S, Rosenberg F (2007) A survey on context-aware systems. Int J Ad Hoc Ubiquitous Comput 2(4):263–277

13. Basu C, Hirsh H, Cohen W (1998) Recommendation as classification: using social and content-based information in recommendation. In: Proceedings of the 15th national conference on artificial intelligence, Madison. AAAI Press, Menlo Park

14. Bates PJ (2003) A study into TV-based interactive learning to the home. http://www.pjb.co.uk/t-learning/contents.htm. Last Accessed 26 Feb 2012

15. Blanco-Fernández Y, López-Nores M, Gil-Solla A, Ramos-Cabrer M, Pazos-Arias JJ (2011) Exploring synergies between content-based filtering and spreading activation techniques in knowledge-based recommender systems. Inf Sci 181(21):4823–4846

16. Blanco-Fernández Y, López-Nores M, Pazos-Arias JJ, Gil-Solla A, Ramos-Cabrer M (2010) Exploiting digital TV users' preferences in a tourism recommender system based on semantic reasoning. IEEE Trans Consum Electron 56(2):904–912

17. Blanco-Fernández Y, López-Nores M, Pazos-Arias JJ, Martín-Vicente MI (2010) Automatic generation of mashups for personalized commerce in digital TV by semantic reasoning. In: Proceedings of the 10th international conference on electronic commerce and web technologies, Linz. Springer, Berlin

18. Blanco-Fernández Y, Pazos-Arias JJ, López-Nores M, Gil-Solla A, Ramos-Cabrer M (2006) AVATAR: an improved solution for personalized TV based on semantic inference. IEEE Trans Consum Electron 52(1):223–231

19. Branting LK (2004) Learning feature weights from customer return-set selections. Knowl Inf Syst 6(2):188–202

20. Bridge D, Göker M, McGinty L, Smyth B (2006) Case-based recommender systems. Knowl Eng Rev 20(3):315–320

21. Burke R (2002) Hybrid recommender systems: survey and experiments. User Model User-Adapt Interact 12(4):331–370

22. Burkow TM (2008) An easy to use and affordable home-based personal ehealth system for chronic disease management based on free open source software. In: Proceedings of the 21st International Congress of the European Federation for Medical Informatics, Göteborg. IOS Press, Lansdale, pp 83–88

23. di Flora C, Ficco M, Russo S, Vecchio V (2005) Indoor and outdoor location-based services for portable wireless devices. In: 25th international conference on distributed computing systems, Columbus. IEEE, Piscataway, pp 244–250

24. Dourish P (2004) What we talk about when we talk about context. Pers Ubiquitous Comput 8(1):19–30

25. Fernández-Luque L, Karlsen R, Vognild LK (2009) Challenges and opportunities of using recommender systems for personalized health education. In: Proceedings of the 22nd International Congress of the European Federation for Medical Informatics, Sarajevo. IOS Press, Lansdale
26. Ferreira-Satler M, Romero F, Olivas J, Serrano-Guerrero J (20011) Sistema de recomendación de información clínica electrónica basado en ontologías borrosas y perfiles de usuario. In: Proceedings of the conference of the Spanish Association of Artificial Intelligence (CAEPIA), Tenerife
27. Flury T, Privat G, Ramparany F (2004) OWL-based location ontology for context-aware services. In: Proceedings of the artificial intelligence in mobile systems (AIMS), Nottingham, pp 52–58. http://www.caepia11.es/index.php?option=com_content&view=article&id=45&Itemid=27&lang=es
28. Freyne J, Berkovsky S (2010) Intelligent food planning: personalized recipe recommendation. In: Proceedings of the international conference on intelligent user interfaces (IUI), Hong Kong. ACM, New York
29. Freyne J, Berkovsky S (2013) Evaluating recommender systems for supportive technologies. In: Martín E, Haya PA, Carro RM (eds) User modeling and adaptation for daily routines. Springer, London, pp 195–217
30. Ganesan P, Garcia-Molina H, Widom J (2003) Exploiting hierarchical domain structure to compute similarity. ACM Trans Inf Syst 21(1):64–93
31. Guo X, Lu J (2007) Intelligent e-government services with personalized recommendation techniques. Int J Intell Syst 22(5):401–417
32. Güler NF, Übeyli ED (2002) Theory and applications of biotelemetry. J Med Syst 26(3):199–220
33. Hammer S, Kim J, André E (2010) MED-StyleR: METABO diabetes lifestyle recommender. In: Proceedings of the 4th ACM conference on recommender systems, Barcelona. ACM, New York, pp 285–288
34. Hepp. M, Leukel J, Schmitz V (2007) A quantitative analysis of product categorization standards: content, coverage and maintenance of eCl@ss, UNSPSC, eOTD, and the RosettaNet Technical Dictionary. Knowl Inf Syst 13(1):77–114
35. Hoens T, Blanton M, Chawla N (2010) Reliable medical recommendation systems with patient privacy. In: Proceedings of the 1st ACM international health informatics symposium (IHI), Arlington. ACM, New York, pp 173–182
36. Hristova A, Bernardos AM, Casar JR (2008) Context-aware services for ambient-assisted living: a case study. In: Proceedings of the 1st international symposium on Applied Sciences on Biomedical and Communication Technologies. IEEE, Piscataway, Aalborg, pp 1–5
37. Im KH, Park SC (2007) Case-based reasoning and neural network based expert system for personalization. Expert Syst Appl 32(1):77–85
38. Kanawati R, Karoui H (2009) A P2P collaborative bibliography recommender system. In: Proceedings of the 4th international conference on Internet and web applications and services, Venice. Springer, Berlin, pp 90–96
39. Kenteris M, Gavalas D, Mpitziopoulos A (2010) A mobile tourism recommender system. In: Proceedings of the IEEE symposium on computers and communications. IEEE, Piscataway, Riccione, pp 840–845
40. Kim JH, Lee JH, Park JS, Lee YH, Rim KW (2009) MED-StyleR: METABO diabetes lifestyle recommender. In: Proceedings of the 4th international conference on computer sciences and convergence information technology (ICCIT), Seoul. IEEE, Piscataway
41. Krulwich B (1997) Lifestyle finder: intelligent user profiling using large-scale demographic data. AI Mag 18(2):37–45
42. Lamber P, Ludwig B, Ricci F, Zini F, Mitterer M (2011) Message-based patient guidance in day-hospital. In: Proceedings of the 12th IEEE international conference on Mobile Data Management (MDM), Lulea. IEEE, Piscataway
43. Lampropoulos AS, Lampropoulou PS, Tsihrintzis GA (2011) A cascade-hybrid music recommender system for mobile services based on musical genre classification and personality diagnosis. Multimed Tools Appl 59(1):241–258

44. Lampropoulou PS, Lampropoulos AS, Tsihrintzis GA (2009) A mobile music recommender system based on a two-level genre-rating SVM classifier enhanced by collaborative filtering. Stud Comput Intell 226:361–368
45. Lin P, Yang F, Yu X, Xu Q (2008) Personalized e-commerce recommendation based on ontology. In: Proceedings of the international conference on internet computing in science and engineering. IEEE, Piscataway, Harbin, pp 201–206
46. Linton F, Schaefer HP (2000) Recommender systems for learning: building user and expert models through long-term observation of application use. User Model User-Adapt Interact 10(2–3):181–208
47. Lundell J, Hayes T, Vurgun S, Ozertem U, Kimel J, Kaye J, Guilak F, Pavel M (2007) Continous activity monitoring and intelligent contextual prompting to improve medication adherence. In: Proceedings of the 29th international conference of the IEEE Engineering in Medicine and Biology Society, Lyon. IEEE, Piscataway
48. Luo H, Fan J, Keim DA (2008) Personalized news video recommendation. In: Proceedings of the 16th ACM international conference on multimedia. Vancouver. ACM, New York
49. López-Nores M, Blanco-Fernández Y, Pazos-Arias JJ, García-Duque J (2012) The iCabiNET system: harnessing electronic health record standards from domestic and mobile devices to support better medication adherence. Comput Stand Inter 34(1):109–116
50. López-Nores M, Pazos-Arias JJ, Garcáa-Duque J, Blanco-Fernández Y (2010) MiSPOT: dynamic product placement for digital TV through MPEG-4 processing and semantic reasoning. Knowl Inf Syst 22(1):101–128
51. López-Nores M, Rey-López M, Pazos-Arias JJ, García-Duque J, Blanco-Fernández Y, Gil-Solla A, Díaz-Redondo RP, Fernández-Vilas A, Ramos-Cabrer M (2009) Spontaneous interaction with audiovisual contents for personalized e-commerce over digital TV. Expert Syst Appl 36(3p1):4192–4197
52. López-Nores M, Blanco-Fernández Y, Pazos-Arias JJ, Gil-Solla A (2012) Property-based collaborative filtering for health-aware recommender systems. Expert Syst Appl 39(8): 7451–7457
53. Manjunath BS, Salembier P, Sikora T (2002) Introduction to MPEG-7: multimedia content description language. Wiley, Hoboken
54. Manouselis N, Drachsler H, Vuorikari R, Hummel H, Koper R (2010) Recommender systems in technology enhanced learning. In: Proceedings of the 4th ACM conference on recommender systems. ACM, New York, Barcelona, pp 203–213
55. Masthoff J (2010) Group recommender systems: combining individual models. In: Recommender systems handbook. Springer, Heidelberg, pp 677–702
56. Montaner M, López B, de la Rosa JL (2003) A taxonomy of recommender agents on the internet. Artif Intell Rev 19(4):285–330
57. Panescu D (2008) Emerging technologies: wireless communication systems for implantable medical devices. Eng Med Biol Mag 27(2):196–101
58. Panniello U, Tuzhilin A, Gorgoglione M, Palmisano C, Pedone A (2009) Experimental comparison of pre- vs post-filtering approaches in context-aware recommender systems. In: Proceedings of the 3rd ACM conference on recommender systems. ACM, New York, pp 265–268
59. Pattaraintakorn P, Zaverucha GM, Cercone N (2007) Web-based health recommender system usign rough sets, survival analysis and rule-based expert systems. Lect Notes Artif Intell 4482: 491–499
60. Pazzani M (1999) A framework for collaborative, content-based and demographic filtering. Artif Intell Rev 13(5):393–408
61. Pazzani M, Billsus D (1997) Learning and revising user profiles: the identification of interesting web sites. Mach Learn 27:313–331
62. Rada R, Mili H, Bicknell E, Blettnet M (1989) Development and application of a metric on semantic nets. IEEE Trans Syst Man Cybern 19(1):17–30
63. Resnik P (1999) Semantic similarity in a taxonomy: an information-based measure and its application to problems of ambiguity in natural language. J Artif Intell Res 11(4):95–130
64. Richardson L, Ruby S (eds) (2007) RESTful web services. O'Reilly Media, Sebastopol

65. Rosaci D, Sarné G (2008) A multi-agent recommender system for supporting device adaptivity in e-commerce. Stud Comput Intell 162:293–298
66. Rosaci D, Sarné G, Garruzzo S (2009) MUADDIB: a distributed recommender system supporting device adaptivity. ACM Trans Inf Syst 27(4):24–65
67. Rudametkin W, Touseau L, Perisanidi M, Gómez A, Donsez D (2008) NFCMuseum: an open-source middleware for augmenting museum exhibits. In: Proceedings of the international conference on pervasive services (ICPS), Sorrento. ACM, New York
68. Saito K, Nakano R (1988) Medical diagnostic expert system based on PDP model. In: Proceedings of the IEEE international conference on neural networks. IEEE, Piscataway, San Diego, pp 255–262
69. Sarwar B, Karypis G, Konstan J, Riedl J (2001) Item-based collaborative filtering recommendation algorithms. In: Proceedings of the 10th international conference on the World Wide Web, Hong Kong. ACM, New York, pp 285–295
70. Schafer JB, Konstan J, Riedl J (1999) Recommender systems in e-commerce. In: Proceedings of the 1st ACM conference on electronic commerce. ACM, New York, Denver, pp 158–167
71. Shambour Q, Lu J (2010) A framework of hybrid recommendation system for government-to-business personalized e-services. In: Proceedings of the 7th international conference on information technology. IEEE, Piscataway, Las Vegas, pp 235–244
72. Sirin E, Parsia B, Wu D, Hendler JA, Nau DS (2004) HTN planning for web service composition using SHOP2. J Web Semant 1(4):377–396
73. Smith D (1992) Expert systems for medical diagnosis: a study in technology transfer. J Tech Transf 17(4):45–53
74. Smyth B, Cotter P (1999) Surfing the digital wave: generating personalized TV listings using collaborative, case-based recommendation. In: Proceedings of the 3rd international conference on case-based reasoning, Munich. Springer, Berlin
75. Snell J, Tidwell D, Kulchenko P (eds) (2001) Programming web services with SOAP. O'Reilly Media, Sebastopol
76. Staab S, Studer R (eds) (2003) Handbook on ontologies. Springer, Berlin
77. Stanojevic M, Vranes S (2009) Semantic classifier for affective computing. In: Proceedings of the international conference on computational intelligence for modelling control & automation, Vienna. IEEE, Piscataway, pp 849–854
78. Sørensen CF, Gimre S, Servold H, Brede S, Wang AI (2005) Development of location-aware applications. In: Mobile information systems II. Springer, Berlin, pp 171–186
79. Tkalcic M, Kosir A, Tasic J (2011) Affective recommender systems: the role of emotions in recommender systems. In: Proceedings of the 5th ACM conference on recommender systems. ACM, New York, Chicago
80. Tkalcic M, Kosir A, Tasic J (2011) Usage of affective computing in recommender systems. Elektrotech Vestn 78(1–2):12–17
81. TV-Anytime forum (2003) TV-Anytime specification series. ETSI standard TS 102 822. http://www.etsi.org/website/technologies/tvanytime.aspx
82. van Pinxteren Y, Geleijnse G, Kamsteeg P (2011) Deriving a recipe similarity measure for recommending healthful meals. In: Proceedings of the international conference on intelligent user interfaces (IUI), Palo Alto. ACM, New York
83. Wiesner M, Rotter S, Pfeifer D (2011) Leveraging semantic networks for personalized content in health recommender systems. In: Proceedings of the 24th international symposium on Computer-Based Medical Systems (CBMS), Bristol. IEEE, Piscataway
84. Yu C, Chang H (2009) Personalized location-based recommendation services for tour planning in mobile tourism applications. E-commerce and web technologies. Lect Notes Comput Sci 5692:38–49
85. Yu Z, Zhou X, Hao Y, Gu J (2006) TV program recommendation for multiple viewers based on user profile merging. User Model User-Adapt Interact 16(1):63–82
86. Yu Z, Zhou X, Yu Z, Zhang D, Chin CY (2006) An OSGi-based infrastructure for context-aware multimedia services. IEEE Commun Mag 44(10):136–142

87. Zhou CL, Zhang ZF (2006) Progress and prospects of research on information processing techniques for intelligent diagnosis of traditional chinese medicine. J Chin Integr Med 4(6):560–566
88. Zhou X, Xu Y, Li Y, Josang A, Cox C (2011) The state-of-the-art in personalized recommender systems for social networking. Artif Intell Rev 37(2):119–132
89. Zimmerman J, Kurapati K, Buczak AL, Schaffer D, Gutta S, Martino J (2004) TV personalization system. Design of a TV show recommender engine and interface. In: Personalized digital television. Targeting programs to individual users. Kluwer Academic Publishers, Dordrecht

Part III
Evaluation

Chapter 7
Requirements Engineering in a Mobile Setting: How Travelers with a Cognitive Impairment Ask for and Use Help

Stephen Fickas, Rik Lemoncello, and McKay Moore Sohlberg

Abstract A requirements-gathering study of getting-lost behavior is described. Two matched groups of subjects, one with and one without acquired cognitive impairments, were asked to navigate a walking route. Two foils were introduced to induce problems in route following. A phone helper was available to assist with problem solving. Both quantitative and qualitative results are reported.

7.1 Introduction

Our group has been involved with assistive technology for travelers with an acquired cognitive impairment (ACI). We have previously studied the type and mode of assistance necessary for walking trips within the community [1]. However, from those studies came evidence that we were ignoring an important issue: how do travelers with a cognitive impairment deal with getting lost or other obstacles that occur within their travels? This was heightened when we realized that much of this population's reluctance to "get out" into the community stemmed from anxiety, i.e., worry and concern about not knowing what to do in problem situations [2].

S. Fickas (✉)
Computer Science Department, University of Oregon, Deschutes Hall, Eugene, OR 97403, USA
e-mail: fickas@cs.uoregon.edu

R. Lemoncello
Speech and Hearing Sciences Department, Portland State University, PO Box 751, Portland, OR 97207-0751, USA
e-mail: rik@pacificu.edu

M.M. Sohlberg
Communication Disorders and Sciences, University of Oregon, 241 HEDCO Education Building, 5284, Eugene, OR 97403-5284, USA
e-mail: mckay@uoregon.edu

E. Martín et al. (eds.), *User Modeling and Adaptation for Daily Routines: Providing Assistance to People with Special Needs*, Human–Computer Interaction Series, DOI 10.1007/978-1-4471-4778-7_7, © Springer-Verlag London 2013

We saw two directions to pursue in our research: (1) we could continue to build better and better prescriptive navigation and way-finding tools that minimized a traveler getting off track. (2) We could begin to explore a new mode of assistance, that of recognizing a travel problem and attempting to remedy it in the field. Clearly we would prefer the former. Who wants to get lost and anxious? However, for those with a cognitive impairment in particular, there are many ways for a trip to go off track, too many to feasibly control or avoid with an assistive device. We felt it was prudent to begin to look at assistance for people who were in a problem state (lost, confused, anxious) during travel. This paper discusses a pilot study to gather information about the way travelers with a cognitive impairment interact with human assistance through phone support. From this, we hope to gather the requirements of a computer-based assistant [3–6].

7.2   The Challenges of Field Evaluation with Impaired Populations

Goodman et al. [7] have suggested field-based mobile-device evaluation procedures for the non-impaired population. It is instructive to look at the metrics proposed and compare each with what we found appropriate for our studies with participants with a cognitive impairment.

1. *Time to complete*. Although we typically record timing information, we find this measure less than useful in evaluating field devices for our population. There are two problems. First, we have found that someone must be available for help. We have used quiet companions in the past. In this study, we used shadow followers. Given that participants were sometimes "interfered with" by the observer, i.e., given feedback when confused or lost, timing information was deemed less than accurate. Further complicating timing information, it is not unusual for us to employ a "foil", an actor in the environment that interrupts the participant to break his or her train of thought, e.g., by asking for a cigarette. But more importantly, we are rarely interested in efficiency. Instead, our interest is whether some technology will enable a person to do something that is currently beyond their means. Of course, timing can't be totally ignored. If a trip takes a person longer than is feasible (e.g., beyond their physical endurance, longer than stores stay open or buses run), then that is an issue. But whether a tool or device is minutes ahead of others is not a priority for us.
2. *Errors*. For us, this is perhaps the key metric in our studies. For each field trial, we spend considerable time developing an evaluation instrument around gradations of errors in navigation. We also video-record each trial to further analyze and validate our written notes. We pilot our evaluation methods to refine them.

3. *Perceived Workload.* Goodman and colleagues note: "Workload is important in a mobile setting as users must monitor their surroundings and navigate, therefore fewer resources can be devoted to an interface. An interface that reduces workload is likely to be more successful in a mobile setting." We would add physical workload to this concern. For instance, we chose a device-on-arm approach in an earlier navigation study [1] to avoid (a) a participant having to carry something in his or her hand over the routes, or (b) having to pull the device in and out of a bag or pocket constantly. However, we observed, and our participants commented on, the problems with a device strapped to their arm. It grew heavy over time. More related to safety than workload, another goal of the device-on-arm was to allow participants to look away from the device (for instance, to watch for traffic), and only glance at it when a new instruction arrived. We did this by beeping on arrival of new directions before they reached a potentially unsafe intersection. Nevertheless, most participants monitored (looked down at) the device more than we would have liked, commenting that they were worried they would miss a direction or not hear the beep. Chewar and McCrickard [8] reported similar issues of participants being extremely cautious of not missing a choice-point direction. In the study reported here, we have finessed many of these issues by using an always-on audio device.

4. *Distance and route.* Goodman and colleagues note that there are various ways one can track a subject, e.g., pedometer, GPS, observation. We do not ask our participants to travel independently while we monitor. Instead, we define "field labs" where routes and distances are known. In this way, routes can be balanced for number and type of choice point, distance, and complexity. This supports controlled studies. We do not see a way of holding the study we report without controlling variables with a set field lab.

5. *Percentage preferred walking speed (PPWS).* We understand the motivation for this metric. If someone is accustomed to walking at a given pace, a device that slows them down will be unpopular. In our studies, we find that most of our participants do not venture far from their facility; there is no baseline for them navigating in unfamiliar surrounds. More generally, our experience is that our participants are much more anxious about getting lost than about how fast they travel.

6. *Comfort.* Of course, in a general sense, comfort is a universal concern. We have discussed how comfort can intersect with workload in a prior point. What we have found particularly heightened in our studies is social comfort: avoid standing out because you are carrying a geeky looking device. Clearly times change, and what might have looked geeky 5 years ago is now the norm. Our approach is to hold small focus groups prior to device selection for each study to gauge participants' perceptions. For this study, in particular, participants were fine with the cellphone earbud in focus groups and during the trial.

The remainder of the chapter describes a study that motivates the points above.

7.3 Study Outline

Participants with a Cognitive Impairment (experimental group) and without a
Cognitive Impairment (control group of age, education, and gender matched peers)
were asked to follow a set of written walking directions. The directions had two
foils: a missing step (a turn) and an incorrect destination description (a bookstore
instead of a bowling alley). Subjects were given an "always on" ear bud (with cellphone in pocket) that connected to a researcher in an office (the phone-helper). The
phone-helper did have knowledge of the general area of travel, but did not have
information about the location of the subject. Hence, the subject was required to
describe his or her location over the phone, as well as any other information about
their problem that might be useful. The phone-helper followed a general script for
helping a subject problem solve. The phone-helper never initiated a conversation,
but only spoke when directly addressed by the traveler. Two other researchers (field
observers) shadowed the traveler, and kept field notes.

All participants were given transport by research staff to the trial site. The route
covered a seven block area of downtown Springfield, OR. Figure 7.1 provides an
overview of the route and the eight-step written directions provided to participants.
There were four steps along the route where challenges were anticipated: initial
orientation (Step 1), a missing step (Step 4), a step with a hidden street sign (Step 7),
and the incorrect destination (Step 8). A series of pilot evaluations with uninjured
adults ensured clear wording of instructions, especially for steps not designed to
present navigational challenges (i.e. steps 2, 3, 5, and 6).

7.4 Research Questions

We will focus on the following questions in this paper.

- **RQ1**. Are there differences in how participants with ACI solve navigational
  challenges compared with age, gender, and education-matched non-injured
  control participants?
- **RQ2**. Do individuals with ACI demonstrate greater delay and less planning
  compared to age, gender, and education-matched non-injured peers when asking
  for assistance due to a missing step with written navigational instructions?
- **RQ3**. Are there differences in preference for re-orientation by telephone between
  participants with or without brain injury?
- **RQ4**. Are there differences in how individuals with ACI or non-injured peers
  describe their current location to an unfamiliar phone assistant at a remote
  location?
- **RQ5**. Are there differences in the quality of potential solutions to on-route
  navigational challenges described by individuals with ACI compared to non-
  injured peers? (Part of the phone-helper's script is to ask the traveler to describe
  what they think a potential solution is to their problem.)

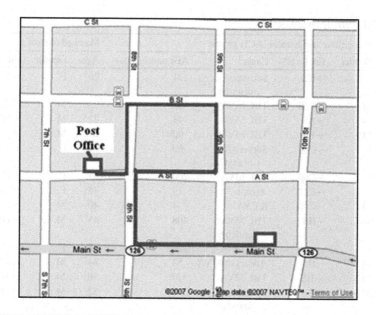

Real Route Directions	*Directions Given to Participants*
1. Start out toward 8th ST	1. Start out toward 8th ST (*orientation)
2. Turn Left onto 8th ST	2. Turn Left onto 8th ST
3. Turn Right onto B ST	3. Turn Right onto B ST
4. Turn Right onto 9th ST	(*missing step)
5. Turn Right onto A ST	4. Turn Right onto A ST
6. Turn Left onto 8th ST	5. Turn Left onto 8th ST
7. Turn Left onto Main ST	6. Turn Left onto Main ST (*hidden sign)
8. End at the entrance to a bowling alley with a blue overhang, about 2 blocks	7. End at the entrance to a bookstore, about 2 blocks; a house with a blue roof. (*wrong destination)

Fig. 7.1 Route map and instructions

7.5 Mechanics

7.5.1 Participants

Two groups of participants completed this study: 18 adults with ACI and 18 matched control participants. Table 7.1 provides further information on our subject pool. The ACI group was drawn from several assisted-living facilities in the area that support those with a cognitive impairment. All members of the ACI group were free to come-and-go independently from their facilities. Each facility had a bus-stop nearby

Table 7.1 Participant profiles

Acquired cognitive impairment (ACI) group					Matched control group		
Age	Gender	Ed. level[a]	Cause[a]	ABI onset (mos)	Age	Gender	Ed. level[a]
19	F	+HS	Seizure disorder	24	20	F	+HS
22	M	−Coll	TBI, MVA	22	22	M	−Coll
23	M	+HS	TBI, MVA	48	22	M	+HS
25	M	+HS	TBI, MVA	90	27	M	+HS
28	F	−Coll	Surgery for brain CA	60	31	F	−Coll
38	F	−Coll	TBI, MVA	200	35	F	−Coll
44	F	+Coll	Anoxia	19	45	F	+Coll
45	M	−Coll	R CVA	4	40	M	−Coll
48	M	−HS	TBI, MVA; epilepsy	408	45	M	−HS
49	F	−Coll	TBI, MVA	120	48	F	−Coll
51	M	−HS	Aneurysm/CVA	52	44	M	−HS
53	M	+HS	TBI, MVA	377	50	M	+HS
55	M	+HS	Syncope, anoxia	312	52	M	+HS
56	M	−Coll	TBI, assault	11	53	M	−Coll
57	M	−Coll	CVA	96	65	M	−Coll
62	F	−Coll	TBI; surgery	480	58	F	−Coll
63	M	−Coll	Brain abscess	240	63	M	−Coll
69	M	+Grad	Surgery for brain CA	240	65	M	+Grad

[a]Ed. levels: −HS (not completed high school), +HS (completed high school), −Coll (began college, but no degree), +Coll (completed bachelor's degree), +Grad (completed graduate school). Cause: *TBI* traumatic brain injury, *MVA* motor vehicle accident, *CVA* cerebral vascular accident – stroke, *CA* cardiac arrest

that would support community travel. Nevertheless, a prior study showed that while there were no policy or procedural barriers to community travel, few residents of these facilities took on independent trips, either by bus or by foot [2].

7.5.2 Scoring

Observational data at each of eight choice points along the route was gathered, and scored on a 6-point scale:

- 5 = correct & independent
- 4 = self-corrected an initial error
- 3 = asked for verification of information
- 2 = asked for assistance

- 1 = required intervention (more than 2 blocks off-track)
- 0 = Unable/Quit

In addition, we scored "directness" at each of eight choice points (1 = direct, 0 = hesitate). We are most interested in how participants did at 4 of these choice points:

- Step 1: Initial orientation ("Face 8th Street")
- Step 4: Missing Instruction (omitted "Turn Right on 9th Street")
- Step 7: Obscure Sign (difficult to see "Main Street" sign)
- Step 8: Wrong Information (told to stop at a bookstore, not a bowling alley)

Additional qualitative data were gathered from four sources: field-observers (2) field notes; phone transcription recordings, and the post-trial interview. These data allowed the researchers to describe and investigate possible group differences in how participants described their current location, generated potential navigational solutions, and opinions about use of a cell phone for pedestrian navigational assistance.

7.5.3 Fidelity of Adherence to Phone Script

Each time participants asked for help using their earbud, the phone-helper asked them a series of scripted questions, and tried to re-orient them with correct information over the phone. Phone conversations were audio recorded and transcribed after each trial. A researcher checked each transcription to ensure that the phone-helper did not deviate from the script when attempting to gather data and re-orient the participant. Fidelity was calculated for a sampling of 21/36 (well above the suggested 25% for single-subject experiments) trials by marking on a checklist if each instruction was delivered correctly and at the correct time, across three different phone helpers and for both groups. Overall, the phone helpers (three different helpers) followed the script with **95.56 %** fidelity (Range: 88–100%) across the sampling.

7.5.4 Data Analysis

Quantitative data were entered into SPSS 16.0. Mixed Model analyses were employed, due to repeated measures for each participant (i.e. 8 choice points per participant). The Mixed Models analysis controls for repeated measures within-participant when investigating between-group differences [9]. To investigate the effects of group and type of direction on wayfinding ability, we ran a Mixed Model analysis for Accuracy and Directness. Chi-Square analyses investigated group differences in Wayfinding Strategies [10]. Significance tests explored relations between all quantitative variables. Effect size measures estimated the practical significance of any statistically significant finding using Cohen's d [11]. Two researchers analyzed qualitative data for themes [12]. The researchers independently analyzed the data, extracted themes as categories, compared results, and reached consensus.

7.6 Results

Descriptive statistics for the two dependent variables included in the Mixed Model analyses revealed non-normal distributions, especially for control group performance (see Table 7.2). However, we conducted no transformations because these non-normal distributions represent hypothesized, naturally occurring phenomena (i.e. the control group performed near ceiling levels with less variance). The overall mixed model was significant, (Wald $Z = 11.66$, p = **.000**).

In the remainder of the section, we will return to each research question, and provide study results for each.

RQ1. Are there differences in how participants with ACI (BI in Table 7.3) solve navigational challenges compared with age, gender, and education-matched non-injured control participants (Con in Table 7.3)

As seen in the table above, there were differences in how participants with ACI solved navigational challenges compared to matched controls. This is a small effect, accounting for only 6% of the variance. Participants with ACI were less independent overall, requiring self-correction, verification, assistance, intervention, or quitting the trial early due to difficulties. While differences between groups were not significantly different at each individual choice point (likely due to reduced power from relatively few choice points and small n), there are a few general trends worth mentioning:

- One participant with ACI was unable to be re-oriented over the phone while another participant with ACI quit the study early due to frustration; all control participants were able to complete the route.
- The field-observer had to intervene (when a participant was >2 blocks off-track) only one time for a control participant, but had to intervene five times for participants with ACI.

Specific to the Missing Direction (Step 4): Participants with ACI were more likely to request assistance (10/18) than control participants, who tended to either ask for verification as they solved it themselves (6/18) or request assistance (6/18).

Table 7.2 Non-normal distributions of data for mixed model analysis

	Accuracy		Directness	
	ACI	Control	ACI	Control
Skewness (SEM)	−0.77[a] (0.20)	−1.41[a] (0.20)	0.46[a] (0.20)	−1.40[a] (0.20)
Kurtosis (SEM)	−0.86[a] (0.40)	0.16 (0.40)	−1.81[a] (0.40)	−0.04 (0.40)

[a]Significance determined as >2 standard errors from mean

Table 7.3 Non-normal distributions of data for mixed model analysis

Strategy	Overall		Step 1		Step 2		Step 3		Step 4		Step 5		Step 6		Step 7		Step 8	
	BI	Con	BI	Con	BI	Con	BI	Con	BI	Con	BI	Con	BI	Con	BI	Con	BI	Con
Independent	82	109	15	16	14	18	13	18	4	5	12	18	14	18	10	16	0	0
Self-corrected	7	3	2	2	0	0	1	0	2	0	1	0	0	0	1	1	0	0
Verifies information	6	6	0	0	2	0	1	0	1	6	1	0	1	0	0	0	0	0
Asks for help	37	25	0	0	2	0	3	0	10	6	2	0	1	0	5	1	14	18
Researcher intervenes	5	1	1	0	0	0	0	0	1	1	0	0	0	0	1	0	2	0
Unable/quit	7	0	0	0	0	0	0	0	0	0	2	0	2	0	1	0	2	0
χ^2 test	$\chi^{2(5)} = 17.41$		$\chi^{2(2)} = 1.03$		$\chi^{2(2)} = 4.50$		$\chi^{2(3)} = 5.81$		$\chi^{2(4)} = 6.68$		$\chi^{2(4)} = 7.20$		$\chi^{2(3)} = 4.50$		$\chi^{2(4)} = 6.05$		$\chi^{2(2)} = 4.50$	
p signif	$p = .004$		$p = .597$		$p = .105$		$p = .121$		$p = .154$		$p = .126$		$p = .212$		$p = .195$		$p = .105$	
Effect size	$\eta^2 = .061$																	

186 S. Fickas et al.

Table 7.4 Dealing with missing step

Group	When asked
ACI group	
Mean (SD)	0.82 (0.61)
	n = 11
Control group	
Mean (SD)	1.83 (0.39)
	n = 12
F test of significance	F(1,21) = 23.42 p = .000
Effect size	d = 1.99

Specific to the Hidden Street Sign (Step 7): Participants with ACI required assistance (6/18) while the majority (17/18) of control participants independently solved the challenge.

Specific to the Wrong Destination (Step 8): Both groups asked for assistance to solve this problem, but two ACI participants were unable to complete this last step accurately.

RQ2. Do individuals with acquired cognitive impairments (ACI) demonstrate greater delay and less planning compared to age, gender, and education-matched non-injured peers when asking for assistance due to a missing step with written navigational instructions?

Each time a participant asked for assistant for the missing step (step 4), we coded this as a 2 if they asked before reaching the intersection of 9th & B, as a 1 if they asked at the intersection, and a 0 if they asked after an unsuccessful search. So, higher scores indicate greater planning.

Table 7.4 shows that control participants demonstrated greater planning and were able to anticipate errors when a step was missing from their set of written directions (M = 1.83), while participants with ACI generally did not anticipate the error or waited to ask for assistance after an unsuccessful attempt to solve the problem (M = 0.82). This is a large effect.

RQ3. Are there differences in preference for re-orientation by telephone between participants with or without brain injury?

Table 7.5 provides a summary of quantitative data related to cell phone use. For 'Ease of Use' and 'Helpfulness,' participants were asked to rate these on a four point scale (1 = not at all; 4 = extremely). Higher scores represent greater ease of use and helpfulness. For 'Use a Phone Again,' this was scored as 0 = no or 1 = yes. Higher scores represent higher endorsement.

Control participants unanimously endorsed the cell phone as easy to use and helpful for accessing navigational assistance. All control participants also indicated they would like to use a similar system in the future if they required navigational assistance. All participants with ABI reported that the assistance they received via the cell phone was helpful to reduce anxiety and re-orient them.

When participants with ACI were off-track or starting from a corner not expected by the phone helper, then they encountered greater difficulty, and the phone helper had to orient the participant to a landmark before giving a left/right direction. A few ACI participants had difficulty with left/right and needed landmark directions,

Table 7.5 Satisfaction data with phone connection to phone helper

Group	Ease of phone use	Helpfulness of phone	Would you use a phone again?
ACI group			
Mean (SD)	3.56 (0.62)	3.72 (0.46)	0.94 (0.24)
	n = 18	n = 18	n = 18
Control group			
Mean (SD)	4.00 (0.00)	3.94 (0.24)	1.00 (0.00)
	n = 17	n = 17	n = 17
F test of significance	$F(1,33) = 8.84$ p = .005	$F(1,33) = 3.04$ p = .091	$F(1,33) = 0.94$ p = .339
Effect size	d = 0.99		

which were harder for the unfamiliar phone helper to give. Our phone helper created a photo map of the streets and tried to use houses, bus stops, or stores to orient participants. It sometimes turned into more of a "trial and error" exercise to get the person re-oriented ("If you got to C, then you went the wrong way. Turn around and go two blocks to get to A.")

RQ4. Are there differences in how individuals with ACI or non-injured peers describe their current location to an unfamiliar phone assistant at a remote location?

When participants asked for assistance over the cell phone, the phone helper asked them to describe their current location. By analyzing the phone transcripts, there were clear qualitative differences in how participants described their location. The descriptions by participants with ACI were more vague or inaccurate.

For the control group, 97% (29/30) of control descriptions provided a clear description of their location, which included two streets of the intersection at minimum, and often included additional modifiers, such as:

- "I'm at 8th & B, I just turned Right onto B."
- "I'm on B, between 8th & 9th."
- "I'm on Main, in front of Alpine Service Imports that services Volvos ... I just passed 11th St ... now I'm at 12th."
- "Right in front of the Sutton Hotel, on Main St, about 1/2 way between 11th and 12th."
- "1100 Main St, in front of Springfield Spas & Tanning."

A small set (3% or 1/30) of control descriptions were vague, e.g., "I'm on Main St" (phone helper assumed correct part of Main and did not ask for clarification).

For the ACI Group, 68% (32/47) of ACI descriptions provided a clear description of their location, which often included two streets at the intersection, sometimes with a modifier, such as:

- "I'm at 8th and B, behind the Post Office."
- "I'm right in front of the Post Office, at the corner of 8th & A Streets."
- "I'm at the Brandt Finance sign, at the corner of 8th & A."

- "I'm at 8th & Main, by a Legit Misfit place and a Subway."
- "There's no Street sign. The Street is just South of A, at the intersection of 8th, and it's the first One-Way sign, with traffic going East to West."
- "I'm at 10th & Main, or the equivalent of 10th & Main. The last street I passed was 9th, so this must be 10th. There's a sign going toward Springfield High School, but no sign identifying the street."
- "I'm on Main St, right by 'Hidden Treasures,' at the corner of Main and . . . right past the 'Alpine Service Imports.' I'm right in the middle of a block . . . now I'm at the corner of 12th & Main".

The ACI Group had a moderate number (23% or 11/47) of vague descriptions. These generally only gave one street or specified a landmark only, such as:

- "I'm on 10th St."
- "On Main St."
- "I'm by the 'Grocery Outlets' and 'Autocraft'."
- "I'm in front of a bowling alley, I guess."

The ACI Group had 9% (4/47) of descriptions that were inaccurate.

RQ5. Are there differences in the quality of potential solutions to on-route navigational challenges described by individuals with ACI compared to non-injured peers?

The phone helper asked participants to provide potential solutions to navigational challenges before providing participants with the correct solution. By analyzing the phone transcripts, there were clear qualitative differences between potential solutions. Participants with ACI gave more vague, inaccurate, or non-solutions. For instance, at Step 4 (Missing Step), 100% (15/15) of solutions generated by control participants were "reasonable". In contrast, 56% (9/16) of solutions generated by participants with ACI were "reasonable" with remaining solutions being vague/inaccurate (31%, 5/16) or non-solutions (13%, 2/16).

Looking at Step 8 (Wrong Destination), 100% (29/29) of solutions generated by control participants were "reasonable". In contrast, 68% (13/19) of solutions generated by participants with ACI were "reasonable" and similar to controls, but 11% (2/19) were vague and 11% (2/19) were non-solutions. We believe it is worthwhile to look in a bit more detail at the potential solutions given at the two foils, step 4 and step 8.

STEP FOUR (Missing Step)

We will first look at the solutions offered by the Control Group (15 generated), and then those generated by the ACI group. The correct solution was to "turn Right on 9th and walk towards A St".

- "Walk towards A and then go Right on A St."
- "I guess I'd have to turn Right onto 9th, go South, to get back up to A St."
- "Take a Right here, because I know A St is South of me."

- "I think somebody gave me the wrong directions. They meant 'Turn Right onto 9th'".
- Two other solutions use a strategy of gathering more information:
- "Walk on B for a while and see if it did run into A St."
- "I was just gonna ask, just now I was thinking, and I saw someone on the street, but they told me to talk on the phone if I was lost." [failed attempt to ask person on street for directions].

We can now compare how the ACI Group did on the same problem (16 generated solutions). Five solutions were similar to the control group and correct. The remaining 11 solutions were unique to the ACI group. We view four to be reasonable solutions, with two examples being "go back to the starting point and start over" and "I think the streets are on a grid so I should be able to use that." Another six solutions we marked as vague, inaccurate or not useful in the current context. These include "look for the bookstore", "go/turn [wrong place/direction]", "go back to a better part of town where people know me better or I know the place better, if at all." The remaining solution was to abandon the entire enterprise: "Look for a bus stop & go back to Eugene".

STEP EIGHT (Wrong Destination)

Solutions offered by the Control Group (29 generated), and those generated by the ACI group (19 generated) had similarities. In the list below, the notation a/b denotes the number of subjects in the control group (a) that offered the solution, and the number of subjects in the ACI group (b) that offered the solution.

- Back-track and try again (9/5)
- Walk a little further and keep looking (8/1)
- Ask someone where is a bookstore (4/5)
- Back-track and look down the side streets as well (3/1)
- Go one block South to see if the other One-Way could also be Main St (2/1)
- Take a Right onto Main instead of Left (1/0)
- Look up "bookstores" in a phone book (1/0)
- Is it Brethren Housing? (has some blue and has a store) (1/0)

We marked six solutions as unique to the ACI group:

- Give up (4)
- "I've got to look for a house with a blue roof" (1)
- "Is there a bookstore?" (1)

7.7   Summary and Discussion

Results of this study confirmed the prevalence of navigational challenges faced by brain injury survivors, even on a short pedestrian route. Participants with ACI demonstrated significantly greater on-route navigational challenges – more frequent errors and hesitations – than matched controls. Participants with and without ACI exhibited different types of problem solving. The ACI group requested assistance over the cell phone more frequently than controls, and required more attempts at re-orientation with concrete, salient directions in order to re-orient in the field. Participants in the control group anticipated errors with greater frequency than those with ACI.

We chose to provide participants with a cellular phone for two reasons: (1) we wanted to capture real-time participant insights relevant to getting lost, and (2) we wanted a flexible means to provide route re-orientation to explore effective strategies. All participants highly endorsed the cell phone as a useful tool for both reorientation and reassurance.

Analysis of the phone helper transcripts revealed several important implications for providing on-route assistance to travelers with ACI. Participants reported they might have quit the route without assistance and support. We also discovered that it was important to explicitly ask the participant to stop walking and remain at a given location while the phone helper attempted to provide assistance. When participants continued to move (e.g. cross a street or face a different direction), left/right directional assistance became irrelevant. It was also important to verify the participant's current location. In one instance, the phone helper was unable to re-orient a participant who reported inaccurate information about his current location. In addition, it was critical to provide specific instructions that utilized landmarks for re-orientation. In several instances during this study, the person with ACI required multiple re-orientations over the telephone when the phone helper assumed to know the participant's location and orientation to provide left/right street directions. We discovered that the only way to successfully re-orient these participants in the field was to provide explicit landmark re-orientation. For example, one participant with ACI required five attempts at re-orientation before the phone helper successfully described salient landmarks (i.e. face the blue house) to get her back on track. It should be noted that the phone helper in this study had access to photographs at each intersection along and near the route. For care providers who do not know the neighborhood or do not have access to such pre-planned information, GIS technology paired with GPS information may provide a useful supplement, such as the Street View images now available in many metropolitan areas provided by Google maps (maps.google.com). Of course, one might argue that the GPS on the phone could reliably place the participant at a certain point and facing, and that there is no need for the phone-helper to ask the participant to self-locate. We will discuss this shortly.

The current study results demonstrated that individuals with ACI perform pedestrian navigational tasks with greater errors and hesitancy than matched controls. Although there was insufficient power to investigate the relation between severity of cognitive impairment and getting lost behavior (due to the small and skewed sample that included only two participants in the severe range), the trend suggested that individuals with more severe cognitive impairments demonstrated greater difficulty. Additional qualitative research, especially in-depth case studies of individuals who are either successful or unsuccessful navigators, may reveal important cognitive

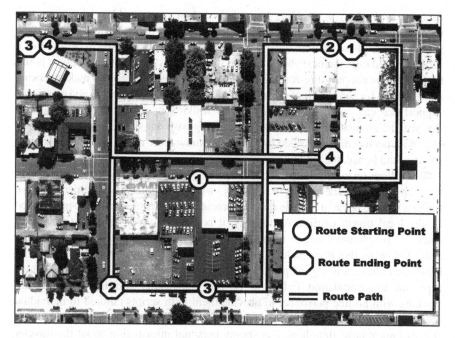

Fig. 7.2 Matched routes of Springfield-1

predictors of navigational performance. Future research must also continue to evaluate the potential effectiveness of various assistive technologies to improve navigational performance. One problem is accuracy: a GPS system carried by the traveler may be able to prompt a traveler to pull a bus-cord (our own work, and that of others [13], has born this out), but not be able to provide location or orientation data accurate enough to place a pedestrian at the correct corner of an intersection, and a specific heading [14]. However, even if a GPS device provided accurate enough data, there remains the issue of two-way interaction. We are dubious that an in-car style of assistant, programmed to replan a route when an error is detected, without feedback from the user, will be effective with either (a) pedestrian situations, in general, or (b) travelers with ACI, in particular. It may be worthwhile to discuss our prior "Springfield-1" trial in this regard [1], which used four matched routes of roughly 300 yards each as shown in the Fig. 7.2 (taken from the paper).

In Springfield-1, we provided perfect, proactive, route-following directions, achieved by using a wizard-of-oz technique to cue instructions at appropriate points. Subjects frequently encountered challenges in following these perfect directions. Researchers stepped in at these points to (a) ask further about what led to the problem, and (b) place the subject back on track. It never crossed our mind to allow subjects to keep walking past the correct choice, and then reroute them around city blocks (as an in-car system would typically do). First, walking is not driving, and blocks can be long. This tends to be a population that does not get out for physical exercise, and taking a rambling tour of the urban core would not be viewed as recreation. In particular, 12 out of 20 of our participants in Springfield-1 had to take significant rest-breaks within the trial. Second, there is every reason to believe that a subject would miss the next choice point if they just missed the current choice point; the problem is not one of re-routing, but debugging why the person is making errors. Also, at least for some, part of the problem is the need for reassurance and emotional support that can overcome their anxiety of walking in an unfamiliar location. In essence, the navigation problems we saw arising with our subjects in Springfield-1, even with perfect directions, led us to want to know more about errors and problem solving, and hence, the study we report here.

Our follow-on to this study has been exploring how we can augment the human in the loop (i.e. the phone helpers in our study) with a computer-based helper. We have found a service point in Eugene that has potential: the travelers' hotline maintained by the local transit district. Admittedly, it is not always on-call. And it focuses solely on problem-solving in relation to public transportation, and not pedestrian route-following (but does include walking to and from transit stops). On the other hand, we believe it is a good place to start given a bus ride is a likely part of most trips with this population. Following up with our results from this study, we are working with hotline personnel to provide them with scripts tailored to individual travelers. On a call to the hotline, the traveler's phone can supply GPS information. Just as importantly, the phone can supply personal information about the traveler (e.g., impairments, ability to use landmarks, solutions that have worked in past) that can allow (we conjecture) hotline personnel to provide efficient problem-solving help. The study has just started, and we hope to report results in a future meeting.

References

1. Fickas S, Sohlberg M, Hung P (2008) Route-following assistance for travelers with cognitive impairments: a comparison of four prompt modes. Int J Hum Comput Stud 66(12):876–888
2. Sohlberg M, Todis B, Fickas S, Hung P, Lemoncello R (2005) A profile of community navigation in adults with chronic cognitive impairments. Brain Inj 19(14):1249–1259
3. Sutcliffe A, Fickas S, Sohlberg M, Ehlhardt L (2003) Investigating the usability of assistive user interfaces. Interact Comput 15(4):577–602
4. Fickas S (2005) Clinical requirements engineering. Invited paper at the 27th international conference on software engineering (extending the discipline track). St. Louis, May 2005
5. Robinson WN, Fickas S (2009) Talking designs: a case of feedback for design evolution in assistive technology. In: Lyytinen K, Loucopoulos P, Mylopoulos J, Robinson W (eds) Design requirements engineering: a ten-year perspective. Springer, Berlin/Heidelberg, pp 215–237
6. Sohlberg MM, Fickas S, Lemoncello R, Hung PF (2009) Validation of the activities of community transportation (ACTs) model of community navigation for individuals with cognitive impairments. J Disabil Rehabil 31:887–897
7. Goodman J, Brewster SA, Gray PD (2004) Using field experiments to evaluate mobile guides. In: HCI in mobile guides workshop at mobile HCI 2004. Glasgow, UK
8. Chewar CM, McCrickard DS (2002) Dynamic route descriptions: tradeoffs by usage goals and user characteristics. In: Proceedings of the international symposium on smart graphics (Smart Graphics '02), Hawthorne NY, June 2002, pp. 71–78

9. Bryk AS, Raudenbush SW (1992) Hierarchical linear models: applications and data analysis methods. Sage, Thousand Oaks
10. Glass GV, Hopkins KD (1996) Statistical methods in education and psychology, 3rd edn. Allyn & Bacon, Boston
11. Cohen J (1988) Statistical power analysis for the behavioral sciences, 3rd edn. Academic, New York
12. Bogdan RC, Knopp-Biklen S (2003) Qualitative research for education: an introduction to theories and methods. Allyn & Bacon, Boston
13. Carmien S, Dawe M, Fischer G, Gorman A, Knitsch A, Sullivan JFJ (2005) Socio-technical environments supporting people with cognitive disabilities using public transportation. ACM Trans Comput Hum Interact 12:233–262
14. Ladetto Q (2000) On foot navigation: continuous step calibration using both complementary recursive prediction and adaptive Kalman filtering. In: Proceedings of the 13th international techinical meeting of the Satellite Division of the Institute of Navigation. Salt Lake City, Utah, Septermber 19–22

Chapter 8
Evaluating Recommender Systems for Supportive Technologies

Jill Freyne and Shlomo Berkovsky

Abstract Recommender systems have evolved in recent years into sophisticated support tools that assist users in dealing with the decisions faced in everyday life. Recommender systems were designed to be invaluable in situations, where a large number of options are available, such as deciding what to watch on television, what information to access online, what to purchase in a supermarket, or what to eat. Recommender system evaluations are carried out typically during the design phase of recommender systems to understand the suitability of approaches to the recommendation process, in the usability phase to gain insight into interfacing and user acceptance, and in live user studies to judge the uptake of recommendations generated and impact of the recommender system. In this chapter, we present a detailed overview of evaluation techniques for recommender systems covering a variety of tried and tested methods and metrics. We illustrate their use by presenting a case study that investigates the applicability of a suite of recommender algorithms in a recipe recommender system aimed to assist individuals in planning their daily food intake. The study details an offline evaluation, which compares algorithms, such as collaborative, content-based, and hybrid methods, using multiple performance metrics, to determine the best candidate algorithm for a recipe recommender application.

J. Freyne (✉)
Information Engineering Laboratory, ICT Center, CSIRO, GPO Box 76, Epping, NSW 1710, Australia
e-mail: jill.freyne@csiro.au

S. Berkovsky
Information Engineering Laboratory, ICT Center, CSIRO, GPO Box 76, Epping, NSW 1710, Australia

Network Research Group, NICTA, Locked Bag 9013, Alexandria, NSW 1435, Australia
e-mail: shlomo.berkovsky@csiro.au; shlomo.berkovsky@nicta.com.au

E. Martín et al. (eds.), *User Modeling and Adaptation for Daily Routines: Providing Assistance to People with Special Needs*, Human–Computer Interaction Series, DOI 10.1007/978-1-4471-4778-7_8, © Springer-Verlag London 2013

8.1 Introduction

Recommender systems have evolved in recent years into sophisticated support tools that assist users in dealing with the decisions encountered in everyday life. Recommender systems were designed to be invaluable tools in decision making situations, where large number of options are available, such as deciding what to watch on television, what information to access online, as well as what to purchase in a supermarket, and what to eat. Recommender systems can play an increasingly valuable role when considered in the context of users with special needs, as illustrated through this chapter.

Evaluating the accuracy and effectiveness of recommender systems is a challenge, which has been faced since their inception [31]. Evaluations are carried out during the design phase of recommender systems to understand the suitability of approaches to the recommendation process, in the usability phase to gain insight into interfacing and user acceptance, and in live user studies to judge the uptake of recommendations and impact of the recommender system.

In this chapter, we present a detailed overview of evaluation techniques for recommender systems covering a variety of methods and metrics suitable for this task. We detail the three typical evaluation paradigms for recommender systems – offline analysis, user studies, and online studies – and provide examples of each paradigm in the context of every day activities and people with special needs. We also detail evaluation metrics suitable for judging algorithm performance in terms of accuracy and important usability dimensions. We highlight the use of various study types and metrics by presenting an evaluation case study of a recommender system for people with special dietary requirements. The evaluation focusses on a meal recommender application for assisting users in planning their daily food intake. The study details an offline evaluation, which compares a set of recommender algorithms, collaborative, content-based, and hybrid algorithms, using multiple performance metrics. Also included is a discussion around suggested scenarios for other evaluation paradigms, including a usability study and a live online evaluation.

The chapter is structured as follows. In Sect. 8.2, we summarise the traditional recommender system evaluation paradigms and metrics. Section 8.3 details a large scale evaluation conducted with an interactive meal planning application and discusses alternative evaluation scenarios and research questions that can be investigated. Finally, Sect. 8.4 concludes the chapter.

8.2 Evaluation Techniques for Adaptive Recommender Systems

Evaluation of the performance of recommender systems generally follows one or more of three paradigms [15, 33]. *Offline evaluations* seek to learn from data that has already been gathered and typically take the form of simulated experiments.

The outcomes facilitate the tweaking and polish of algorithms and processes used to generate recommendations. *User studies* typically involve a small cohort of participants undertaking specific tasks on a prototype system and outcomes include feedback on a variety of areas, including interfaces, algorithm performance, and general system acceptance. *Online evaluations* learn by monitoring real users "in the wild", as they interact with a live system and the outcomes include real-time, longitudinal data that facilitates understanding of algorithm performance and system appeal. Each paradigm and analysis provides researchers with different information pertaining to a multitude of possible system components, from algorithm performance, through preferred user interaction mechanisms, to real-world impact. While many systems employ one or, perhaps, two types of analysis, there is a logical evolution from offline evaluation, through user studies, to online analysis.

8.2.1 Offline Experiments

Much of the early work in the recommender systems domain focused on offline algorithm accuracy evaluations and preference predictions in a variety of application domains, e.g., movies, restaurants, television, and books. For most recommender system designers, offline algorithmic analysis is the first crucial step in designing an adaptive system with recommendation support. There are a large number of tried and tested recommender system algorithms and approaches, which are well documented in the literature. These include content-based algorithms [20], social or collaborative algorithms [18, 19], and complex machine learning algorithms [28, 35] and there are many variations of each. This phase of evaluation is primarily conducted offline with datasets collected for the purpose of simulated experiments, such that a high degree of control remains with the researcher as to what is analysed.

Offline analyses typically focus on the predictive power of approaches and algorithms in accurately determining the opinions of users [7, 16]. This is achieved using simulated user interactions, such as providing ratings or selecting items from an item repository. Often, portions of user profiles are withheld from the algorithms, with ratings being predicted and the predictions then compared to the real ratings. The advantages of offline experiments include the provision for a large selection of algorithms to be evaluated at low cost and without the requirement for real-time user input. Offline analyses facilitate thorough investigation of various components of algorithmic performance, including coverage, accuracy, execution speed, the susceptibility to issues such as the cold start problem, and many other dimensions which impact directly on algorithm performance and are difficult to evaluate in deployed systems.

The quality and applicability of the knowledge gained from offline experiments is often highly correlated with the quality, volume, and closeness of the evaluation dataset to the data which would be collected by the intended recommender system. This is a key consideration for offline experiments. If the data gathered comes from users, who are not typical of the intended audience, if the items do not have the same features, or if the system has different functionality or context, then the lessons learned are less clear. There exists several publicly available datasets for recommender system evaluation; the most widely used are the MovieLens [14], EachMovie [22], and Moviepilot [32] movie rating datasets. While the availability of these datasets has proven invaluable in the development of recommender systems algorithms, their use in the design of adaptive systems similar to those discussed in this book is often limited due to a miss match in domain and recommendation functionality.

There are numerous examples of offline evaluations in recommender systems [3, 6, 15, 23]. Burke's investigation into hybrid recommender systems is a typical example of an offline analysis comparing multiple recommender systems algorithms [6]. The aim of the analysis was to judge how effective each algorithm (collaborative filtering, collaborative heuristic, content-based and knowledge-based) is at recommending restaurants to users of the Entree restaurant recommender system. As the evaluation did not call for exact rating predictions, rank accuracy metrics (see Sect. 8.3.2.3) were used to compare the algorithms. The data set was collected from the Entree system itself and user ratings were extracted from the system logs. The obtained results showed that the performance of the algorithms varied, but that the collaborative algorithms generally performed best. Burke used these findings in further analyses of the performance of hybrid recommender algorithms.

In the domain of daily routines, a detailed analysis of recommender systems in television program scheduling can be found in the Neptuny's ContentWise recommender system [2]. With more and more digital entertainment options available at the touch of a button, the experience of watching television has changed drastically in recent years. Internet Protocol Television (IPTV) delivers traditional TV channels and on demand TV over broadband networks, meaning that users can draw from a huge repository of programs and create their own schedules and playlists. The challenge for providers is that viewing becomes interactive and there are a range of opportunities and challenges for personalization and recommender technologies to assist users in finding and engaging with relevant content [2]. The ContentWise recommender system was integrated into a live IPTV provider's service and the data gathered through the live site has facilitated analyses, which involved three versions of the ContentWise recommender system: item-based collaborative filtering, LSA content-based algorithm, and collaborative SVD algorithm. The data used in the analyses was based on the views recorded during 7 months of user activity from a video on demand catalogue. The analyses concentrated on evaluating the predictive accuracy metrics using recall (see Sect. 8.3.2.3). The results showed differences in the performance across the algorithms, with the collaborative algorithm outperforming other algorithms.

8.2.2 User Studies

While investigating which techniques and algorithms work best in certain domains, their accuracy and predictive power is only one of many measurable components that contribute to the success and impact of the adaptive system [34]. Previously gathered information can provide insight into user behaviour patterns, but it is often difficult to accurately simulate how users will interact with a system and even more challenging to effectively judge the real-world impact of a system. Many researchers have argued that the predictive accuracy of a recommendation algorithm might not correlate with the user perceived value of the recommendations or the general appeal of the service or system, which is often impacted by the visual and interaction design, language, tone and general usability [5,8]. Thus, researchers frequently turn to user studies to observe interactions of real users with the systems in order to obtain real-time feedback on performance and perceived value.

User studies typically involve the recruitment of a small cohort of users to complete specific tasks and provide feedback on a prototype system [21,27]. User studies can gather qualitative and quantitative feedback on the system performance, often logging each and every interaction, monitoring task durations, completion rates, as well as gathering explicit feedback on interface, performance, and preferences relating to user experience. In systems, where change or awareness is sought, users are often requested to fill out questionnaires before, during, and after exposure to a system or technology. This user feedback can be used to confirm researcher's hypotheses and inform changes in the service design and interaction methods. For example, they can determine the most appropriate layout of a recommendation engine in a larger system or the type of rating scale that users find intuitive. More importantly, researchers can acquire real-time feedback on various aspects and functionality of the service provided by the system.

In the area of recommender systems for information access, the ASSIST social search and navigation system was evaluated in a classroom-based usability study [10]. ASSIST was designed to recommend Web search results and navigation paths within a repository of research papers by exploiting recommender algorithms and visual cues. The purpose of the study was to assess the actual and perceived value of social support in search, and the integration of social search and social browsing. The study gathered quantitative and qualitative feedback from participants. Two versions of the system were created: a control system that had no recommendation functionality and an experimental system that provided users with a host of social support features. Thirty students were recruited and randomly assigned to the experimental groups. The students were asked to spend 1 hour using the system in order to locate papers pertaining to the introduced topics and provide a short explanation justifying the relevance of each, before filling out a questionnaire relaying their experience with the system and their views of the various features provided. The evaluation examined the output quantity and quality, as well as rank accuracy metrics of the recommendations, while also facilitated an understanding of real user interactions, the impact of visual cues, and the critique from the students involved. Results showed that users found more relevant results when supported by the recommender system but feedback on the visual cues reported that there were too many cue types which were not intuitive to all users.

Pixteren et al. [26] in their work on intelligent meal planning assistance, modelled the similarity of recipes by extracting important features from the recipe text. Based on these features, a weighted similarity measure between recipes was determined and this provided the foundation for their recipe recommender engine. In order to judge the accuracy of the models, they conducted a user study, in which real users were asked to provide their opinion on the similarity of recipes that was then compared to various predictive models. Over a period of 2 weeks, 137 participants were recruited through emails and message boards. Participants were presented with 20 consecutive recipe pairs and for every pair they were asked to rate the similarity on a 7-point scale. The recipe presentation interface showed the title, cuisine, preparation time, ingredients, and directions. The recipe similarity measure derived by the authors was compared to that of a baseline similarity metric, cosine similarity, and the users' explicit similarity score. Results showed that the accuracy of the derived similarity metric outperformed that of the baseline algorithm.

The opportunity for diverse and detailed feedback through user studies is of immense value. However, user studies come at a heavy cost in terms of user time and (if the participants are not volunteers) potential financial costs, which can limit the number of system dimensions being investigated. Revisiting the recipe recommender example of [26], we note that the evaluation mainly concentrated on model accuracy and ignored other dimensions, such as algorithm accuracy. In a similar vein to the offline experiments, care must be taken when recruiting test subjects of user studies, to ensure that they represent the intended audience of the resulting live system.

8.2.3 Online Evaluations

The most realistic assessment of a recommender system can be achieved by an online evaluation or live user study. This typically involves a group of trial users, who use the system in true information overload conditions and are assisted by the system in performing self selected tasks. It should be noted that live online evaluations generally follow a number of offline and/or user studies, or are exploited in situations, where the performance can more accurately be measured in real-world scenarios, such as with systems that influence long-term user behaviour [13]. Only an online study with real users, who are self motivated to try a system and use it in a natural manner, can enable researchers to monitor the true system impact in its intended environment [17]. In addition, research which applies recommendation technology to new application domains or populations where datasets do not exist, or to complex environments that cannot be simulated, also require online experimentation [11].

In online studies, users are often exposed to various instantiations of a system, which may focus on different algorithms, interfaces, or other variables. While several dimensions of a system can be experimented upon, typically most variables are kept stable and only the one being investigated is adapted. To evaluate the dependent variable, user interactions with the system are monitored over a period of time and then analysed. For example, the uptake or rejection of recommendations, the ranking or position of the selected items in the recommendation lists, and the resulting user behaviour can be examined to determine the outcomes of the evaluation. The recruitment of users for online evaluation can be on a voluntary basis, through random selection from an existing user base on a pre-existing site, or all system users can be involved in a trial.

Vigourous research into recommender system performance in online studies has been carried out by the GroupLens research group on the live MovieLens recommender system [18]. The research platform, which was established in 1997 and now has over 100,000 users is an ideal platform for small and large scale live evaluations in movie recommendations. The MovieLens team has carried out multiple user evaluations, a number of which have looked at the practicality of obtaining accurate user models with minimal user effort and the impact of this data in the recommendation process [29, 30]. Ideally, systems need to elicit high-value user information that holds important knowledge about user preferences in its early interactions with users. For example, acquiring a rating for movie that received mixed reviews, which acts as an informative differentiator in a dataset is more valuable than acquiring a positive rating for a movie that is liked by most users. Movielens researchers devised several strategies to select movies that new MovieLens users should rate before they receive recommendations. An online study was conducted for 20 days and 381 users were involved. To assess their efforts, each user was randomly assigned to a condition and asked to rate 15 movies in order to complete their registration. The movies presented for rating were determined by varying algorithms. In line with previous offline analyses, two algorithms showed performance benefits for users, in that users were shown fewer titles of movies before they found the 15 that they could rate. However, the data gathered by a lesser preforming algorithm (in terms of selecting movies the user could rate) led to the generation of more accurate recommendations and users did not perceive rating the additional movies as effort. Thus, it was deemed the best suited algorithm for this environment. Without the completion of the live analysis in this case, the authors may have misplaced emphasis on user effort and possibly compromised the performance of the final system.

The analysis of the ContentWise system for IPTV video on demand recommendations, discussed in Sect. 8.2.2, continued with an online evaluation that examined the success of each algorithm on the live site. In the online user evaluation, the authors concentrated on responses of real users to recommendations provided by the system and on the recall of these algorithms, as measured by the uptake of recommendations. The impact of the presence of recommendation technology on the system was also measured, as reflected by the number of recommended movies that have actually been viewed within a certain time period after being recommended. Authors monitored user interactions with the system for 24 h and 7 days from the recommendation delivery. Results showed a 24% success rate over the 7 days, but noted differences in success rates between popular and unpopular content, with higher success rates achieved when less popular content was recommended. This could be caused by either the fact that a user has already watched a popular recommended movie or was not interested in the movie at all.

Results also showed a 15% increase in viewing rates associated with the presence of the recommender system. This type of information can only be ascertained through a live analysis.

8.3 Case Study: Analysis of Recommender Algorithms to Support Healthy Eating

To illustrate the considerations and practicalities involved in evaluating a recommender system for daily routines, in particular in the context of supporting dietary choices, one of the most common daily routines we present the following case study. We open our discussion by motivating the urgent need for digital tools supporting users in fighting obesity, before presenting a large scale offline study that provides an understanding of the applicability of several recommender algorithms for the purposes of recipe recommendation. We detail the challenges surrounding data collection, algorithm selection, evaluation metrics, and the obtained results. Finally, we discuss future studies demonstrating the user study and online paradigms, which would compliment the lessons learned from the offline evaluation.

8.3.1 Obesity and Daily Routines

Food and diet are complex domains for adaptive technologies, but the need for systems that assist users in embarking on and engaging with healthy living programs has never been more real. With the obesity epidemic reaching new levels, many practitioners are looking for novel and effective ways to engage users and sustain their engagement with online solutions for effective change in everyday life.

A huge challenge facing dieters is to break habits around exercise and food consumption, in order to balance energy intake and expenditure levels. This can be a daunting task, which is often circumvented by dietary providers supplying one size fits all meal plans. While this might be a short-term solution, it is not conducive to long-term behaviour changes due to two primary factors: (1) specified plans are often restrictive and may be too difficult or repetitive for dieters to maintain, and (2) users may not acquire diet management skills that influence the long-term success of the dietary change. On the flip side, asking users to plan from scratch is often equally daunting, given the range of existing food options and combinations available to them.

With the move to digital recording through online or mobile applications, diet solution providers have access to rich records, which encapsulate user preferences for foods and recipes and offer rich input for adaptive support systems. The goal of the presented study was to design and evaluate an adaptive meal planner application that exploits this rich digital record acquired to assist users in planning meals which not only conforms to the preferences of individual dieters in terms of the foods they like, their cooking skills, budget, and other parameters but also to the rules and guidelines of a particular diet. This tool can assist dieters in acquiring the necessary skills and communicate the implications of certain dietary choices through real-time visual feedback.

8.3.2 *Recommender Strategies for Dietary Planning*

The domain of food is varied and complex and presents many challenges to the personalization research community. To begin with, thousands of food items exist, so the initial range of choices is immense. Secondly, food items are rarely eaten in isolation, with a more common consumption tending to be in combination, in the form of meals. Given the number of food items, the number of resulting combinations is exponentially large. More complexly, users' opinion on ingredients can vary quite significantly based on several factors. Specifically, the content or ingredients of a meal is only one component that can impact a user's preference. Other components include the cooking method, ingredient availability, complexity of cooking, preparation time, nutritional values, and ingredient combination effects. Finally, cultural and social factors are often crucial in eating and cooking considerations. Add to this the sheer number of ingredients, the fact that eating often occurs in groups, and that sequencing is important, and the complexity of challenge becomes evident.

Recommender systems offer a promising means to address this challenge. They can simplify the task of selecting and planning meals and provide recommendations for meals that both satisfy diet requirements and comply with user preferences. Most traditional recommendation algorithms can be exploited for meal recommendation purposes. For example, a content-based recommender could exploit user preferences for specific ingredients or cooking methods and select meals that include these, whereas a collaborative recommender would find people with similar culinary tastes and select meals they liked. Likewise, a variety of hybrid solutions can be implemented and deployed by a meal recommender.

Figure 8.1 shows a sample user interface to illustrate the recipe recommender. The individual's daily plan is shown in the centre, a structured tree of recipes is on the left, and the recommended recipes are on the right. Users can drag-and-drop their preferred recipes to/from the daily plan and the recommended list changes accordingly. The key to maintaining a diet is often not in the appropriateness of individual meals or dishes to the diet, but in the appropriateness of the combination of meals included in a daily plan. Hence, items in the recommended list are filtered by their compliance with the daily dietary guidelines and the user's current plan, i.e., only items, which would keep users compliant with the diet plan for the day, are shown in the recommendation list. Hence, it is important for the recommender

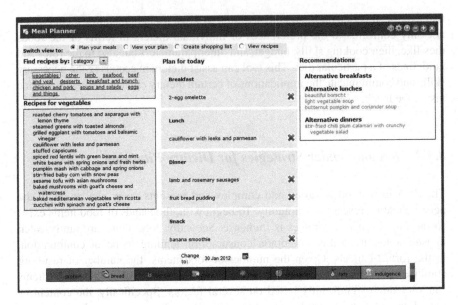

Fig. 8.1 Recipe recommender interface

system to not only be aware of the individuals preferences, but also of the context in which the recommendations are being delivered, so that it can adapt appropriately.

8.3.2.1 The Data

To gather ratings required for the offline analysis, users of Amazon's Mechanical Turk[1] crowdsourcing tool were requested to provided explicit preference information on a set of recipes. Online surveys, each containing 35 randomly selected recipes were posted and users could answer as many surveys as they chose. Users were asked to report on how much each recipe appealed to them on a 5-Likert scale. A set of 343 recipes from the Total Wellbeing Diet recipe books [24, 25] and an online meal planning service Mealopedia[2] was acquired. Each recipe had a common structure, containing a *title, ingredient list*, and *cooking instructions*. Two indicators of recipe complexity (the *number of ingredients* in a recipe and the *number of steps* required to cook it) were automatically extracted from this information. We collected 101,557 ratings of 917 users, such that each user rated on average 109 recipes, with the minimum number of ratings per user being 35 and the maximum being 336. The distribution of recipe rating scores over the entire set of users is shown in Table 8.1.

---

[1]http://www.mturk.com

[2]http://www.mealopedia.com

Table 8.1 Distribution of user ratings

Not at all	Not really	Neutral	A little	A lot
15%	15%	20%	25%	25%

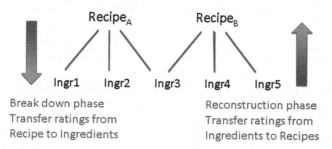

Break down phase
Transfer ratings from
Recipe to Ingredients

Reconstruction phase
Transfer ratings from
Ingredients to Recipes

Fig. 8.2 Recipe – ingredient breakdown and reconstruction

8.3.2.2 The Algorithms

In the study, we analysed the applicability of four personalized recommender algorithms: content-based filtering, collaborative filtering, and two hybrid approaches.

A classic example of a cognitive personalization is a *content-based* (CB) recommender system, whose user models represent the degree to which various domain features (in this case ingredients) are liked by the user. CB recommenders promote items, whose features match the features that are preferred by the user [1, 4, 20, 20]. CB filtering examines the ingredients of the recipes and the user's preferences for these ingredients in order to predict the probability that the user will like other recipes in the dataset.

The dataset in this case study represented user preference information on recipes rather than individual ingredients. A number of approaches to working with this data were considered. For example, it would be possible to try identify the effect of recipe complexity and obtain alternative preferences for ingredients through use of a logistic regression. Similarly, general population levels of ingredients could be obtained and exploited. However, previous research showed that simple conversions from recipe ratings to ingredient ratings provided sufficiently good accuracy levels, such that in this study the same method of conversion of recipe preferences into ingredient preferences was used [12]. This content based recommendation process firstly converts the rating for a recipe r_i provided by user u_a to ingredient scores, as schematically shown in Fig. 8.2. The pre-processing step assigns the ratings provided by u_a to each ingredient according to Eq. 8.1. All cooking processes and combination effects are ignored and all ingredients are considered to be equally important. Ratings gathered on recipes are transferred equally to all ingredients, and vice versa, from ingredients to their associated recipes. Once completed, a content-based algorithm shown in Eq. 8.2 is applied to predict a score for the target recipe r_t based on the average of all the scores provided by u_a on ingredients $ingr_1, \ldots, ingr_j$ making up r_t.

$$score(u_a, ingredient_i) = \frac{\sum_{l \ s.t. \ ingr_i \in r_l} rat(u_a, r_l)}{l} \qquad (8.1)$$

$$pred(u_a, r_t) = \frac{\sum_{j \in r_t} score(u_a, ingr_j)}{j} \qquad (8.2)$$

Collaborative filtering (CF) algorithms exploit statistical techniques to identify common behavioural patterns amongst a community of users [1, 9, 18, 19]. The recommendations are based on the notion that users who agreed in the past, are likely to agree again in the future. Thus, CF uses the opinions of like-minded users to predict the opinion of a target user. User opinions can be either expressed explicitly on a predefined scale of values or inferred implicitly from the observed user activities. The main stages of CF are to recognise commonalities between users and compute their similarity; select a set of most similar users referred to as neighbours; and aggregate the opinions of the neighbours to generate recommendations. A key advantage of CF algorithms is that they are domain agnostic and require no knowledge of domain features and their relationships. We implemented a standard CF algorithm that assigns predicted scores to recipes based on the ratings of a set of N neighbours. Briefly, N neighbours are identified using Pearson's correlation similarity measure shown in Eq. 8.3 where the similarity of users u_a and u_b is determined by considering the scores provided by each user for the set of items, I_{ab} rated by both u_a and u_b. The prediction for recipe r_t not previously rated by the target user u_a is generated using Eq. 8.4 which considers the ratings provided by N weighted by their similarity to u_a as in Eq. 8.4.

$$sim(u_a, u_b) = \frac{\sum_{i \in I_{ab}} (u_{a_i} - \overline{u_a})(u_{b_i} - \overline{u_b})}{\sqrt{\sum_{i \in I_{ab}} (u_{a_i} - \overline{u_a})^2} \sqrt{\sum_{i \in I_{ab}} (u_{b_i} - \overline{u_b})^2}} \qquad (8.3)$$

$$pred(u_a, r_t) = \frac{\sum_{n \in N} sim(u_a, u_n) rat(u_n, r_t)}{\sum_{n \in N} sim(u_a, u_n)} \qquad (8.4)$$

Two *hybrid* strategies that combine CB and CF recommendation techniques were also implemented. These break down each recipe rated by u_a into ingredients and exploit CF to reduce the sparsity of the ingredient scores by predicting scores for ingredients with no available information. The *hybrid_recipe* strategy identifies a set of neighbours based on ratings provided on recipes as in Eq. 8.3 and predicts scores for unrated ingredients using Eq. 8.4 (applied to ingredients scores rather than recipe ratings). The *hybrid_ingr* strategy differs only in its neighbour selection step: user similarity is based on the ingredients scores obtained after the recipe break down rather than directly on the recipe ratings. In both cases, the CB prediction shown in

Eq. 8.2 is used to generate a prediction for r_t using the denser ingredient score data. In addition, we implemented a baseline algorithm *random* that assigns a randomly generated prediction score to a recipe.

8.3.2.3 The Metrics

There is a plethora of approaches appropriate for evaluating the performance of recommender systems. The decision on which approach or combinations of approaches to use is informed by the goals and settings of the evaluation. The work of Herlocker et al. [15] and Shani and Gunawardana [33] set out classifications for recommender system performance measurements. Two primary categories of evaluation metrics are suggested to compare the accuracy of different recommender algorithms: predictive accuracy metrics and classification accuracy metrics.

Predictive accuracy metrics show how close a recommender system's predictions are to real ratings given by users. These are deemed to be particularly important in illustrating to users through visual cues the predicted values of items or in ranking items according to their relevance. This category includes the well known and commonly used metric of Mean Absolute Error (MAE) and similar metrics, such as Normalised Mean Absolute Error (NMAE), Mean Square Error (MSE), and Root Mean Square Error (RMSE).

MAE measures the absolute deviation between a predicted rating, $pred(item_i)$, and the true rating, $rat(item_i)$ for user u_x and item $item_i$ as shown in Eq. 8.5.

$$MAE = \frac{\sum_{i \in I} |\ pred(item_i) - rat(item_i)\ |}{I} \tag{8.5}$$

MAE is seen as the standard accuracy prediction metric, as it quantifies prediction errors, is easy to comprehend, and has well studied statistical properties that allow significance testing to be easily computed. Other metrics in this category often appear in addition to or as a substitute for MAE. For example, NMAE normalises the MAE values with respect to the range of ratings and allows direct comparisons across datasets, whereas MSE and RMSE square the error before averaging it to penalise large prediction errors.

Classification accuracy metrics measure the frequency with which a recommender system makes correct and incorrect decisions about whether an item is relevant or irrelevant. These metrics do not predict actual ratings, but concentrate on classifying items into the relevant/irrelevant category. The key to using these metrics is that the user preference information must be represented in a binary relevance form, although this is often too coarse-grain in recommender systems. In order to compute the classification accuracy metrics, the typical 5 or 7 point rating scale is reduced into the binary relevance indicator. Decisions regarding the cut off point are often subjective and depend on the system functionality. Furthermore, different users may have their own cut off points; some may class a 3 and above on a 5 point rating scale as positive, whereas others 4 and above.

Popular metrics in this category include Precision, Recall and F-measure (FI), which were originally used in information retrieval systems, but have been successfully adopted in recommender systems. Precision measures the proportion of relevant recommendations among all the recommendations (Eq. 8.6). Recall measures the proportion of relevant recommendations among all potentially recommendable items (Eq. 8.7). In many cases, knowledge of both precision and recall is required to effectively judge performance. Thus, both measures can be combined into the F1 metric, which represents their harmonic mean assigning equal weights to precision and recall is shown in Eq. 8.8.

$$precision = \frac{I_{rs}}{I_s} \tag{8.6}$$

$$recall = \frac{I_{rs}}{I_r} \tag{8.7}$$

$$F1 = \frac{2 \times precision \times recall}{precision + recall} \tag{8.8}$$

Two other evaluation metrics should be mentioned. Rank accuracy reflects an algorithm's ability to produce a list of recommended items, ordered according to the user's preferences. Although rank accuracy metrics are more sensitive than classification accuracy metrics in that they order all items in terms of their predicted preference, they are not intended to judge predicted rating accuracy but just the relative relevance of items to an individual. Coverage reflects an algorithm's ability to generate recommendations regardless of their accuracy. It is computed by considering the proportion of items or users for which the algorithm can generate any prediction. Item space coverage refers to the percentage of items, for which a recommender can make recommendations, and user space coverage refers to the percentage of users for which the algorithm can make recommendations.

8.3.3 Offline Evaluation

The metrics selected in the case study evaluation were informed by the nature of the data gathered (more than 100,000 ratings on a set of recipes) and the intended type of analysis (offline evaluation of the applicability of several recommendation algorithms for recipe recommendations). A leave-one-out strategy was employed for the majority of the experiments. For each iteration, one $\{u_i, r_t, rat(u_i, r_t)\}$ tuple was withheld from the data and the algorithms were applied to predict the rating $rat(u_i, r_t)$. A set of 20 CF neighbours was selected and their ratings were aggregated in a weighted manner. Cut off points of 3 and 4 were used as classification accuracy relevance indicators.

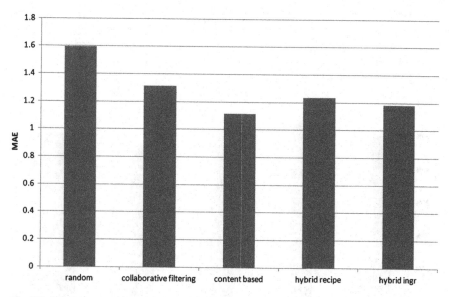

Fig. 8.3 MAE scores

The MAE [15], precision, recall, F1, and coverage scores obtained by each algorithm and averaged across the entire population of users is presented. Figure 8.3 shows the average MAE of the predictions for each algorithm presented in Sect. 8.3.2. The accuracy of the CF and CB recommenders is similar, with an improvement in accuracy of 0.05 over CF obtained by CB. A comparison between the CF algorithm, which treats each recipe as one entity and ignores its ingredients, and the CB algorithm, which considers the ingredients, shows that even the uniformly weighted break down and reconstruction offer improvement in accuracy. The two hybrid strategies $hybrid_{recipe}$ and $hybrid_{ingr}$ produce MAE scores of 1.23 and 1.18, respectively. Hence, the $hybrid_{ingr}$ algorithm is the best performing of the traditional recommender algorithms.

Given the context of recipe recommendations, the prediction accuracy isn't the only suitable metric. In this recommender, the aim is to assist users in planning healthy and appealing meal plans, but the plans will contain a variety of meals over a period of time. Thus, the system should be able to identify a set of appealing meals rather than just the single most appealing meal. In line with this, classification accuracy analyses were carried out to judge each algorithm's ability to produce an accurate positive and negative classification of recipes.

Figure 8.4 shows the classification accuracy of the algorithms. This shows what portion of the predicted scores is converted into correct binary relevance indicators, regardless of their relevant/irrelevant value. Figure 8.4 shows the performance of the algorithms with two cut off points: a strict one that categorises meals with predicted scores of 4 and higher as relevant and a lenient one that categorises meals with

%endfigure

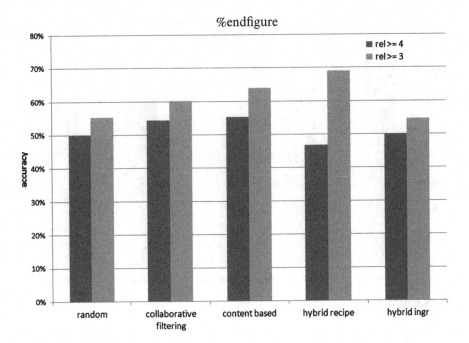

Fig. 8.4 Classification accuracy

scores of 3 and higher as relevant. Different trends were observed, depending on the cut off points. When the strict cut off was in place, the best performing algorithm, with a classification accuracy of 55% was CB, whereas when the lenient cut off was in place, the $hybrid_{recipe}$ algorithm achieved the highest accuracy at 70%.

For a full comprehension of the algorithms' potential, the overall classification accuracy is not sufficient, as only the relevant predictions will determine the recommendations delivered to the user. Thus, *recall*, *precision*, and *F1* measures were calculated for the top 1, 3, 5, and 10 predictions generated by each algorithm. Figure 8.5 shows the average precision of the algorithms when k (1, 3, 5, and 10) recommendations are generated for each user in the dataset.

High precision of the CB and CF algorithms and low performance of the hybrid methods were observed. Figure 8.6 shows the average recall[3] of the algorithms for the same values of k. We observe the CB and CF algorithms again outperforming the hybrid approaches. Combining precision and recall into F1, the trend is further illustrated in Fig. 8.7 that CB and CF algorithms outperforms others. However, when only one recommendation is generated, the algorithms behave similarly and their differences become more apparent as the number of recommendations grows.

---

[3]Note that the number of relevant items varies across users, as each profile contains a different number of ratings.

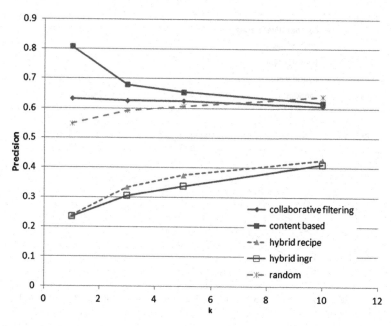

Fig. 8.5 Precision

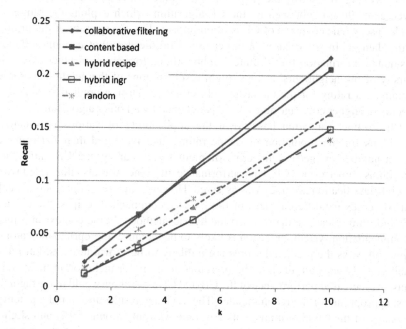

Fig. 8.6 Recall

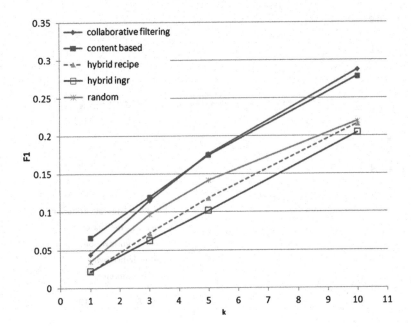

Fig. 8.7 F1 measure

Finally, Fig. 8.8 shows the item space coverage of the algorithms. The lowest coverage of 96% is obtained by the CF algorithm, which exploits the ratings of similar users. The coverage of CF is often impacted by the sparsity of the profiles in the dataset. In some cases, a target user's profile does not contain sufficient or suitable information for accurate neighbourhood formation; in other cases, the sparsity of the neighbours' ratings might result in none of the neighbour profiles containing a rating for the target item. In either scenario, a prediction cannot be generated. Higher coverage above 99% is obtained by all other algorithms.

This offline evaluation has shown the applicability of various personalized algorithms for the prediction of recipe ratings and measured their performance over a number of metrics. In terms of prediction accuracy, the CB and hybrid algorithms outperformed CF. This performance difference was also illustrated when general classification accuracy was assessed. However, in terms of precision, recall, and F1 scores for different sizes of the set of recommended recipes, the CB and CF algorithms clearly outperformed the hybrid methods. In the context of a meal recommendation system, precision is likely to be the most appropriate indicator of applicability, as the predicted scores are unlikely to be shown to users, but rather small sets of meals are likely to be presented to users for inclusion in their plans. Thus, the increased performance of the CB and CF algorithms would make them the most appropriate for the recommender. The coverage results uncovered a potential weakness of the CF algorithm, as its coverage was only around 90%, and slightly prioritised the appropriateness of the CB algorithms.

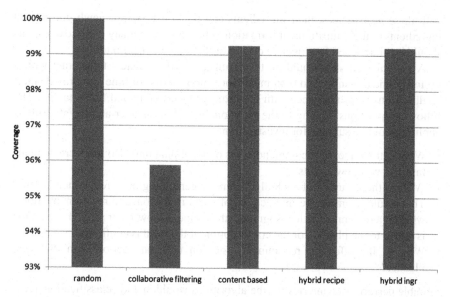

Fig. 8.8 Algorithm coverage

8.3.4 Possible Future Directions

The results of the offline analysis provided information regarding the strengths and weaknesses of each algorithm in the candidate algorithm set, indicated that no algorithm performs badly, and that different algorithms win out for different scenarios. We noted that it was unlikely that predictions scores would be shown to users and that groups of recipes would rather be presented as recommendations, but the dieters may have another opinion on how a meal recommender system should work. We conclude this chapter with a discussion of future studies, which would compliment and strengthen the lessons learned from the conducted offline study. Naturally, these future studies follow the user study and online evaluation paradigms.

8.3.4.1 User Study

There are many avenues for analyses of the suggested meal recommender, which could be achieved through directed user studies. These include interface options, such as plan creation mechanisms, diet compliance visualisations, usage frequencies, the convenience of shopping lists and diet summaries, as well as the straightforward algorithm performance evaluation with real dieters. Understanding the user requirements of planners is also crucial. For example, users may want to add their own recipes to the systems. If so, how should the recommender deal with these new recipes, their ingredients and the conversion of newly introduced ingredients to their nutritional information? The answers to many of these questions should be understood for effective design of the recommender interface.

A natural next step would be to recruit a cohort of dieters to interact with a prototype meal planner and plan meals for a short period of time and provide their feedback on their experience with the prototype's usability and functionality. The following questions relating to the functionality of the planner and the algorithms applied would be suitable for investigation:

- What is the effect of recommendations on meal planning? Do users create plans faster or with fewer edits?
- What is the accuracy of each algorithm for generating meal recommendations? This would examine the interactions of users in response to recommendations: whether a recommendation is ignored, the recipe is browsed or printed, the recipe is added to the planner, or the consumption of the meal is confirmed.
- What is the effect of recommendations on user satisfaction with the meal planner?

Suitable performance metrics for the algorithms would include classification accuracy metrics, ranking accuracy metrics, as well as the indicators of the time spent planning, dietary compliance, and overall user satisfaction.

8.3.4.2 Online Evaluation

As mentioned previously, offline and usability evaluations can inform researchers about the accuracy and usability of the planner. However, only real users can interact with the system independently and allow researchers to can get a true understanding of the performance of the technology. For example, an online study could ascertain not only if users receive good recommendations, but whether the recommendations are acted upon, i.e., cooked and eaten. In terms of behaviour change and long-term health goals, a longitudinal online study is the only way to investigate the impact of the meal planner on weight loss.

If we consider suitable online evaluations of the meal planner, the following questions relating to the impact of the presence of personalization would be suitable for investigation:

- What is the effect of recommendations on the compliance with the diet? Do personalized suggestions make diet compliance easier?
- What is the effect of recommendations on user satisfaction with the meal planner?
- What is the effect of long-term system usage of personalized recommendations? Do personalized recommendations sustain engagement with the system?

Real dieters, embarking on real diets could be recruited for the purpose of the online evaluation through a live site, and their interactions with the system would be monitored over an extensive period of time. Users could be exposed to various algorithms or interfaces at different times or assigned one algorithm or interface for the entire duration of the study. The metrics suitable to compare algorithm performance would include ranking and classification accuracy metrics, general success measures, such as uptake, days planned, average diet compliance, and other indicators that could reflect the overall impact of the recommendation component.

8.4 Conclusions

Recommender systems play a key role in assisting user decision making in situations where a large number of options is available. They can also be helpful in assisting users with special needs in planning and supporting their daily routines. In this chapter, we focused on the evaluation techniques of recommender systems and detailed three widely used evaluation paradigms: offline analyses, user studies, and online studies. We provided examples of each paradigm and detailed on specific evaluation metrics suitable for judging various aspects of an algorithm's performance.

We exemplified the use of offline evaluations with a case study of a meal recommender for users with special dietary requirements. The case study compared the performance of collaborative, content-based, and hybrid recommender algorithms with respect to several evaluation metrics and allowed us to derive conclusions regarding the appropriateness of the algorithms for meal recommendations. We also discussed scenarios for other evaluation paradigms, such as a user study and online evaluation, and the research questions that can be successfully addressed by these evaluations.

References

1. Adomavicius G, Tuzhilin A (2005) Toward the next generation of recommender systems: a survey of the state-of-the-art and possible extensions. IEEE Trans knowl Data Eng 17: 734–749
2. Bambini R, Cremonesi P, Turrin R (2011) A recommender system for an iptv service provider: a real large-scale production environment. In: Recommender systems handbook. Springer, Boston, pp 299–331
3. Berkovsky S, Freyne J (2010) Group-based recipe recommendations: analysis of data aggregation strategies. In: Amatriain X, Torrens M, Resnick P, Zanker M (eds) RecSys. ACM, New York, pp 111–118
4. Billsus D, Pazzani M (1998) Learning collaborative information filters. In: Proceedings of the fifteenth international conference on machine learning, vol 54. Morgan Kanfinan Publishers Inc. San Francisco, CA, USA, p 48
5. Bollen D, Knijnenburg B, Willemsen M, Graus M (2010) Understanding choice overload in recommender systems. In: Proceedings of the fourth ACM conference on recommender systems. ACM, New York, pp 63–70

6. Burke R (2007) The adaptive web, chap. In: Hybrid web recommender systems. Springer, Berlin/Heidelberg, pp 377–408. URL http://dl.acm.org/citation.cfm?id=1768197.1768211
7. Burke R, Hammond K, Young B (1996) Knowledge-based navigation of complex information spaces. In: Proceedings of the national conference on artificial intelligence, AAAI Press, Oregan USA, pp 462–468
8. Cremonesi P, Garzotto F, Negro S, Papadopoulos A, Turrin R (2011) Comparative evaluation of recommender system quality. In: Proceedings of the 2011 annual conference extended abstracts on human factors in computing systems. ACM, Vancouver, pp 1927–1932
9. Desrosiers C, Karypis G (2011) A comprehensive survey of neighborhood-based recommendation methods. In: Recommender systems handbook. Springer, Boston, pp 107–144
10. Farzan R, Coyle M, Freyne J, Brusilovsky P, Smyth B (2007) Assist: adaptive social support for information space traversal. In: Proceedings of the eighteenth conference on hypertext and hypermedia, HT '07. ACM, New York, pp 199–208. doi:http://doi.acm.org/10.1145/1286240.1286299. URL:http://doi.acm.org/10.1145/1286240.1286299
11. Farzan R, DiMicco J, Millen D, Geyer W, Brownholtz E (2008) Results from deploying a participation incentive mechanism within the enterprise. In: Proceedings of the SIGCHI conference on human factors in computing science (CHI2008), ACM Press, Florence, Italy
12. Freyne J, Berkovsky S (2010) Intelligent food planning: personalized recipe recommendation. In: Proceedings of the 2010 international conference on intelligent user interfaces (IUI 2010), ACM Press, Hong Kong, China, pp 321–324
13. Freyne J, Berkovsky S, Baghaei N, Kimani S, Smith G (2011) Personalized techniques for lifestyle change. In: Proceedings artificial intelligence in medicine, AIME, Bled, Slovenia, 2–6 Jul 2011, pp 139–148
14. Herlocker J, Konstan J, Borchers A, Riedl J (1999) An algorithmic framework for performing collaborative filtering. In: Proceedings of the 22nd annual international ACM SIGIR conference on research and development in information retrieval. ACM, New York, pp 230–237
15. Herlocker JL, Konstan JA, Terveen LG, Riedl JT (2004) Evaluating collaborative filtering recommender systems. ACM Trans Inf Syst 22(1):5–53. doi:http://doi.acm.org/10.1145/963770.963772
16. Koenigstein N, Dror G, Koren Y (2011) Yahoo! music recommendations: modeling music ratings with temporal dynamics and item taxonomy. In: Mobasher B, Burke RD, Jannach D, Adomavicius G (eds) RecSys. ACM, Chicago, pp 165–172
17. Kohavi R, Longbotham R, Sommerfield D, Henne R (2009) Controlled experiments on the web: survey and practical guide. Data Min Knowl Dis 18(1):140–181
18. Konstan J, Miller B, Maltz D, Herlocker J, Gordon L, Riedl J (1997) GroupLens: applying collaborative filtering to Usenet news. Commun ACM 40(3):87
19. Koren Y, Bell R (2011) Advances in collaborative filtering. In: Recommender systems handbook. Springer, Boston, pp 145–186
20. Lops P, Gemmis M, Semeraro G (2011) Content-based recommender systems: state of the art and trends. In: Recommender systems handbook. Springer, Boston, pp 73–105
21. Masthoff J (2004) Group modeling: selecting a sequence of television items to suit a group of viewers. User Model User-Adap Interact 14(1):37–85
22. McJones P (1997) Eachmovie collaborative filtering dataset, DEC systems research center. http://www.research.compaq.com/src/eachmovie/
23. McNee S, Albert I, Cosley D, Gopalkrishnan P, Lam S, Rashid A, Konstan J, Riedl J (2002) On the recommending of citations for research papers. In: Proceedings of the 2002 ACM conference on computer supported cooperative work. ACM, New York, pp 116–125
24. Noakes M, Clifton P (2005) The CSIRO total wellbeing diet book. Penguin Group, Australia
25. Noakes M, Clifton P (2006) The CSIRO total wellbeing diet book 2. Penguin Group, Australia
26. van Pinxteren Y, Geleijnse G, Kamsteeg P (2011) Deriving a recipe similarity measure for recommending healthful meals. In: Proceedings of the 2011 international conference on intelligent user interfaces, IUI 2011, ACM Press, Palo Alto, CA, USA, pp 105–114

27. Pu P, Chen L (2006) Trust building with explanation interfaces. In: Proceedings of the 11th international conference on intelligent user interfaces, IUI '06. ACM, New York, pp 93–100. doi:http://doi.acm.org/10.1145/1111449.1111475. URL:http://doi.acm.org/10.1145/1111449.1111475

28. Quinlan J (1992) Learning with continuous classes. In: Proceedings of the 5th Australian joint conference on artificial intelligence, Citeseer, pp 343–348

29. Rashid A, Karypis G, Riedl J (2008) Learning preferences of new users in recommender systems: an information theoretic approach. ACM SIGKDD Explor Newslett 10(2):90–100

30. Rashid AM, Albert I, Cosley D, Lam SK, McNee SM, Konstan JA, Riedl J (2001) Getting to know you: learning new user preferences in recommender systems. In: Proceedings of the 7th international conference on intelligent user interfaces, IUI '02. ACM, New York, pp 127–134. doi:http://doi.acm.org/10.1145/502716.502737. URL:http://doi.acm.org/10.1145/502716.502737

31. Ricci F, Rokach L, Shapira B, Kantor P (2010) Recommender systems handbook. Springer, New York

32. Said A, Berkovsky S, De Luca EW (2010) Putting things in context: challenge on context-aware movie recommendation. In: Proceedings of the workshop on context-aware movie recommendation, CAMRa '10. ACM, New York, pp 2–6. doi:http://doi.acm.org/10.1145/1869652.1869665. URL:http://doi.acm.org/10.1145/1869652.1869665

33. Shani G, Gunawardana A (2009) Evaluating recommender systems. Recommender systems handbook. Springer, Boston, pp 257–297

34. Swearingen K, Sinha R (2001) Beyond algorithms: an hci perspective on recommender systems. In: ACM SIGIR 2001 workshop on recommender systems, Citeseer

35. Wang Y, Witten I (1996) Induction of model trees for predicting continuous classes. Working paper series ISSN:1170-487X

Chapter 9
Automated Usability Evaluation of Model-Based Adaptive User Interfaces for Users with Special and Specific Needs by Simulating User Interaction

Michael Quade, Grzegorz Lehmann, Klaus-Peter Engelbrecht, Dirk Roscher, and Sahin Albayrak

Abstract Adaptive applications have the potential to help users with special and specific needs. However, evaluating the usability of such adaptive applications tends to become very complex. This chapter presents an integrated concept for the automated usability evaluation of model-based adaptive user interfaces. The approach is supposed to be used complementary to custom usability evaluations at an early stage of development. Interaction of a user is simulated and evaluated by combining a user model with user interface models from a model-based development framework, which is capable of providing different adaptation alternatives based on user attributes and the context of use. The main benefit of the approach is that no additional descriptions of the application's UI and tasks need to be created for the usability evaluation because they are already available from the development process. As a result, different design alternatives and adaptation variants can be compared under equal usability evaluation criteria. Further, the complexity and costs for applying automated usability evaluation to adaptive user interfaces for users with special and specific needs can be reduced.

M. Quade (✉) • G. Lehmann • D. Roscher • S. Albayrak
DAI-Labor, Technische Universität Berlin, Ernst-Reuter-Platz 7, Berlin 10587, Germany
e-mail: michael.quade@dai-labor.de; grzegorz.lehmann@dai-labor.de;
dirk.roscher@dai-labor.de; sahin.albayrak@dai-labor.de

K.-P. Engelbrecht
Quality and Usability Lab, Telekom Innovation Laboratories, Technische Universität Berlin,
Ernst-Reuter-Platz 7, Berlin 10587, Germany
e-mail: klaus-peter.engelbrecht@telekom.de

E. Martín et al. (eds.), *User Modeling and Adaptation for Daily Routines: Providing Assistance to People with Special Needs*, Human–Computer Interaction Series,
DOI 10.1007/978-1-4471-4778-7_9, © Springer-Verlag London 2013

9.1 Introduction

Recently, former stand-alone computer systems are evolving into everyday appliances and become parts of our daily lives [60]. Characterized by a multitude of physical interaction devices and networked applications, smart environments offer opportunities for providing assistance to users with special and specific needs, e.g. in the domain of Ambient Assisted Living. However, this change also poses a big challenge, because applications that make up smart environments need to present or query required information properly and tailored to the users' needs and abilities (see Chap. 2). Otherwise, the applications might not be used to their full extent or, even worse, they might not be used at all. This challenge is currently approached by the development of adaptive applications, which aim at providing user interfaces (UI) that adapt to users instead of requiring users to adapt to the UI. While this is generally preferred, it is particularly important when addressing users with special needs and abilities.

For the development process, model-based UI development has become a well-established approach for engineering adaptive applications, e.g. as proposed in [4, 40]. Here, the core idea is to create user interfaces based on different models of desired interaction means, target users, tasks and the user interface elements. The main benefit of applying model-based UI development is the significantly raised reusability and lowered complexity of the implementation process. Further, there exist model-based UI development approaches allowing the execution of the underlying models during development [9]. As a result the user interface can be simulated based on information of e.g. the task model and the context of use. In general, model-based development of user interfaces promises to lower the costs and time during development of adaptive applications.

The growing flexibility of UIs provides a challenge not only for the development, but also for usability evaluations of such systems. User tests, which usually provide the best evaluation results, are even more expensive and time consuming in the domain of adaptive applications and users with special needs. Moreover, detailed information about the context of use and the abilities of the end users, e.g. vision, hearing and motor capabilities; and their influence on the interaction process are difficult to foresee by the designer of an adaptive application. On the other hand, usability evaluation methods based on expert evaluations require evaluators, who know the specific domain and applied method in detail which is a challenging task in this specific domain.

Automated usability evaluation (AUE) emerges as a paradigm allowing exhaustive and at the same time cheap testing. While there are AUE methods which assist in capturing user interaction in laboratories, most promising approaches are based on *predictive analytical modeling* and *predictive simulation* [24]. Based on underlying psychological theories, concepts and models, these approaches have proven to correctly predict cognitive usability criteria, e.g. execution time predictions and learning time estimations. However, there still exist main barriers to the adoption of AUE by the interaction design industry:

Costly and time-consuming modeling process. Current AUE approaches require additional specific descriptions of the user, UI and tasks. In most cases, such descriptions of the UI and the tasks do not exist or cannot be automatically derived from the final UI by automatic routines or the source code. Therefore, the required models need to be provided by the evaluators themselves, which is a time consuming and potentially error-prone task.

Complexity of modeling process. Although some AUE methods are very powerful for specific evaluation purposes, they are hard to apply for complex tasks and more general usability evaluations. So far, they are not widespread because they require highly skilled evaluators, who must put high effort in creating the required models. Further, the methods are usually used for analyzing expert interaction only and therefore need to be adapted to users with special and specific needs.

In this chapter we will address the described barriers of automated usability evaluation of adaptive UIs by investigating how already existing models from the development process can be integrated with a simulated user interaction for the purpose of automated usability evaluation. The main benefit of this concept lies in directly using existing UI models to bypass manually creating specific AUE models of the application and thereby assisting the designer during evaluation.

In the following section we give an overview of usability in general, before we highlight current AUE approaches and model-based UI development. We continue with general requirements for automated usability evaluations and present our approach. Further, we highlight a case study and specific implementation details. Finally, we conclude with a discussion and an outlook on future work.

9.2 Related Work

We start this section by describing the term usability and current evaluation methods. Further, we investigate existing model-based AUE methods and inspect their models and evaluation results. We conclude with a survey on model-based UI development for adaptive applications and refer to how they are currently evaluated.

9.2.1 Usability Evaluation Methods

The term *usability* has been used since about the 1980s to describe the quality of interactive systems from a user-centered design perspective [38]. In ISO 9241-110, usability has been defined as "... the extent to which a product can be used by specified users to achieve specified goals with effectiveness, efficiency and satisfaction in a specified context of use" [15]. The same norm details dialog principles which result in effective, efficient, or satisfactory interfaces, e.g. conformity with user expectations, suitability for learning, or error tolerance.

Although these dialog principles exist, interface design is usually approached in a trial and error manner [32]. While interface designs are partly informed by prior knowledge about the users, in most cases they are actually created more or less intuitively. Afterwards, they are tested and either changed, discarded, or kept, depending on the evaluation results. This procedure is optimized by following the *Usability Engineering Lifecycle* [45], which basically states that tests should be conducted early and frequently while a maximum of diversity should be ensured.

Principally, the usability of a system can be tested by observation of users (*user tests*) or inference based on prior knowledge about users (*expert evaluation*). In both cases, *formative* testing aims at finding problems in the UI in order to improve it, whereas *summative* testing targets the estimation of the systems quality, e.g. to compare two versions of a UI, or to prove the achievement of design goals.

Usually, the best way to conduct usability evaluations is carrying out tests with real users, e.g. by applying the *Think Aloud* method where participants are asked to tell what is on their mind while interacting [44]. Observations are usually captured in video recordings, log files and annotations of the videos. In addition, questionnaires are available to quantify the users' subjective experience of the interaction, comprised under *satisfaction* in ISO 9241-110. Unfortunately, carrying out user tests is time consuming and expensive. Another common problem of user tests is that evaluations need to be as close as possible to the *context of authentic use* [1], i.e. users might behave unnaturally in a laboratory environment when being given specific instructions.

To save time and money, usability experts can check the application against predefined criteria, e.g. by using *Heuristic Evaluation* [43, 46], or by analyzing steps and knowledge required to conduct a task, e.g. *Cognitive Walkthrough* [49]. However, this still requires several professionals with expertise in typical user behavior [45] and provides only an educated guess of the problems real users will encounter. For example, in an examination of different usability studies conducted in [42], the authors found that designers and evaluators are often the same persons, which obviously limits the objectivity of the evaluation. Farenc et al. [17] list other typical problems designers run into when applying guidelines and evaluation methods due to missing standards and completeness of existing approaches.

Especially the potentially high complexity of the context of use, and as a possible result the explosion of the applications' state space [64], leads to problems in evaluating the usability of adaptive applications. Additionally, considering users with specific needs, adequate sample groups might be hard to acquire for user tests. In difference, approaches based on expert evaluations require evaluators who have deep knowledge in the domain and the applied method.

9.2.2 Automated Usability Evaluation (AUE)

In contrary to manually conducting usability evaluations, automated usability evaluation is carried out with assistance of computer-aided tools. However, aspects like qualitative and subjective information, e.g. user satisfaction or the usability of a certain "Look and Feel" are hard to measure and to predict. Thus, todays AUE methods are not able to fully substitute custom usability evaluations. Instead, they should be used complementary, e.g. during early stages of development in order to structure the interaction process or when custom evaluations are too costly or too hard to apply.

In [24] a general taxonomy of AUE is introduced. The authors categorize 128 different AUE approaches depending on:

- the *usability evaluation method* (testing, inspection, inquiry, analytical modeling and simulation)
- the *level of automation* (non-automatic, automatic capture, automatic analysis and automatic critique)
- the human *effort* (minimal effort, informal use, model development and formal study).

Regarding this taxonomy, the approach proposed in this chapter can be categorized as following: *automatic analysis, model development, simulation* by using *analytical modeling*. Further, the authors also list the main benefits of AUE, some of which are:

- Uncover various types of errors more consistently.
- Increase the coverage of evaluated features.
- Enable comparisons between alternative designs.
- Predict times and errors across an entire design.
- Reduce the need for evaluation expertise.
- Can be embedded directly into the design process.
- Reduce the cost of usability evaluation.

When it comes to applying AUE methods, there are also costs which have to be weighed against these benefits. As stated above, these costs lie especially in the time-consuming and complex creation and maintenance of the underlying models. An example gives that designers usually start by sketching mock-ups of different UI versions with their preferred tools in an early stage of development. Thus, an import-functionality would be desirable in order to minimize the effort of the designer when evaluating these first mock-ups. However, importing from different mock-up tools is an aspect which most of the AUE tools do not support sufficiently even though recently work has been targeted on this aspect, e.g. in [23]. Still, the problem remains that the interaction logic of the application cannot be provided when using mock-ups, i.e. the task model of the application is missing. In [28] some of the costs are generalized, which a designer needs to invest when choosing to incorporate a specific AUE into the *Usability Engineering Lifecycle*:

- Learning and understanding the modeling theory.
- Learning how to use the modeling tool itself.
- The time it takes to create the model in the modeling theory with the help of the modeling tool.

- Obtaining the knowledge to create an appropriate cognitive model in the task domain for the intended user group.

Regarding the approach described in this chapter, we expect to decrease the first three costs because main parts of these steps are already included in the development process of the application when utilizing a model-based UI development framework and executable application models.

Below, a survey of different automated usability evaluation approaches is given which are performed at development time with the goal of predicting values of human performance. Basically, the described approaches are implementations of cognitive theories with the help of a structured *user model* and a *task* description (respectively goals) for the interaction process. We focus mainly on these models and the required information for the simulated interaction process. Further, we highlight the corresponding usability evaluation criteria and existing tools for the creation of the models.

9.2.2.1 GOMS Method and GOMS-Based Evaluation Tools

GOMS is based on models of *goals, operators, methods* and *selection rules* [14]. In general, GOMS models can be used to provide information about the required knowledge for fulfilling a task with a given application. Therefore GOMS focuses mainly on the *task model* and the *user model*. Furthermore, GOMS can be used to predict execution times and the required time to learn interaction with the UI. In a GOMS model, the direction of interaction is represented with the help of *goals*. These goals can be divided into hierarchically ordered sub-goals to break down the complexity of interaction. In order to model how a human user would try to achieve these goals, *operators* are being performed on a perceptual, cognitive or motor-act level. Effects of these operators can lead to changes in the internal mental state of the modeled user or changes in the external environment, i.e. the *application model* and the *model of the context of use*. Similar to the more basic Keystroke-Level model (KLM) [13], which can also be applied for disabled people, see e.g. [31], execution times are bound to these operators in order to predict the overall execution time. The execution times are based on (internal) cognitive operators and (external) movements of the hands. Therefore, Fitts' Law [19] is used, which describes a function including the size and distance of the UI elements. Thus, layout specific information needs to be provided using a specific description. Another similarity between the GOMS approach and KLM are the *methods* which describe sequences of operators in order to achieve sub-goals. If more than one method can be used to achieve a goal, the *selection rules* are applied. These rules represent the user's knowledge depending on the current task.

In [29], the authors list different GOMS analysis methods for different areas of application. Tool support for GOMS models is implemented e.g. by USAGE[1] [11].

---

[1]UIDE System for semi-Automated GOMS Evaluation.

With USAGE an NGOMSL[2] model of the UI is generated and executed. This model can be run on a provided set of user tasks and estimates execution time and learning time. In USAGE, goals and tasks cannot be ordered hierarchically and are therefore limited to relatively low-level goals and tasks. GLEAN[3] [33] uses GOMSL[4] for describing the user task and interaction steps. The evaluation process relies on the correct identification of the task. However, complex tasks tend to be hard to model and to validate against collected data. Modeling the simulated devices is a further challenge of this approach [36]. Further tools based on GOMS are reviewed in [6] according to different aspects like cognitive plausibility, required design information and available modeling constructs.

9.2.2.2   Cognitive Architectures: ACT-R, EPIC and Related Tools

The *Adaptive Control of Thought-Rational* (ACT-R) [3] is an architecture used to describe cognitive aspects of human-computer interaction. ACT-R is based on different internal modules (of the *user model*) which are able to process different information in parallel and serially. A manual module is controlling the hands of the modeled user for interaction while perception is achieved with the help of a visual module from a description of the UI, i.e. a basic *application model*. Rudimentary vocal and aural systems complement the visual module. Further modules consist of an intentional module which processes the current goals and intentions of the user and a declarative module for retrieving information from memory. A central production system is coordinating all other modules. Within each cycle, the central production system is able to recognize patterns in the internal buffers which contain information from the external world (*application model* and *context of use*) and the internal state (*user model* and *task model*). As a result, production rules are fired and the internal buffers are updated accordingly. To better reflect human limitations all of these modules and processes underlie several restrictions.

G2A [2] is a tool which allows automatically generating different ACT-R models from a given GOMS model. The approach allows for the evaluation of different ACT-R models by varying mappings from the GOMS model to different ACT-R production rules. This becomes possible, because GOMS models are specified on a higher level of abstraction than ACT-R production rules.

In a similar way, the *ACT-Simple* framework [53] and the closely related CogTool [30] are both based on a compilation approach to produce ACT-R models. Additionally, CogTool eases the complexity for creating required ACT-R models by manually demonstrating interaction on a storyboard of the UI. This storyboard consists of mock-ups or screenshots of the UI. In the background a KLM model is generated from the input sequences the designer has specified. Additional

---

[2]Natural GOMS Language.
[3]GOMS Language Evaluation and Analysis.
[4]GOMS Language.

mental operators [14] are added automatically by CogTool. Finally, the resulting KLM model is compiled together with information from the storyboard into an ACT-R model which can be used to evaluate expert interaction. The main benefit of modeling with CogTool is that creating the models becomes more intuitive and applicable for designers. An approach towards applying CogTool to the field of mobile devices is described in [27]. The CogTool-Explorer [56] focuses on predicting human interaction for novice users. The main difference of CogTool-Explorer to the initial CogTool is that the designer does not directly specify the interaction but provides goals of the modeled user in form of a textual description. Based on the concepts of information scent and label-following, the user model compares the semantic similarity of a Web UI and the specified goal description. Therefore, CogTool-Explorer extends the initial CogTool with SNIF-ACT[5] 2.0 [20] and provides different strategies for interaction.

Similar to ACT-R, another cognitive architecture is the *Executive Process-Interactive Control* (EPIC) architecture [35]. In contrary to ACT-R, the perceptual and motor mechanisms of EPIC have an equal status with cognition in accounting for human performance. This is a direct consequence of the assumption, that limitations on human ability are not central but structural, i.e. the ability to fulfill tasks might be limited directly by peripheral, perceptual and motor mechanisms but not by a pervasive limit of cognitive-processing capacity. Several steps are required for constructing the models in EPIC. On the one hand, the *task model* needs to be specified by the designer. Therefore, production rules, which represent the task procedures, have to be specified and task-specific information for perception and actions need to be added. On the other hand, the simulated UI (*application model*) with its own attributes and characteristics for interaction with the processors of the user model needs to be defined. A comparison between modeled keyboard and touchscreen interaction with EPIC is made in [34].

9.2.2.3 Programmable User Model

The idea for a *Programmable User Model* (PUM) was first described in [63]. The basic concept of this analytical evaluation approach is to program a *user model* capable of simple human problem solving strategies and common sense knowledge. This user model needs to be extended by the designer in order to be able to interact with a *model of the application under study* in its specific domain. The main idea behind this concept is to show that interaction with the UI would be intuitive and therefore easy to implement into a PUM. The designer needs to consider what knowledge is required for a goal-directed interaction and if the intended user has to have this knowledge in advance (*task model*). Following the maximum rationality hypothesis [41], an enhanced PUM approach was implemented by assuming that human users interact in a rational way when having a goal to obtain [8]. In this

---

[5]Scent-based Navigation and Information Foraging in the ACT cognitive architecture.

enhanced approach, the knowledge of the state of the world is formalized as beliefs which can be altered through operations. In detail, these operations are represented by beliefs about actions and their effects. Interaction is simulated with the help of operations. All operations that match to the goals of the user will be performed.

9.2.3 Model-Based UI Development for Adaptive Applications

Adaptive applications are commonly described as being able to adapt to the current context of use in order to cope with the increasing complexity and diversity of current software systems [25]. One approach to address this problem is model-driven engineering (MDE). Based on the notion of models as a basis for software engineering, it represents the shift from object-oriented to model-driven thinking. MDE has been researched as a possible approach to reduce the complexity of UI development [59] and thus the notion of model-based UI development emerged.

According to the CAMELEON reference framework [12], model-based UI development aims at expressing different aspects of the UI using a set of models. CAMELEON identifies several levels of UI model abstraction according to which we will structure the models described in our approach. These models include:

- *Concepts* and *Task Models*, which consist of descriptions from the designer and define possible actions of the user and the application. The tasks can be ordered e.g. by temporal or hierarchical relations to reflect the interaction process.
- *Abstract User Interface* (AUI), which is an intermediate model, and independent from the specifications of the target UI and platform. The AUI channels the models from the concepts and tasks to a logical structure.
- *Concrete User Interface* (CUI), which is still an intermediate model that cannot be run independently, but specifies the final look of the UI.
- *Final User Interface* (FUI), which is the actual source code that can be compiled and run on a runtime infrastructure.

A main benefit of using this framework is that utilizing formal UI models conforming to CAMELEON takes the design process to a computer-processable level, on which design decisions become understandable for automatic systems. Currently, there exist UI description languages, e.g. UsiXML [37] and TERESA [39], which utilize models conforming to CAMELEON in order to generate the final UI code from models and adapt the UI by transforming their executable models.

One of the research topics in the field of model-driven UI engineering is UI plasticity. Plasticity denotes the capability of a UI to adapt, while preserving pre-defined usability properties [57]. In the following we present several model-driven approaches, which aim at the provision of plastic UIs and thus incorporate usability evaluation measures into the UI development and adaptation process.

Sottet et al. [54] propose UI model adaptation mappings augmented with information about their impact on usability properties specified at development time, e.g. according to criteria specified in [5]. The mappings help the designer to select appropriate UI adaptations that best match the context and usability requirements of the application. At runtime of the application the mappings can be used to optimize the selection of automatic adaptations or to negotiate possible modifications with the user, e.g. based on predefined trigger events.

The SUPPLE system [21] refers to UI adaptation as an optimization problem. SUPPLE focuses on an algorithm for minimizing execution times for users with different motor impairments by building up a user model for motor abilities based on training data.

In [18] an AUE is connected to executable models of an application at development time. The final UI is simulated and evaluated for a specific user model.

Some approaches utilize UI models for improving the effectiveness and quality of interaction by providing users with information about available functionality, the context of use, or performed adaptations. Xplain [22] addresses the design of self-explanatory, adaptive UIs in which the user gets answers about the design and behavior of the interactive system. Although Xplain does not evaluate the usability of the UIs, it makes the design rationale accessible and understandable at runtime.

The approach presented in [48] aids the process of engineering interaction techniques. A special focus is set on the evaluation of interactive techniques with regard to pre-defined usability and user experience requirements. Each interaction technique is modeled using the Interactive Cooperative Objects (ICO) formalism. Because ICO is based on Petri nets, the modeled interaction technique can be simulated and tested automatically. A simulation environment generates model-based simulation log data, which is then evaluated by experts.

The TERESA [39] authoring tool supports the user-centric development of interactive applications based on concurrent task trees (CTT) and UI models. The tool enables an early evaluation of the designed applications by means of simulation. For example, the simulation of the task tree enables the designer to detect possible dead-ends or unreachable states.

9.2.4 Conclusion

As we have shown in the above sections, there exist adaptive applications which are able to adapt their UI and underlying task structure to the observed context of use. Usually, these mechanisms are based on assumptions of the predictive context of use, as well as different rules and mappings that are predefined. So far, to our knowledge, executable UI models conforming to CAMELEON have not been integrated directly for providing information to an automated usability evaluation. Thus, in this chapter we propose an approach of model-based interaction simulation in order to automatically evaluate usability criteria. As outlined above, the expected benefits of this approach are a reduction of evaluation costs in general and more specifically a reduction of the complexity of creating the required models for an automated usability evaluation. The next section discusses in detail the requirements and focuses on the problem scope addressed by our approach.

9.3   Problem Scope and Requirements

In order to conduct automated usability evaluations of adaptive applications by using simulated user interaction, basic requirements need to be specified first. Conforming to the definition of usability stated above we need to identify and provide detailed information about the *criteria for evaluation*, i.e. the evaluation method and the measurements, the *application under study*, the *user* as part of the *context of use* and a specific *task* or set of goals which the user tries to fulfill.

In the following subsections, we discuss these five requirements and their formalisms with a focus on information required for automated usability evaluation methods.

9.3.1   Criteria for Evaluation

Usually, different usability evaluation methods predict and uncover different types of usability criteria [61]. However, AUE allows reasoning about human performance measures mainly, e.g. the task completion time or the number of required interaction steps. In contrary to these measures, there also exist quality-related measures, e.g. frustration and joy of use, which currently cannot be predicted accurately using an AUE. Therefore, the choice of the targeted measure directly influences the different types of information required to conduct the evaluation. Additionally, this information needs to be structured conforming to a specific model or description language.

In the case of evaluating adaptive applications, the system response to user input also depends on the context of use (as described below), leading to a multitude of unique situations for which an appropriate system response needs to be ensured. Thus, methodologically, simulation-based evaluation is required to enable extensive testing of possible interaction paths.

9.3.2   Application Under Study

As in AUE user and application interactions are usually modeled abstractly, a formal description of the application under study needs to be provided. More specifically, detailed information about the UI and its interaction logic is required and needs to be provided in a computer-processable way, e.g. by using models. This usually comprehends all UI elements along the path of interaction and their specific attributes required for an AUE, e.g. type, size, position, color and label. This way, it allows e.g. the calculation of execution times of specific interaction paths by using the GOMS method.

If interaction paths are to be created automatically with the help of user simulation, a connection needs to be established between the UI elements and the application task the user is currently performing. This allows reasoning about the effects of using the UI elements, i.e. their purpose within the task; and simulating a goal-directed path through the application.

9.3.3 User

As different users may interact with the application differently, information about users which is relevant for the interaction behavior needs to be specified and taken into account during evaluation. Users may differ in their expertise regarding the application and its UI, but also regarding the domain of the task. In addition, they may have different preferences regarding interaction techniques (e.g. using the mouse or keyboard shortcuts). Finally, regarding users with special needs, physical and psychological abilities of the users have to be taken into account, especially when it comes to disabilities such as motor impairments [31, 58].

Most AUE methods expect that the user is an expert in the domain of the application and therefore only optimal interaction paths are evaluated. Some other approaches, e.g. CogTool-Explorer, model novice users, but expect that the user has no knowledge of the domain at all. A main difference between modeling expert users and novice users is that in the latter case interaction problems due to a wrong understanding of the application can be accounted for. These errors have usually been excluded from AUE methods, but due to advances of the methods as well as availabilities of large corpora on the Internet recently have gained increasing attention [7, 55, 56]. As adaptivity of interactive applications aims at simplified usage, as a requirement, ideally the expertise of the targeted user group should be modeled accurately.

Unfortunately, errors due to a lack of experience with the application or domain are hard to predict. An exception is the simulation of browsing behavior, where category labels are evaluated based on semantic similarity between goal concepts and UI element labels, e.g. as in [7, 56]. If errors cannot be predicted automatically, at least known errors can be modeled and their consequences can be evaluated using a simulation approach. In this case, meaningful results are expected if either:

- the error type and its preconditions are known, but the design cannot easily be completely inspected manually for all instances of the error, or if
- the error types, preconditions and respective application states are known, but removing them leads to conflicts with other constraints on the design.

Mainly the first case is relevant for the evaluation of adaptive applications, as adaptation is usually not defined explicitly for all cases, but inferred from general adaptation rules or mechanisms [54]. A precondition to practical applications of the AUE method is then to develop knowledge about error types and their precondition, either in a general way, or during the task analysis phase preceding the design of the actual interface under test.

Wood and Kieras pointed out that the user behavior following an error can be hard to predict [62]. It involves, among other things, that the user notices that an error has occurred and reasons about recovery possibilities. Therefore, the description of the user also requires including some kind of mental representation of the application (and the world), which allows predicting expected consequences of actions and comparing them to the actual outcome. Such an internal description of the application could be called a *mental model* [47].

9.3.4 Context of Use

When applying any usability evaluation method a formal description of the current context of use is required in order to get an objective view on the outcome, because surrounding factors may influence the interaction. Usually, this includes information about the platform, the environment and the user [12].

Information about the platform also includes the interaction devices, e.g. keyboard, mouse, touchscreen or monitor. In some cases this information can be integrated into the information about the application under study, because maybe no sharp distinction can be made between software and hardware components.

Information about the environment may include surrounding factors, e.g. acoustic or lighting condition. In case of adaptive applications, the modeled surrounding factors should at least include those which are sensed by the system. If the user is performing other actions besides the current task, e.g. driving a car while interacting with a navigational application, constraints arising from this secondary task need to be modeled as well [52].

9.3.5 Task

The goals the user tries to achieve during interaction are also required in order to evaluate an application's usability. These may be specified in form of a task the user wants to perform. When conducting usability tests with real users, goals are usually predefined and the participants receive a description of the task to be performed. Like real-user tests, AUE simulations are based on predefined tasks. However, in most cases more different tasks can be tested in the latter case.

If the task is to be used in simulations, the actions performed by the user to reach the goal state are sometimes not contained in the task description, i.e. they may be determined on the fly based on general rules describing how users would try to proceed.

9.4 Approach

Based on the five requirements stated above, we present an integrated approach which suits these requirements and provides evaluation results based on existing AUE methods. Again, we start by addressing the *criteria for evaluation* and proceed with the information about the *application under study*. As shown in Fig. 9.1, we make use of application models conforming to the CAMELEON reference framework which is described above. More specifically, one of our assumptions is, that the application models need to be computer-processable, i.e. executable, in order to simulate the UI and for tracing information within the models. Further, a *user* model capable of interaction simulation with the provided application models is described. We also describe how information from the *context of use* can be accessed during the simulated user interaction and the usability evaluation. Finally, we conclude with a description of how different *tasks* can be made available for simulation using already provided connections between UI development models in combination with the proposed AUE method.

In the following we continuously refer to the environment for model-based automated usability evaluation depicted in Fig. 9.1 and describe the different components in more detail.

9.4.1 Criteria for Evaluation

In our approach, the evaluation is based on user interaction simulations. Different interaction paths are simulated automatically based on the information provided in the underlying models of the application and the user. Each simulated interaction is logged, and from the log, different performance criteria can be predicted using a specific AUE method, as depicted in Fig. 9.1.

In general, meaningful criteria, which have proven useful in summative usability evaluation, can be calculated with the described approach. Efficiency can be predicted in terms of interaction turns, task duration or the number of non-goal-driven interaction steps. Further, effectiveness can be used as criteria by measuring task success rates, i.e. the ratio of successfully accomplished tasks to overall simulated tasks. All of these measures can be used for a comparative analysis of different design alternatives, e.g. shorter task durations are generally preferred but depending on the user's needs and abilities fall behind accessibility.

In addition, the interaction logs can be used for a formative evaluation (i.e. finding interaction problems or inadequate application responses). However, tracing the simulated interaction path needs to be done manually by the designer.

9.4.2 Application Under Study

The application under study and its UI are described within the models defined by the application designer. By having clearly defined syntax and semantics, the models provide computer-processable information about the design decisions and can be utilized for simulation purposes. By interpreting the models it becomes possible to simulate and evaluate the behavior of the application under a varying context of use.

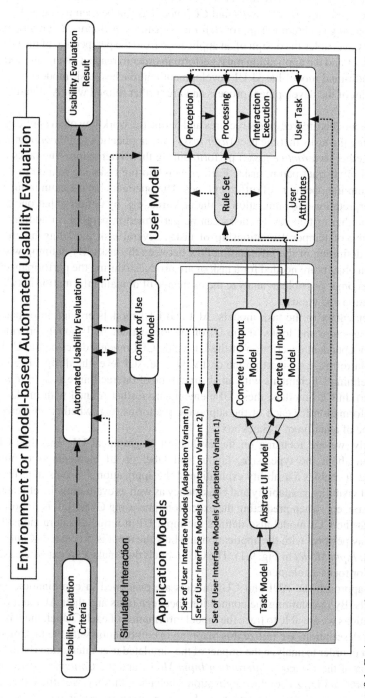

Fig. 9.1 Environment for model-based automated usability evaluation based on user interaction simulation with UI models conforming to the CAMELEON reference framework

In terms of the CAMELEON reference framework, our approach focuses on the utilization of *task model*, *AUI model* and *CUI model* as can be seen in Fig. 9.1.

Task modeling is a common approach for user-centric development of interactive applications. It enables the design of an application from the perspective of the tasks, which the user and the application must perform in order to reach a given interaction goal. In traditional model-based UI development approaches, task models are the starting point of the development process and are further refined with AUI and CUI models.

The task models are tree-like structures and define the workflow of an application by describing the tasks that the user (*user tasks*), the application (*application tasks*) or both together (*interactive tasks*) perform during their interaction. The tasks can be grouped in abstract parent tasks. Further, neighboring tasks are related to each other by temporal operators of different types. The operators have a main influence on the interpretation and simulation of the task tree, e.g. by defining that one task precedes another or that several tasks can be performed in parallel. In addition to the modeling of temporal relationship of tasks, several task modeling notations enable the definition of the information flow between the tasks. By defining which information objects are needed for a task or are produced during the performance of a task, it becomes possible to analyze the exchange of domain information between the application and the user.

Complementary to the task models, AUI and CUI models provide information about the structure and looks of the UI of an application. AUI models provide a platform independent description of the UI, while CUI models describe the UI for different platforms, e.g. smart phone or TV. On the AUI level the designer refines tasks by defining UI elements with an abstract type of interaction (e.g. *Selection* or *Navigation*). In CUI models, these UI elements are further refined with modality-specific information for each of the supported platforms (e.g. whether an element has the type of a button or a checkbox).

Currently, we are focusing on the evaluation of graphical UIs and thus CUI information about the type, size, layout and label of UI elements is of most importance. It enables a usability evaluation of the application's visuals in terms of UI element visibility, readability and consistency as well as evaluating the efficiency of interaction, e.g. when predicting the execution time using GOMS. It is important to note that the CUI model also defines the input UI in terms of interactions that the user may perform with the application and how the input is processed (*Concrete Interaction Input Model* in Fig. 9.1). The CUI models thus make explicit when users may click or focus an element.

In our approach the AUI and CUI models are examined in combination with task models. By maintaining the connections between tasks and their AUI and CUI representations we are able to trace the model information of each GUI element back to the task description. We utilize this mapping in combination with the task model simulation in order to analyze the impact of the simulated user interaction (based on information of the *Concrete Interaction Input Model* and the *Concrete Interaction Output Model* in Fig. 9.1) on the application's behavior. Further, we utilize the task model of an application to calculate the task sequences envisioned in the application by its designer. In general, by simulating the task performance, it becomes possible to detect potential usability problems, like too long interaction paths, interaction loops, unreachable or untimely reachable tasks, wrong task sequences, dead ends or missing domain information access.

9.4.3 User

In general, simulations of human performance can be done on the cognitive level with architectures like ACT-R or EPIC, which however require a very detailed and task-specific model of the user and the cognitive procedures. On the other hand, it yields detailed results regarding cognitive requirements for the tasks. As a main goal for the evaluation described in this chapter is to evaluate the application reactions to different adaptations (i.e. combinations of different user interfaces, user-specific characteristics and context of use), a user model on the behavioral level would be sufficient as there is not much additional information about the internal processes and procedures required. Consequently, if the interaction is modeled on the behavioral level, the simulated interaction traces can be evaluated using several AUE criteria, such as execution time prediction or estimations of learnability. However, in order to predict accurate execution times and learnability, some elements from cognitive theory need to be included. Therefore, a combined approach of behavioral and cognitive level is required to suit our needs.

The user model in our approach conforms to the concept of the *model human processor* [41] which structures the internal processes into *perception* of information, *processing* of information and interaction *execution*. During each step, interaction is started by a simulated perception process (see Fig. 9.1). The perception is based on the modeled description of the UI in the *Concrete Interaction Output Model*, containing e.g. text from labels and layout information from all graphical UI elements. In the same manner, the user model retrieves possible interactions with the UI from the *Concrete Interaction Input Model*. In the subsequent processing step, interactions are chosen depending on whether or not they move the interaction process towards the current goal. To find goal-directed interactions, the perceived information is compared to the current goal of the user model, implementing the principle of label following [50], i.e. if labels of UI elements are semantically similar to a goal description, they are chosen for interaction. More details of the implemented semantic processing approach can be found in [55]. In the last step, the execution of the selected interaction is simulated, e.g. pressing a specific button. In this way the user model generates input events for the *Concrete Interaction Input Model* and as a result the application model is updated accordingly (see bottom of Fig. 9.1).

As we have concluded above, most AUE approaches focus on expert interaction only. However, when extending these approaches to users with special and specific needs it becomes important to take interaction errors into account. In order to simulate user errors due to unexpected combinations of user characteristics, application attributes, and context of use features [28] we make use of a probabilistic approach based on rules [51]. These rules are applied at all three phases of interaction: perception, information processing and interaction execution. The conditional part of these rules describes trigger points for rules to fire, e.g. the user has a tremor and there is a small button on a touch display. The consequences part describes the effects of the conditions on the simulated interaction process, e.g. reducing the probability that the user performs the interaction correctly. Several such rules could be defined based on usability expert knowledge or experimental data, e.g. as described in [5]. After all rules, which apply in the given state, have been evaluated, the probabilities of all possible input interactions of the state are normalized and the interaction to be performed is chosen using a Monte Carlo method (see [51] for more details). This way, non-expert interactions can be evaluated and effects of interaction errors can be revealed when simulating different iterations.

The described approaches for user error generation are not complete. For example, errors in the user's understanding of the task cannot be described this way. However, simulating interaction problems as described above is a first step towards a better simulation of novice user behavior and for users with special and specific needs.

9.4.4   Context of Use

As stated above, in model-based UI development the context of use is defined as a combination of the environment, the platform and the user. The adaptation of the UI based on the context of use is defined as modifications of its models at different levels of abstraction defined in the CAMELEON reference framework. Often the adaptations are defined as model transformations in a separate model and are bound to definitions in a context model. In other approaches the models already inherit context of use dependency definitions, e.g. some task modeling notations enable the declaration of the context of use in which a task is available. However, for our AUE approach it is not important how the adaptations are defined, but how to trigger them based under a varying simulated context of use.

As depicted in Fig. 9.1, we utilize a context model, which is connected to the models of the application and which can be queried by the AUE method. The designer is able to alter the context model and consequently simulates different situations to which the application under study reacts. The simulated context of use may lead to the adaptation of the application, visible to our evaluation components as a new variant of the application's models. This way, different adaptations of the UI can be evaluated by the designer.

9.4.5   Task

As depicted in Fig. 9.1, a task model is required in order to simulate interaction between user model and application model. In our approach, a task model of

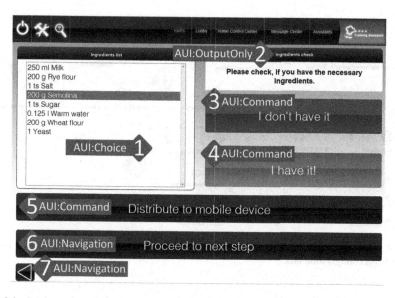

Fig. 9.2 Graphical user interface for the recipe ingredients configuration task, annotated with AUI model information. The numbers correspond with those of the task model (Fig. 9.3)

the user defines which information has to be transferred between user model and application model for changing the applications state towards the goal of the task. The underlying task model of the deployed user model is structured with the help of attribute-value pairs, which can be ordered hierarchically. Each attribute of a pair defines the category of the information while the value provides a specific assignment to this attribute. An example gives the attribute-value pair of available ingredients in the household when interacting with an interactive cooking assistant (see Fig. 9.2), e.g. <ingredient, 250 ml milk> where the attribute is "ingredient" and the value is a specific allocation.

Currently, in our approach the user task model is being derived from the task model of the application. So first of all, different paths to a goal state have to be generated. Such a goal state is predefined by the designer and contains a list of attribute-value pairs which the user model tries to transfer to the application model in order to fulfill the task. We call the resulting list the *solution path* which contains all relevant information. This solution path is being calculated by traversing the task model of each application (see e.g. Fig. 9.3). Based on the applications task tree structure and the temporal operators between the tasks we are calculating the *enabled task sets* (ETS), which can be performed at a given point of time. Starting with the initial ETS of the task model and by simulating the tasks, we are building a graph of all reachable states. Each node of the graph represents an ETS, while each edge represents a performed task. Thus, for any target end task selected for the evaluation we can determine the possible solution paths and the tasks the users have to accomplish in order to reach their goals. Each solution path contains all subtasks

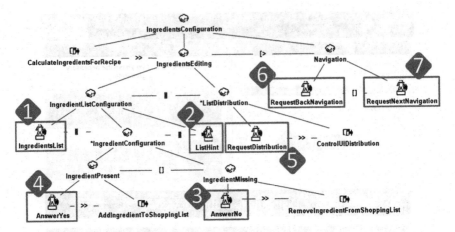

Fig. 9.3 Excerpt from the cooking application's task model, showing the sub-tree for recipe ingredients configuration task

the user model needs to pass through. By using mappings between task model via AUI to the CUI and the domain model all relevant attributes for the attribute-value pairs can be identified. The specific assignments, e.g. from the domain model, are used as values to complete each attribute-value pair.

However, not all interaction steps require a manipulation of the underlying application variables. We call these steps navigational steps, e.g. when the user model needs to select "Next" in order to proceed in the dialogue. These steps can be identified using the AUI type *Navigation*. The corresponding UI elements and their labels are derived by using mappings to the CUI. This way, all navigational steps are identified and the solution path is created and transferred as a list of attribute-value pairs to user task model.

If an error occurs during interaction, i.e. the user leaves the calculated solution path; a new solution path to the predefined goal state is being calculated and transferred to the user model in order to maintain the goal directed interaction according to the maximum rationality hypothesis. In case no such interaction can be found, before ultimately canceling the task, path search can be applied to look for interactions leading to a sub goal, or another state on the goal-directed path [26].

9.4.6 Conclusion

The described approach allows for evaluating adaptive model-based applications compatible with the CAMELEON reference framework by integrating the UI models into an automated interaction simulation and usability evaluation. The approach enables the evaluation of the application with regard to selected user tasks and a specific context of use. By including information about the user into the simulation it becomes possible to evaluate non-expert behavior and the influence and effects of special and specific needs on the interaction process.

With the help of a case study, in the following section we will describe how an application can be evaluated using our approach.

9.5   Case Study

This section describes how we applied our approach to an example application implemented in a model-based UI runtime architecture. To provide the required application models depicted in Fig. 9.1, we utilize a model-based runtime system for ubiquitous UIs, called the Multi-Access Service Platform (MASP) [10]. MASP UIs are defined by the designer as sets of models compatible with the CAMELEON reference framework, spanning task and domain models, as well as AUI and CUI models. The models are held at runtime to dynamically derive the final UI, i.e. the models are executable. As a result, modifications to the models are directly reflected as changes in the UI and interaction with the UI leads to changes in the underlying models. Further, the concept for the user model stems from the MeMo workbench for semi-automated usability evaluation [16]. For the purpose of this example, we have connected the user model of MeMo with the underlying task and UI models of the MASP runtime framework in order to simulate user interaction. Finally, in our case study, we are using the *ACT-Simple* framework [53] and CogTool [30] in order to demonstrate how our approach can be connected to further AUE approaches. This combination allows predicting execution times of different UIs based on simulated user interaction without having to model the application for each AUE approach separately.

As example application, we chose an interactive cooking assistant, which provides a cooking recipe database and assists the user in choosing and preparing meals during everyday life in a smart home environment (Fig. 9.2).

The cooking assistant adapts its UI to different interaction devices which may all have different sizes of the screen and different input devices, e.g. a touchscreen in the kitchen, a smartphone and a TV. Further, the cooking assistant is also able to adapt to the context of use, e.g. the observed distance of the user to the screen. Conforming to this distance important parts of the UI are enlarged for a better perception and an additional voice input and output can be triggered. Further, different kitchen appliances can be controlled, e.g. the oven, the hood or a bread machine. This suits especially for users with disabilities, e.g. motor-impairments, as it allows the whole preparation process to take part with a single interaction device in an assistive way.

The application consists of several interactive steps leading to the final goal of preparing a meal. One of the interactive steps is the configuration of a shopping list with ingredients needed for the meal. The corresponding graphical user interface is shown in Fig. 9.2 where the UI elements are annotated with information about the type of the AUI elements. Further, the numbers of each AUI element correspond with the annotations of tasks from the task model in Fig. 9.3 in order to highlight the connection from *task model* to *AUI model* which is depicted in Fig. 9.1. We will use this interactive step of the cooking assistant as an excerpt to describe how the whole application is modeled within the MASP runtime architecture and how information from these models is used for the automated usability evaluation process.

9.5.1   Description of the UI Models

The ingredients needed for the meal are listed on the top left (1) of Fig. 9.2. The list is a representation of the interactive task *IngredientsList* (see Fig. 9.3). On the level of the AUI model the element is declared as a *Choice* interaction, meaning that the user selects an element from a set of alternatives. On the top right, the application provides a text hint (2), declared as a non-interactive *OutputOnly* element in the AUI model. By tapping on the red (3) or green (4) button, the user informs the application about the availability of the ingredients in the household. In the AUI model both interactions are modeled as *Commands*, because the user triggers a functionality of the application by pressing the button. This is also visible in the task model (bottom of Fig. 9.3), where system tasks follow both interactive tasks: *AnswerYes* and *AnswerNo*. Depending on the user's input, the application performs the *AddIngredientToShoppingList* or *RemoveIngredientFromShoppingList* task. The same applies to (5) with its corresponding interactive task *RequestDistribution* and its following *ControlUIDistribution* system task. Both buttons (5) and (6) navigate from the ingredients mask to other UI masks and are thus modeled as *Navigation* elements.

The AUI specification of the tasks is further refined in the CUI model – (1) is declared as a *GraphicalList*, (2) as a *Label*, while tasks (3)–(7) are *Buttons*. In addition to the output description, the CUI model also defines the mapping between the input provided by the user and the UI elements. The input definition for (3)–(7) is intuitive – any *Selection* events (mouse clicks, touch taps) within the UI elements of these tasks triggers the execution of the underlying commands, respectively navigations. In case of (1) the *Selection* events are interpreted as the choice of the list element at which the input occurred. Finally, as (2) is a label, the CUI model does not define any input events.

9.5.2   Process of Interaction Simulation

As described above, at first the user model retrieves the user task from the application task model, e.g. selecting a meal and checking all required ingredients. Here, the designer may want to evaluate how different adaptation variants of the application behave in case some ingredients are not available. With the help of mappings from the task model to the AUI and the CUI model we can identify

Iterate over List of Ingredients

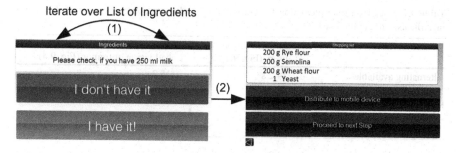

Fig. 9.4 Depicted is an adaptation variant of the recipe ingredients configuration task including fewer, but enlarged, UI elements for users with bad vision or motor-impairments. At first the application queries all required ingredients (1) and then presents the result as a shopping list of ingredients which are not available in the household (2)

which attribute-value pairs need to be exchanged to fulfill the task. Further, by using the AUI model and the CUI input model, the user model is provided with information on whether to make a choice, e.g. interacting with the ingredient list in Fig. 9.2, or which UI elements have to be selected when the user model intends to proceed to the next UI mask (button labeled "Proceed to next step" has the AUI type *Navigation*). Likewise, the attributes from the UI elements are gathered from the Concrete Interaction Output Model and are used during the perception, processing and execution phase of the user model. In case rules are triggered based on user or UI attributes, deviations from the solution path may occur.

9.5.3 Exemplary Results of Automated Usability Evaluation Process

In our case study, we describe how the time prediction of CogTool can be used as usability evaluation criteria for a specific task of the cooking application. Therefore, the interaction path of the simulated user interaction is automatically transferred as input to the ACT-R compiler (used e.g. in CogTool). This includes the UI elements in the order of their visit by the user model and the used interaction devices. In our case study there is touch interaction only. Thus, due to order, size and position of the UI elements, the execution time prediction can be used as criteria for comparing different design alternatives.

An alternative adaptation variant of the ingredients configuration task (shown in Fig. 9.2) is depicted in Fig. 9.4. Here, the designer chose to split up the single tasks and to sequentially query the user for the required ingredients (see left of Fig. 9.4). The resulting user interface consists of fewer UI elements within each UI mask and as result provides several benefits for users with special and specific needs. The user interfaces only presents one information at a time, it allows for a better perception and better interaction capabilities, e.g. for users with bad vision

Table 9.1 Execution time prediction for the initial UI and the adaptation variant of the recipe ingredients configuration task

	Initial GUI for expert users (Fig. 9.2)	Adaptation variant for users with bad vision or tremor (Fig. 9.4)
Alternating available ingredients	14.2 s	15.2 s
First four ingredients available and last four ingredients unavailable	9.8 s	15.2 s

or motor-impairments. However, it strictly leads the user through the whole list of ingredients and queries the availability in the household. It does not show the overall list and does not provide any shortcuts, e.g. in case the user knows that the last four ingredients are all not available in the household a click on the button "Distribute to mobile device" would directly transfer these items to the shopping list on the smartphone. In our case study we expect the user to know which ingredients are available in the household and therefore do not take into account any time required for checking ingredients in the kitchen.

The results of the execution time prediction with the ACT-R compiler from CogTool are shown in Table 9.1. In order to better compare the results in this case study no interaction errors were modeled based on user characteristics.

It can be seen, that the initial version of the GUI suits well for users without specific needs because it allows a faster interaction process. This is a direct result of fewer mental operators because the UI mask stays the same while it changes in the adaptation variant. It further allows directly switching to the shopping list in case some of the listed ingredients are not available. On the other hand, the adaptation variant for users with special and specific needs, in our case users with bad vision or motor-impairments, only takes around 1 s longer which seems to be a good trade-off between the usability and the accessibility of the application, i.e. it provides a good efficiency in terms of ISO 9241-110. However, it does not allow shortcuts, which should be considered for further iterations in the development process of the application.

So far, these interaction execution times do not reflect further implications caused by different motor-impairments, as described e.g. in [31, 58]. However, with the help of the rule based approach such findings can be included, because similar to our approach the underlying models also rely on the model human processor and can therefore be applied on each phase separately. Keates et al. [31] propose to add an additional time of around 50% for the motor function time and 20 ms for each cognitive process due to extra effort for planning and controlling each movement. Thus, according to [31] the whole interaction execution time for users with motor-impairments would increase from 15.2 to 16.6 s. We are planning to further analyze the literature on these issues and the effects on different adaptation variants specifically for user with special and specific needs and to include the results in a future implementation state of our approach.

9.6 Conclusion and Future Work

In this chapter we have investigated existing automated usability approaches and summed up their requirements with a focus on evaluating the usability of model-based adaptive applications. On the basis of this analysis, we have introduced an integrated approach for the automated usability evaluation of executable UI and task models stemming from a model-based UI development process compatible to the CAMELEON reference framework. Further, we have demonstrated the feasibility in a case study related to users with special and specific needs when interacting with an application within a smart home environment.

The main benefit of our approach is that designers are able to evaluate the resulting application and its different adaptation variants at an early stage of development based on the same models utilized within the development process. Our assumption is that this significantly reduces the time, effort and complexity of evaluating user interfaces for different interaction devices and user groups, e.g. regarding adaptations for users with special and specific needs. We are planning to further analyze these savings in the next iteration of our implementation.

Further, we will extend our approach by integrating more automated usability evaluation methods in order to gain a wider range of evaluation criteria from which to choose. We will also investigate how different user behavior may be generated, i.e. how errors can be simulated based on user attributes and on the level of the user task in order to evaluate different interaction strategies of the user model. Therefore, we intend to expand the rule-based approach which helps to evaluate more diverse states of the application based on user input, e.g. due to inferences from different adaptations which are hard to foresee by the designer.

References

1. Abowd GD, Mynatt ED (2000) Charting past, present, and future research in ubiquitous computing. ACM Trans Comput Hum Interact 7(1):29–58
2. Amant RS, Freed AR, Ritter FE (2005) Specifying ACT-R models of user interaction with a GOMS language. Cogn Syst Res 6(1):71–88
3. Anderson JR, Bothell D, Byrne MD, Douglass S, Lebiere C, Qin Y (2004) An integrated theory of the mind. Psychol Rev 111(4):1036–1060
4. Balme L, Demeure A, Barralon N, Coutaz J, Calvary G (2004) CAMELEON-RT: a software architecture reference model for distributed, migratable, and plastic user interfaces. In: Markopoulos P, Eggen B, Aarts E, Crowley JL (eds) Ambient intelligence, vol 3295, lecture notes in computer science. Springer, Berlin/Heidelberg, pp 291–302. ISBN:978-3-540-23721-1, doi:10.1007/978-3-540-30473-9_28, URL:http://dx.doi.org/10.1007/978-3-540-30473-9_28
5. Bastien JMC, Scapin DL (1993) Ergonomic criteria for the evaluation of human-computer interfaces. Technical report RT-0156, INRIA, Institut National de Recherche en Informatique et en Automatique
6. Baumeister LK, John BE, Byrne MD (2000) A comparison of tools for building GOMS models. In: CHI '00: Proceedings of the SIGCHI conference on human factors in computing systems. ACM, New York, pp 502–509

7. Blackmon MH, Kitajima M, Polson PG (2005) Tool for accurately predicting website navigation problems, non-problems, problem severity, and effectiveness of repairs. In: CHI '05: Proceedings of the SIGCHI conference on human factors in computing systems. ACM, New York, pp 31–40

8. Blandford A, Butterworth R, Curzon P (2004) Models of interactive systems: a case study on programmable user modelling. Int J Hum Comput Stud 60(2):149–200

9. Blumendorf M, Albayrak S (2009) Towards a framework for the development of adaptive multimodal user interfaces for ambient assisted living environments. In: Stephanidis C (ed) Universal access in human-computer interaction. Intelligent and ubiquitous interaction environments, vol 5615, Lecture notes in computer science. Springer, Berlin/Heidelberg, pp 150–159. ISBN: 978-3-642-02709-3, doi:10.1007/978-3-642-02710-9_18, URL:http://dx.doi.org/10.1007/978-3-642-02710-9_18

10. Blumendorf M, Lehmann G, Roscher D, Albayrak S (2009) Ubiquitous user interfaces: multimodal adaptive interaction for smart environments. In: Kurkovsky S (ed) Multimodality in mobile computing and mobile devices: methods for adaptable usability. IGI-Global, Hershey, pp 24–52

11. Byrne MD, Wood D, Sukaviriya PN, Foley JD, Kieras DE (1994) Automating interface evaluation. In: Plaisant C (ed) CHI conference companion. ACM, New York, p 216

12. Calvary G, Coutaz J, Thevenin D, Limbourg Q, Souchon N, Bouillon L, Florins M, Vanderdonckt J (2002) Plasticity of user interfaces: a revised reference framework. In: TAMODIA '02: Proceedings of the first international workshop on task models and diagrams for user interface design. INFOREC Publishing House, Bucharest, pp 127–134

13. Card SK, Moran TP, Newell A (1980) The keystroke-level model for user performance with interactive systems. Commun ACM 23:396–410

14. Card SK, Moran TP, Newell A (1983) The psychology of human-computer interaction. Lawrence Erlbaum Ass. Publ., Hillsdale. ISBN 0898592437

15. DIN, Deutsches Institut für Normen (2008) Ergonomie der Mensch-System-Interaktion - Teil 110: Grundsätze der Dialoggestaltung, DIN EN ISO 9241-110. Beuth Verlag, Berlin

16. Engelbrecht KP, Quade M, Möller S (2009) Analysis of a new simulation approach to dialog system evaluation. Speech Commun 51(12):1234–1252

17. Farenc C, Palanque P, Vanderdonckt J (1995) User interface evaluation: is it ever usable? In: Anzai Y, Ogawa K, Mori H (eds) Proceedings of 6th international conference on human-computer interaction HCI international'95, vol 20B, Advances in human factors/ergonomics series. Elsevier Science B.V., Amsterdam, pp 329–334

18. Feuerstack S, Blumendorf M, Kern M, Kruppa M, Quade M, Runge M, Albayrak S (2008) Automated usability evaluation during model-based interactive system development. In: HCSE-TAMODIA '08: Proceedings of the 2nd conference on human-centered software engineering and 7th international workshop on task models and diagrams. Springer, Berlin/Heidelberg, pp 134–141

19. Fitts PM (1954) The information capacity of the human motor system in controlling the amplitude of movement. J Exp Psychol 47(6):381–391. http://www.ncbi.nlm.nih.gov/entrez/query.fcgi?cmd=Retrieve&db=pubmed&dopt=Abstract&list_uids=13174710, (reprinted in J Exp Psychol: General 121(3):262–269, 1992)

20. Fu WT, Pirolli P (2007) Snif-act: a cognitive model of user navigation on the world wide web. Hum Comput Interact 22:355–412

21. Gajos K, Weld DS (2004) Supple: automatically generating user interfaces. In: IUI '04: Proceedings of the 9th international conference on intelligent user interface. ACM Press, New York, pp 93–100

22. Garcá Frey A, Calvary G, Dupuy-Chesa S (2010) Xplain: an editor for building self-explanatory user interfaces by model-driven engineering. In: Proceedings of the 2nd ACM SIGCHI symposium on engineering interactive computing systems, EICS '10. ACM, New York, pp 41–46

23. Harris BN, John BE, Brezin J (2010) Human performance modeling for all: importing UI prototypes into CogTool. In: Proceedings of the 28th of the international conference extended abstracts on human factors in computing systems, CHI EA '10. ACM, New York, pp1 3481–3486
24. Ivory MY, Hearst MA (2001) The state of the art in automating usability evaluation of user interfaces. ACM Comput Surv 33(4):470–516
25. Jameson A (2008) Adaptive interfaces and agents. In: Sears A, Jacko JA (eds) The human-computer interaction handbook: fundamentals, evolving technologies and emerging applications, 2nd edn. CRC Press, Boca Raton, pp 433–458
26. Jameson A, Mahr A, Kruppa M, Rieger A, Schleicher R (2007) Looking for unexpected consequences of interface design decisions: the MeMo workbench. In: Proceedings of the 6th international conference on Task models and diagrams for user interface design, TAMODIA'07, Toulouse, France. Springer, Berlin/Heidelberg, pp 279–286, 8 p. ISBN:3-540-77221-9, 978-3-540-77221-7, URL:http://dl.acm.org/citation.cfm?id=1782434.1782466
27. John B, Suzuki S (2009) Toward cognitive modeling for predicting usability. In: Jacko J (ed) Human-computer interaction. New trends, lecture notes in computer science, vol 5610. Springer, Berlin/Heidelberg, pp 267–276
28. Bonnie EJ, Tiffany J (2010) Exploration of costs and benefits of predictive human performance modeling for design. In: Proceedings of the 10th international conference on cognitive modeling, Philadelphia, pp 115–120
29. John BE, Kieras DE (1996) The GOMS family of user interface analysis techniques: comparison and contrast. ACM Trans Comput Hum Interact 3(4):320–351
30. John BE, Prevas K, Salvucci DD, Koedinger K (2004) Predictive human performance modeling made easy. In: CHI '04: Proceedings of the SIGCHI conference on human factors in computing systems. ACM Press, New York, pp 455–462
31. Keates S, Clarkson J, Robinson P (2000) Investigating the applicability of user models for motion-impaired users. In: Proceedings of the fourth international ACM conference on assistive technologies, ASSETS '00. ACM, New York, pp 129–136, http://doi.acm.org/10.1145/354324.354354
32. Kieras D (2003) Model-based evaluation. In: The human-computer interaction handbook: fundamentals, evolving technologies and emerging applications. Lawrence Erlbaum Associates, Inc., Mahwah, pp 1139–1151
33. Kieras D (2006) A guide to GOMS model usability evaluation using GOMSL and GLEAN4. Unpublished manuscript. ftp://ftp.eecs.umich.edu/people/kieras/GOMS/GOMSL_Guide.pdf
34. Kieras D, Meyer D, Ballas J (2001) Towards demystification of direct manipulation: cognitive modeling charts the gulf of execution. In: CHI '01: Proceedings of the SIGCHI conference on human factors in computing systems. ACM, New York, pp 128–135
35. Kieras DE, Meyer DE (1997) An overview of the epic architecture for cognition and performance with application to human-computer interaction. Hum Comput Interact 12(4):391–438
36. Kieras DE, Santoro TP (2004) Computational GOMS modeling of a complex team task: lessons learned. In: CHI '04: Proceedings of the SIGCHI conference on human factors in computing systems. ACM, New York, pp 97–104
37. Limbourg Q, Vanderdonckt J, Michotte B, Bouillon L, López-Jaquero V (2005) USIXML: a language supporting multi-path development of user interfaces. In: Bastide R, Palanque P, Roth J (eds) Engineering human computer interaction and interactive systems, vol 3425, lecture notes in computer science. Springer, Berlin/Heidelberg, pp 200–220. ISBN:978-3-540-26097-4, doi:10.1007/11431879_12, URL:http://dx.doi.org/10.1007/11431879_12
38. Mahlke S (2008) User experience of interaction with technical systems. Theories, methods, empirical results, and their application to the development of interactive systems. Ph.D. thesis, TU Berlin
39. Mori G, Paterno F, Santoro C (2004) Design and development of multidevice user interfaces through multiple logical descriptions. IEEE Trans Softw Eng 30(8):507–520

40. Myers B, Hudson SE, Pausch R (2000) Past, present, and future of user interface software tools. ACM Trans Comput Hum Interact 7(1):3–28
41. Newell A (1990) Unified theories of cognition. Harvard University Press, Cambridge
42. Nielsen CM, Overgaard M, Pedersen MB, Stage J (2005) Feedback from usability evaluation to user interface design: are usability reports any good? In: Human-computer interaction – INTERACT 2005. Lecture notes in computer science, vol 3585. Springer, Berlin/Heidelberg, pp 391–404
43. Nielsen J (1992) Finding usability problems through heuristic evaluation. In: CHI '92: Proceedings of the SIGCHI conference on human factors in computing systems. ACM Press, New York, pp 373–380
44. Nielsen J (1993) Noncommand user interfaces. Commun ACM 36(4):83–99
45. Nielsen J (1993) Usability engineering. Morgan Kaufmann Publishers Inc., San Francisco
46. Nielsen J, Molich R (1990) Heuristic evaluation of user interfaces. In: CHI '90: Proceedings of the SIGCHI conference on human factors in computing systems. ACM Press, New York, pp 249–256
47. Norman DA (1983) Mental models, chap. In: Some observations on mental models. Erlbaum, Hillsdale, pp 7–14
48. Palanque P, Barboni E, Martinie C, Navarre D, Winckler M (2011) A model-based approach for supporting engineering usability evaluation of interaction techniques. In: Proceedings of the 3rd ACM SIGCHI symposium on engineering interactive computing systems, EICS '11. ACM, New York, pp 21–30
49. Peter GP, Lewis C, Rieman J, Wharton C (1992) Cognitive walkthroughs: a method for theory-based evaluation of user interfaces. Int J Man-Mach Stud 36(5):741–773. ISSN:0020–7373, doi:10.1016/0020-7373(92)90039-N, URL:http://www.sciencedirect.com/science/article/pii/002073739290039N
50. Rieman J, Young RM, Howes A (1996) A dual-space model of iteratively deepening exploratory learning. Int J Hu Comput Stud 44(6):743–775
51. Ruß A, Quade M, Kruppa M, Runge M (2012) Rule-based approach for simulating age-related usability problems. In: Wichert R, Eberhardt B (eds) Ambient assisted living. Advanced technologies and societal change, vol 5, AAL-Kongress 2012. VDE, Springer, Berlin, pp 149–166
52. Salvucci DD (2009) Rapid prototyping and evaluation of in-vehicle interfaces. ACM Trans Comput Hum Interact 16:33
53. Salvucci DD, Lee FJ (2003) Simple cognitive modeling in a complex cognitive architecture. In: CHI '03: Proceedings of the SIGCHI conference on human factors in computing systems. ACM Press, New York, pp 265–272
54. Sottet J-S, Calvary G, Coutaz J, Favre J-M (2008) A model-driven engineering approach for the usability of plastic user interfaces. In: Gulliksen J, Harning MB, Palanque P, Veer GC, Wesson J (eds) Engineering interactive systems. Springer, Berlin/Heidelberg, pp 140–157, 18 p. URL:http://dx.doi.org/10.1007/978-3-540-92698-6_9, doi:10.1007/978-3-540-92698-6_9
55. Steinnökel P, Scheel C, Quade M, Albayrak S (2011) Towards an enhanced semantic approach for automatic usability evaluation. In: Proceedings of the computational linguistics-applications conference, Jachranka, Poland, pp 85–91. ISBN:N 978-83-60810-47-7
56. Teo L, John BE (2011) The evolution of a goal-directed exploration model: effects of information scent and GoBack utility on successful exploration. Top Cogn Sci 3(1):154–165
57. Thevenin D, Coutaz J (1999) Plasticity of user interfaces: framework and research agenda. In: Human-computer interaction, INTERACT'99: IFIP TC. 13 international conference on human-computer interaction, 30 Aug–3 Sept 1999. IOS Press, Edinburgh, pp 110–117
58. Trewin S, Pain H (1999) Keyboard and mouse errors due to motor disabilities. Int J Hum Comput Stud 50(2):109–144, http://dx.doi.org/10.1006/ijhc.1998.0238
59. Vanderdonckt J (2008) Model-driven engineering of user interfaces: promises, successes, failures, and challenges. In: Proceedings of ROCHI 08
60. Weiser M (1991) The computer for the 21st century. Sci Am 265(3):66–75

61. Whiteside JL, Bennett J, Holtzblatt K (1988) Usability engineering: our experience and evolution. Elsevier Science Publishers, B. V., Amsterdam, pp 791–817
62. Wood SD, Kieras DE (2002) Modeling human error for experimentation, training, and error-tolerant design. In: Proceedings of the interservice/industry training, simulation and education
63. Young RM, Green TRG, Simon T (1989) Programmable user models for predictive evaluation of interface designs. In: CHI '89: Proceedings of the SIGCHI conference on human factors in computing systems. ACM, New York, pp 15–19
64. Zhang J, Cheng BHC, Goldsby H (2007) Amoeba-rt: run-time verification of adaptive software. In: Giese H (ed) Models in software engineering, workshops and symposia at MoDELS 2007, Reports and revised selected papers. Lecture notes in computer science, vol 5002. Springer, Nashville, pp 212–224

Index

E. Martín et al. (eds.), *User Modeling and Adaptation for Daily Routines: Providing
Assistance to People with Special Needs*, Human–Computer Interaction Series,
DOI 10.1007/978-1-4471-4778-7, © Springer-Verlag London 2013